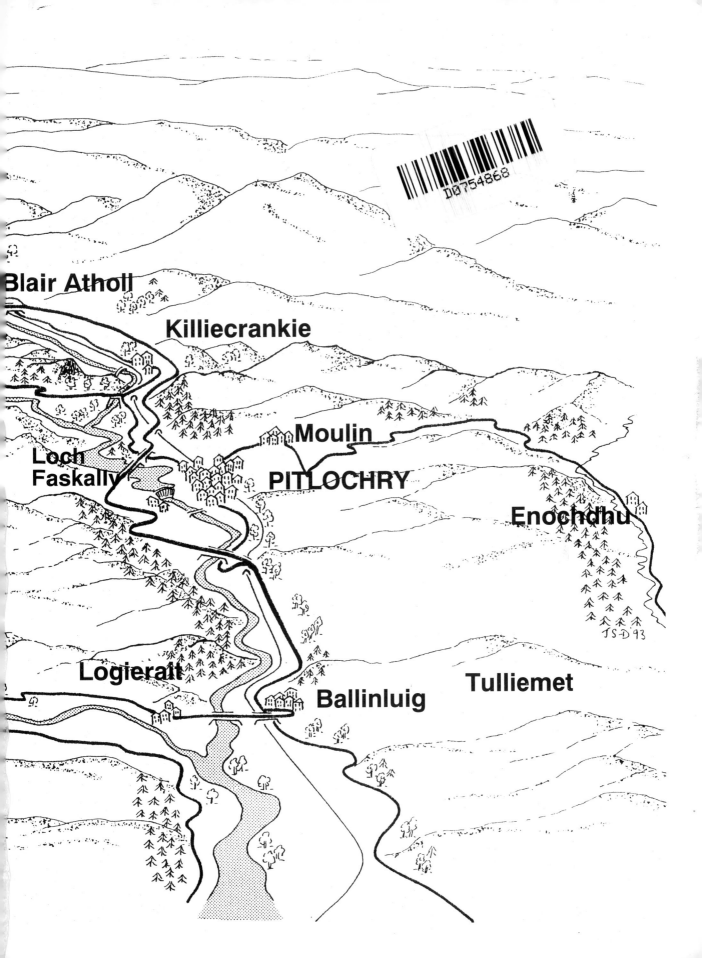

Pitlochry

Heritage of a Highland District

Colin Liddell

Perth and Kinross District Libraries
1993

© Colin Liddell, W. S.
1993

Published by
Perth and Kinross District Libraries

ISBN 0 905452 14 3

Printed by
Cordfall Ltd
041 332 4640

Contents

Foreword 7

Introduction 9

1 The Natural Setting 11

2 Early Inhabitants 19

3 The First Millenium AD (From Pictland into Scotland) 27

4 The Origins of Moulin 39

5 Centuries of Unrest 45

6 The Origins of Pitlochry 61

7 The Eighteenth Century 65

8 The Nineteenth Century 77

9 The Twentieth Century 97

10 The Smaller Villages 121

11 Roads, Ferries and Bridges 131

12 Religious Sites in the District 139

Bibliography 148

Index 152

Foreword

by
**Major Sir David H. Butter, K.C.V.O., M.C., of Pitlochry,
H.M. Lord-Lieutenant of Perth and Kinross.**

Reading this excellent and informative book about Pitlochry and its heritage has shown to me what great interest it will generate to those of us who are lucky enough to live in this beautiful part of Highland Perthshire.

There is also a fund of information contained within the pages of this book for our visitors who will be keen to learn all about the history, the ecology, the local stories and the changes which have taken place around Pitlochry over the past centuries.

There is no doubt that a tremendous amount of detailed studying and research has been carried out by Colin Liddell to achieve this very readable book and I commend it to you, either to learn more about the local history of this district, or to enhance your visit here.

David Butter.

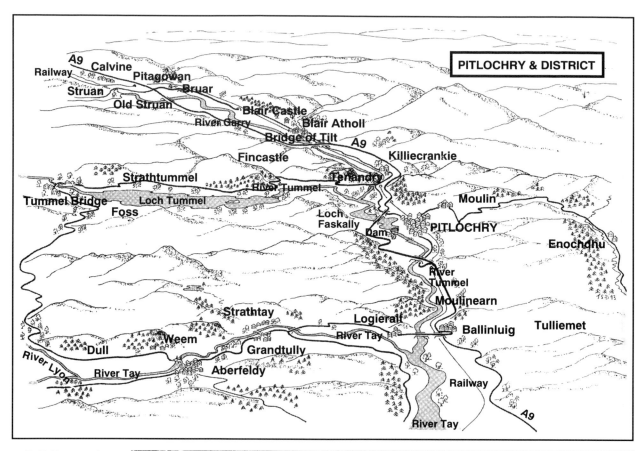

(Left) Excerpt of an aerial map of Highland Perthshire

Introduction

Pitlochry is at the geographical heart of Scotland, with the main north-south communication links passing through or beside the town (or 'village' as the locals perhaps not incorrectly still refer to it), including:

- the A9 trunk road, upgraded in the nineteen seventies and following closely the line of the Great North Road built two hundred and forty years earlier by General Wade;
- the London to Inverness railway line, introduced after much resistance in the eighteen sixties; and
- the natural flow of the River Tummel, albeit over the famous Dam built in the nineteen forties.

Pitlochry is also at the centre of Highland Perthshire, the name now given informally to the original Perthshire Highland Region, embracing the nine historic Parishes of Blair Atholl, Dull, Dunkeld & Dowally, Fortingall, Kenmore, Little Dunkeld, Logierait, Moulin and Weem.

Other parts of Highland Perthshire have been well documented, including for instance the Atholl Estates, the cathedral city of Dunkeld and historic Glenlyon. The purpose of this book is to centre on Pitlochry and its immediate district, stretching from Tummel Bridge in the south-west to Logierait in the south-east and from Struan in the north-west to Enochdhu in the north-east, about 125 square miles all told.

This book thereby attempts to update many local works, in particular the celebrated book *"Pitlochry District"* by Hugh Mitchell, F.S.A. (Scot), which was published by Lachlan Mackay, Bookseller and Stationer of Pitlochry, in 1923 and which has been out of print for many years.

It is perhaps fitting that this book should be written now, seventy years later, by a current partner of the local law firm which was founded by Hugh Mitchell's father in Dysart Cottages, Pitlochry in 1838 and in which Hugh Mitchell himself was a partner for over fifty years until his death in 1928.

Anyone who has heard two versions of a road accident is likely to appreciate that history can at times be delightfully inexact. Whether there be few facts or many, their interpretation can lead to endless possibilities. History is always in a state of flux as it becomes revisited and reassessed, sometimes in the light of new evidence which then has to fit into a perceived jigsaw puzzle, or in undermining existing perceptions, which prompts the creation of new perceptions. At the least, this book repeats some of the best known and most documented legends and stories of the district, without attempting to conclude that, because of longevity alone, they are either definitive or correct in every respect. It tries to allow the atmosphere of bygone days to shine through!

Gaelic names present a similar problem. The language which was once the only one known here was essentially a spoken one, only comparatively recently committed to writing. There are many place names which, depending on phonetics, could have quite different meanings. For example, the names 'Atholl', 'Logierait' and 'Pitlochry' have at least two possible meanings apiece. A proper judgement probably cannot be made as to which is the correct derivation in each case, although some writers have perhaps accepted that particular version which best befits their story. At times this is not unreasonable; a name is usually nothing other than a descriptive label given to a place probably just because of some pertinent association or fact.

Many of the sites and local artefacts which are mentioned throughout this book are located on land in private ownership, or for some reason or another are relatively inaccessible. This book is not intended to be an invitation to explore. It might hopefully encourage those who have special sites or artefacts on their land to preserve them, at the least, and perhaps, where appropriate, to consider sharing them with a wider public. The point of citing these is to show that this district has a long and vital history and that many aspects of that past are still in existence, at least in some shape or form, as part of the rich tapestry which makes up Highland Perthshire today.

Indeed, our heritage may be richer than we currently realise. In recent years, some surprising discoveries have been made, sometimes because of reinterpretation of something which has been staring us in the face all the while (such as the huge neolithic barrow 'found' at Bridge of Allan in 1989), sometimes because it is unearthed (such as a neolithic stone axehead found near Bridge of Cally in the earthen spoil of a rabbit warren), sometimes because we do not appreciate properly just what is around us. The Royal Commission on the Ancient and Historical Monuments of Scotland have conducted a fascinating and fruitful study between Alyth and Enochdhu. Who knows what they or others may discover if a similar study were to be extended further westwards into this district?

It is always more difficult to write an objective history of one's own time and so, within the chapter on the twentieth century, I have allowed some current themes and personal opinions to make an appearance. I must stress that these are mine alone.

This book, in short, is the story of a Highland district from the earliest recorded time until the present, its geography, its people and the vestiges of its past which still exist and touch us today. The pace of change has been great and is seemingly ever-quickening. This change has often caused conflict as new uses eradicate old. It is perhaps pertinent at the end of a millenium to view this change in some perspective and, thereby, to see how much of our local heritage has been maintained, how much has been altered – for better or worse – or how much has been lost forever. Nothing less than our culture is at stake.

It is now becoming acknowledged that the way our past is imprinted on the landscape, that link between local history and local countryside, is a 'cultural landscape'. An understanding of yesterday – our cultural landscape and our heritage – can assist us in the preparations we undertake today for tomorrow.

The Pitlochry Archive is a good local source, but (without criticising it in any way) it could be very much better. To be so, it needs your help. If you have photographs, souvenirs or other items of local interest, please consider lodging them within the Archive, to be retained carefully for the enlightenment of and study by those who follow us, be they schoolchildren, students or others. Such sharing would aid learning.

My thanks go to those who have encouraged me to write this book and to those whose knowledge and wisdom have kept me on the right tracks. Any errors which remain either in fact or in interpretation are mine alone. I should stress that I would always welcome corrections or more information; indeed, I would judge this book a success if it does nothing other than provoke such a response!

I am indebted to the Perth & Kinross District Libraries (Jim Guthrie in particular) who are kindly publishing this book, to Cordfall Limited (John Stewart and Laura Waters in particular) who printed it and to everyone (too many to name here but hopefully all listed in the Acknowledgements on page 151) who has made a contribution great or small. I have met with such enthusiasm and generosity at every turn which has helped to make this book a joy to create.

It has been fascinating to discover so much about this part of Scotland during my researches in which I was inspired initially as a child by my father's keen interest and enthusiasm. My special thanks go to my wife Katrina and our children Iona and Bryony, who accompanied me on many a field trip and who suffered the writer's work through all its stages. This book is dedicated to them.

Colin Liddell
Pitlochry
1993

CHAPTER ONE
The Natural Setting

Mountains

The highest mountain in the vicinity of Pitlochry is Ben-y-Vrackie (2,757' / 840m), which dominates the northern skyline. From the summit, one can marvel not only at the immediate district but also, on a clear day, at each of Arthur's Seat in Edinburgh, the North Sea off Montrose, Ben Nevis by Fort William and Ben More on the Isle of Mull.

Within one's vista is a landscape which has changed little over the last ten thousand years. It is one unusually rich in variety. To the far north lie the bare uplands of the Braes of Atholl, leading up into the forbidding Drumochter Pass, whilst closer below are the grassy slopes of Blair Atholl and the Pass of Killiecrankie. To the far west, beyond the majestic profile of Schiehallion (3,547' / 1,083m), lie the bleak marshlands of Rannoch Moor and, beyond, the three distinctive peaks of Buachaille Etive Mor above Glencoe whilst, nearer to hand, the dark expanse of Loch Tummel glitters in the sun. To the south are fertile and richly wooded valleys, which stretch away, row upon row, towards the Trossachs. Finally, to the east are the rolling moorlands above Dunkeld and the productive farmlands leading to Perth and beyond.

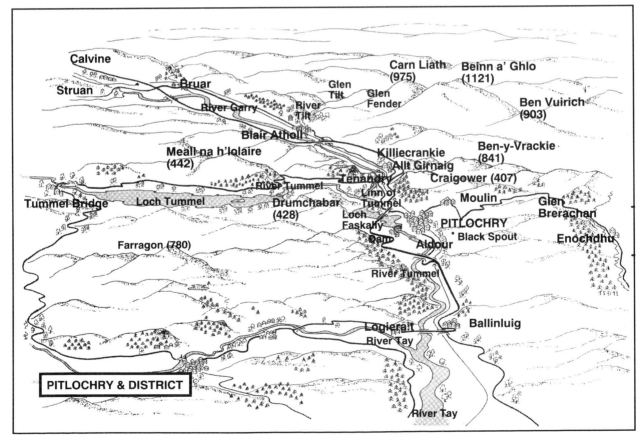

PITLOCHRY & DISTRICT

Ben-y-Vrackie (known until about the First World War simply as Ben Vrackie) means 'speckled hill', because of the white quartz rocks which used to be scattered across its slopes and which were visible from quite a distance. Almost all of these were taken away at the end of the nineteenth century to enhance the houses and gardens of Pitlochry. Yet, after a snowstorm, the Ben still looks speckled enough, albeit black on white now, the black being the rockier crags where the snow cannot settle. Ben-y-Vrackie is unique in the Grampian range in being an isolated volcano, which discharged through a vent on its eastern shoulder. Its remains are about half a mile in diameter.

Craigower ('the goat's rock') is an outcrop (1,335'/407m) situated due north of Pitlochry. From its summit, now in the ownership of the National Trust for Scotland, there are panoramic views of the locality. It is reached by a path, which starts at Moulin, follows for part of the way what was the old North Road, leads at the top end of the Golf Course into a plantation of larch, Norway spruce and some native Scots pine and then climbs to the well-signposted viewpoint. In times past, Craigower was a beacon hill, used to pass messages by fire, perhaps between Dunkeld and Blair Atholl, or between east and west.

Ben Vuirich (2,961'/903m) lies to the north-east of Ben-y-Vrackie. It is part of a large 'deer forest' (as the relatively bare moorland on which deer herds roam is called). There must for long have been deer there as its name comes from the Gaelic *beinn buireadh* ('hill of the rutting'), the rut being the mating season for deer, when the stags roar and bellow. Ben Vuirich is the only wholly granite mountain in the Grampians. Its vein of granite extends southwards through Pitlochry in the form of mica schist. Most of the Victorian houses of Pitlochry have been built of this stone, obtained from the long-exhausted quarry at Aldour, to the east of the town.

The foundations of the landscape visible from the top of Ben-y-Vrackie were begun over five hundred million years ago. Massive earth movements, caused by significant shifting of continental land masses, created the Caledonian mountain range, which has since been eroded to such an extent that the hills we see today are literally the inner core of their former grandeur.

Minerals

The rocks which remain here are very old. To the north are the ancient granites of the Moine series, evident in Rannoch Moor. To the south is the slate associated with the Highland Boundary Fault which runs immediately to the north of Dunkeld. In this district are the more recent and varied rocks of the Dalradian series, where softer sandstone has been eroded over the years to leave schists, quartzites and limestones as the surface rocks.

The prevailing rock is black schist, a rough friable stone of a dark grey hue; it is really solidified mud from earlier erosion. It has been broken up by violent earth movements, the principal movement in this district being from south-west to north-east. The pressure was so great that many of the surface rocks became folded. At Loch Tay that folding was so severe that the rock formations there have actually been inverted and are now completely upside down.

Small deposits of gold have been found in the district, principally in the Allt Girnaig burn at Killiecrankie. Other deposits have been found to the west of Aberfeldy and by Tyndrum.

The largest known deposit in Europe of barytes (barium sulphate, mixed with other minerals such as quartz and iron pyrites), used as an additive to drilling fluids in the North Sea oil fields, is mined in the hills around Farragon (2,559'/780m) – which derives either from the Gaelic *feargan* ('a warrior') or from St. Fergus – between Loch Tummel and the Upper Tay Valley. Barytes is also used as an aggregate for the type of heavy concrete used to shield against radiation. Its particular property is its high specific gravity, making it three times heavier than coal and two times heavier than granite.

Bog iron can be found throughout the district, giving a red skein to the water. The Red Well, north-east of Balnakeilly House, was famous down the centuries for its health-giving waters (because of the salts of iron that the water dissolves out of the rocks). In Rannoch, the deposits of iron ore were so plentiful that they were smelted and forged at "bloomeries" into what were reputed to have been the finest examples of the Highland claymore, which derives from *claidheamh* ('sword') and *mòr* ('large').

The most famous of these were made by Andrea Ferrara at *allt na cheardaich* ('burn of the forge') in Rannoch.

Limestone, used as a fertiliser, is still quarried commercially at Blair Atholl. It used to be quarried round the corner in Glen Tilt, where it was so pure that it had become marble. The quarry is situated near the cottage known as Marble Lodge. It was in operation from about 1815, after it had been brought to the attention of the Duke of Atholl two years earlier by the Scottish Geological Survey; production stopped in 1844 when it became uneconomic, because of cheaper marble being imported from abroad. Some of the older houses in the district still have mantelpieces of the pale green Glen Tilt marble, but it can most readily be seen within Blair Castle; the font at Tenandry Church is also made from this local marble.

The Ice Ages

As much an influence on the shaping of our landscape as the continental and volcanic movements of a younger Earth were the great glaciers of ice. More than once, they wended their slow and powerful progression eastwards from the great ice fields of Rannoch Moor, gouging out the various straths, leaving deep lochs in the middle and gravel terraces to the sides.

The first, or 'Great' ice age, took place some twenty-five thousand years ago. A large glacier came down the strath of the Tummel from the immense ice fields of Rannoch Moor. To the west of Pitlochry, the glacier's face must have been almost three hundred metres high. The ends of its moraines are still clearly visible, the northern end at Craigower and the southern end at Drumchabar (on the south side of the river, where there is now a ruined clachan atop the hill, opposite Faskally House). The Pass of Killiecrankie, its steep sides of mica-schist rock strengthened by bands of quartzite, was one of the few places which withstood this glacial onslaught.

Where this glacier swept past and collected the one from the north a small moraine was formed, on the end of which the Pitlochry Hydro Hotel now stands. In turn, this combined glacier met the one coming down the Tay valley to the south of Ballinluig, around Kinnaird and Guay, where the valley has been pushed to its widest. Its distinct terminal moraine is visible immediately above Dalguise.

Other signs of glacial movement can be seen in the natural 'terracing' along many valley sides (particularly noticeable in Glen Brerachan, near Enochdhu), in the scratching marks and scars on exposed rocks and in the rounded and typically ice-worn higher slopes.

Panorama from the smaller Creag Dhubh ('black crag'), to the south-west of Cluniemore House, looking due north over Drumchabar, Loch Faskally and Faskally House in the foreground, the Garry Bridge, Craig Fonvuick ('rock in the land of pigs') and the Pass of Killiecrankie in the middle distance and Creag Eallaich ('white crag'), Glen Girnaig and Carn Liath ('grey-topped mountain') in the background

Terracing is also evident within Pitlochry itself. Both Lower Oakfield and Higher Oakfield are, for instance, terraces which were formed by the loch of melted ice that backed up from Dunkeld, dammed there by the harder rock of Craig a Barns ('the spiky hill' – 1,106'/337m). Terracing closer to Dunkeld itself shows that for a long period of time the water remained at precisely 354'(108m) above current sea-level.

All over the landscape are rocks which have been carried within the glaciers and then deposited during their passage, particularly when the melting process began at the end of each ice age. Thus it is possible to match the origin of many particles of rock found in the district which are in fact alien to it; for instance, the distinctive pinkish granite of Ben Vuirich, about five miles north-east of Pitlochry has been found as far afield as Angus and Fife, whilst granite masses from Rannoch Moor lie on the hills around Pitlochry.

The 'Great' ice age was followed by a semi-tropical age. At that time the mountains were still significantly higher than they are now, perhaps by some three to five hundred metres. There was no North Sea; Britain was still connected to the Continent of Europe. On the west, what were later to become the islands of the Hebrides still formed part of the mainland. The country was covered with deciduous trees – oaks, hazels, elms and, higher up, pines.

A lesser ice age ensued, which reduced the height of the mountains almost to what we see now and formed both the North Sea and English Channel. A typical moraine of this lesser ice age can be seen up the length of West Moulin Road between Pitlochry to Moulin.

After the glaciers receded for a second time, about eleven thousand years ago, there began the temperate clime which has continued up to the present day. Initially, it was much warmer than it is now. Trees were able to grow freely at about 3,000' (1,000m) above sea level, compared with a maximum of about 1,500' (500m) now. There were human settlements at higher elevations than now, practising rudimentary agriculture, where now only heather and bracken will grow.

The weather was more sharply divided season by season than it is now. In the Church of Scotland's Statistical Account for the Parish of Moulin in 1845 the local minister laments:

The temperature is very different from what it was some sixty or seventy years ago. In exchange for the great and long-continued heat of summer and the excessive cold of winter which was then experienced, we have now very little of the fine summer weather and, with few exceptions, the winters are generally mild and temperate. Of late, during the summer months, the temperature has ranged from 45 to 75 degrees and in winter from 20 to 50 degrees. The air is not humid.

The Romans also had something to say about our climate, almost two thousand years ago. Agricola wrote of *"damp with continual showers, and overcast with clouds"*, which may sound all too familiar a forecast today. Julius Caesar, writing a couple of centuries earlier, thought that Britain's climate was milder than he had experienced in France. Evidently, there have been considerable climatic changes in the past, which will doubtless continue in the future.

Rivers and Lochs

Whilst the landscape of this district has changed little for thousands of years, the same cannot be said about the waters which flow through it. They have been greatly changed by the works of man during the twentieth century, in his harnessing the power of water to create hydro-electricity for the National Grid. The rivers and lochs here are important, not only for this new energy but also for being perhaps the most critical element of nature so much sought after and admired by visitors who flock to this district from all over the world.

These waters have always been a means of travel. It is thought that for the early inhabitants of Scotland the ribbons of interconnecting rivers, lochs and lochans were the major, sometimes only, routes used to traverse a countryside densely covered by the famous Caledonian forest. When the new A9 trunk road was being constructed between Dunkeld and Pitlochry in about 1976, a dug-out canoe was discovered by the river bank; the alluvial clay above this find has been carbon-dated to 6400 BC. In the age before bridges, not so long ago, ferries plied across these waters, as vital communication links between riparian communities. Nowadays, water-borne travel is more leisure-orientated, with sailing boats, windsurfers, kayaks and racing rafts in abundance.

River Tummel

The principal river is the Tummel, which rises in the Black Mount near the head of Glencoe, almost in sight of the Atlantic Ocean. All its water has already flowed for over fifty miles, through the lochans of Rannoch moor (where the height differential over eleven miles is a mere twenty metres) and on through Lochs Rannoch (either from *raineach* meaning 'bracken' or from *ratheanach* meaning 'watery') and Tummel (*teimheil* meaning 'dark' or 'shadowy'), by the time it has reached Pitlochry.

Its passage has been significantly altered by being harnessed in 1950 within the largest Hydro-Electric Scheme in Britain. The Scheme's creations include the scenic Lochs Faskally, Errochty and Eigheach; Dunalastair Reservoir, its height being carefully maintained to preserve the rich birdlife sustained on its wetland; the Pitlochry Dam, seven other dams and six power stations; and the Fish Ladder at Pitlochry Dam, famous the

(Top) The Falls of Tummel as they were in their heyday before 1950. (Bottom) Linn of Tummel in spate in 1993

world over. Loch Tummel itself was raised five metres, its length doubling from three miles to seven. [The Scheme is mentioned in more detail in Chapter Nine.]

The famous Falls of Tummel were described by John Ruskin as "*the only perfect waterfall*" and were visited in their heyday by Queen Victoria on 17th September 1844. They nearly ceased to exist when Archibald Butter of Faskally proposed in 1844 to dynamite the Falls so as to improve the salmon fishing in the river above; this plan did not proceed. However, the Falls were diminished in their effect as a result of the Hydro-Electric Scheme in 1950, partly because of a reduction in the amount of water coming down the river (most of it travelling by pipe instead from the eastern end of Loch Tummel to the Clunie Power Station) and partly because of an increase in the water level below the Falls (with Loch Faskally starting at that point).

Whilst the Falls were never dynamited, the problem of the fishing was addressed in 1910 by the construction of a salmon ladder on the north side of the Falls (precursor of the world famous one built forty years later at the Pitlochry Dam), part of which is through a tunnel twelve metres long. This ladder noticeably improved the quantity of salmon above the Falls, not only by saving them from having to leap up the formidable Falls themselves, but also by letting them avoid being caught in the wicker baskets which the locals, whilst clinging to the slippery face of the Falls, used to lower on ropes made of birch twigs.

When the Falls were reduced in size, they were renamed the Linn of Tummel (either from the Gaelic *linne* meaning 'a pool' or more appropriately from the Scots *linn* meaning 'waterfall'). They were gifted by the Barbour family to the National Trust for Scotland, along with the adjoining woodland of some fifty acres beside the confluence of the Rivers Garry and Tummel. A little upstream from the Linn of Tummel is the Coronation Bridge, a footbridge which connects it with the Foss/Pitlochry public road. The bridge is so called because it was dedicated on 22nd June 1911, the day that King George V and Queen Mary were crowned.

(Top) The River Garry near Calvine

(Bottom) The Cuilc above Pitlochry, looking north over the Golf Course towards Baledmund House with Creag Chuinnlean ('crag of the corn stubble') and Ben-y-Vrackie behind

River Garry

The River Garry rises from Loch Garry, which lies in a deep ravine between high hills near the northern county boundary at Drumochter. It is not clear whether the name derives from *garaidh* ('a den'), or as suggested by the Reverend James McLagan in 1793 from *gath ruith* ('the flight of the dart' – on account of its swift and turbulent nature), or simply and most probably from *garbh* ('rough stream').

After flowing nearly thirty miles and receiving in its course many tributary burns – including the Bruar (*bruir* meaning 'noisy'), the Tilt (*teilt* meaning 'boiling') the Fender (*fiodabhar* meaning 'bright') and the Girnaig (*gairneag* meaning 'young and noisy') – the Garry unites with the Tummel, just to the north of Loch Faskally. The Tummel in turn joins the River Tay (*tatha* meaning 'the silent one', which may have been the name of a water goddess) at Ballinluig and, having the deeper channel, is in fact the larger of the two.

The Cuilc

Within Pitlochry, the only pond, apart from the old mill ponds, is the Cuilc, its name deriving from the Gaelic word meaning 'sedges' (a grass-like reed with jointless stems). It is in fact an old marl pit. Marl is soil containing clay and carbonate of lime, a much-prized fertiliser. At one time the Cuilc was considerably larger and discharged to the west but, in the fifteenth century, a deep cutting was made and the water diverted to its current course eastwards in order to supplement the supply for the meal mill in Pitlochry.

The Black Spout

To the east of Pitlochry is the impressive waterfall known now as the Black Spout (and in Gaelic as *sput dhubh*), to the south of which there are the remains of a Pictish fort. The waterfall is approximately sixty metres high. A sturdy viewing platform was provided in 1989, not before time, as a number of accidental falls were recorded over the years. In May 1933, there was some excitement caused by a motor cyclist and pillion passenger performing what was described in the local paper as *"a daring ascent"* of the sheep path running along the verge of the ravine.

Trees

The landscape, spectacular though it is with ancient mountains and noble lochs, is brought to life by the abundance of trees throughout Highland Perthshire.

Thousands of years ago, trees grew at a height of up to 3,000' (900m) above sea level, whereas now any species of tree struggles to grow anywhere above 1,500' (450m), even though the straths here are neither exposed nor steep. In addition, elevations are surprisingly modest for a part of 'the Highlands', Pitlochry's main street being for instance only around 330' (100m) above sea level and the 1,000' (300m) mark being attained only once the road levels out onto Moulin moor. Relatively speaking, it is still an ideal environment for trees.

When the Romans came, there were so many trees that they called the country 'Caledonia', their word for 'woods'. Yet, during the largely undocumented three hundred years after their departure, most of these trees disappeared. Effectively, by 800 AD, much of the Great Wood of Caledon was no more. There are still a few remains of that ancient and splendid forest, notably at Mar Lodge, Glen Feshie and, more locally, the Black Wood of Rannoch.

Climatic changes at that time may have been the cause in that there was suddenly a significant growth of peat. Peat throttles the root systems of trees. When the Bog of Allan near Stirling was drained at the beginning of the nineteenth century, a Roman road was uncovered under some four metres of peat, which would indicate an average growth of about thirty centimetres of peat per century, but it was doubtless quicker than that in more humid times.

There were also determined efforts to reduce the dense woodlands, for reasons which pertain the world over, wherever forest, jungle and woodland is cut back and felled. These included the telling demand for additional pasture land, even in quite early times, exacerbated of course once sheep were introduced in large numbers. Felling took place deliberately to keep wild animals at bay, by denying them their shelter, notably the wolf which was the scourge of the Highlands not only for humans but particularly for their livestock. Cut wood was also in heavy use (perhaps more so than peat) to heat primitive hearths, as well as by which to cook, to see (splinters of resinous pine heartwood, called "stocks", being used as candles), to distil whisky and, transformed into charcoal, to smelt.

The Black Spout waterfall east of Pitlochry

The indigenous trees of Highland Scotland include Scots pine, oak, silver birch, ash, aspen, alder, rowan and hazel. One of the best examples of a venerable oak wood can still be seen on the hillside between the Garry Bridge and Tenandry Church, to the south of the Pass of Killiecrankie. Killiecrankie itself is well known for its aspen wood. Rowan trees were planted for good luck beside dwellings; many sole examples stand guard yet over remote ruins in the hills. Hazels and oaks predominated at the lower elevations. Interesting examples of these have been found over the years.

At the turn of the twentieth century, digging tests were carried out in the field above the road leading to the houses in Robertson Crescent, Pitlochry. Beneath fully a metre and a half of boulder clay were uncovered the trees from a buried forest, mainly hazels and oaks, with a surprising accumulation of large hazelnuts forming a layer almost thirty centimetres thick. It would seem that this wood was trapped not by retreating ice but by a sudden deluge of water released from above, which levelled the trees as it tore down the valley.

Also at the beginning of the twentieth century, a prehistoric oak was discovered whilst the original Pitlochry public water supply was being laid. This fallen tree was discovered within peat at the foot of Lettoch Farm. It had a diameter of almost a metre and was followed by the workmen for a length of over six metres without its end being reached. It was left where it was, its being cheaper to alter the line of the pipe.

The Statistical Account of 1793 shows that, as well as peat, timber was being used extensively for fuel. Oak bark was sold for tanning leather, indeed being the principal export from the district after linen yarn. Alder was used for furniture, to such an extent that it was often called "Scotch mahogany".

By the latter part of the eighteenth century, landowners had begun laying out some plantations of larch, spruce and Scots firs. The larch had been introduced by James Menzies of Culdares from the Austrian Tyrol in about 1738. John, fourth Duke of Atholl transformed the Atholl Estates during his lifetime, being responsible for the planting of nearly twenty-seven and a half million trees, mostly Scots fir and oak. When he succeeded to the title in 1774, the plantations covered about 1,100 acres; by the time of his death in 1830, they exceeded 16,500.

These plantations were encouraged, to replace the woodland destroyed in the sixteenth and early seventeenth centuries, *"by fire or otherwise"*. The author of the 1793 Account lamented that *"places still bear the names of woods were there is not a tree now"*. Happily, these places have since regained their foliage and their names once more are appropriate, such as Faskally (*fas choille* which means 'a growing wood') and Killiecrankie (which may derive from *coile chrionaich*, – 'withered brushwood' – as the author of the 1793 Statistical Account avers, or more probably from *coille chritheann* – 'wood of aspen' – as Hugh Mitchell suggests). The Killiecrankie area is famed for its aspen wood.

The main cause of the destruction of Scotland's forests between 1715, in the aftermath of the first Jacobite Rebellion, and about 1850 was not so much *"fire"* but more *"otherwise"*, in that many of the Highland lairds, keen to adopt English ways and eager for English money, sold off their forests, or at least their growing timber, at absurdly low prices.

Much of that "cheap" wood built the ships of the English navy, until iron began to be used instead; seven hundred and seventy-two larch trees, with an average age of fifty-nine years, were used to build the *Athole* frigate of twenty-eight guns in 1816. However, the coming of iron did not represent much of a reprieve; forestry continued to be felled, to be transformed into charcoal, after which it was transported south to fire the iron smelters. Wood was also much used in the construction of the railways, not only in the smelting of the tracks, but for the sleepers in between. The land freed of growing timber was transformed into yet more pasture for sheep.

By the time of the next Statistical Account, published in 1845, there were several kinds of new plantation. As well as natural woods of oak and birch, there were woods of ash, aspen, Scots fir, spruce and larch.

New afforestation continued unchecked until the two World Wars saw a renewal of large-scale felling. It was not until after the creation of the national Forestry Commission in 1935 that land became systematically drained, ploughed and planted. Over 12,000 hectares of forestry lie between Logierait and Rannoch Station, not all spruce either, but a good mix of larch and Scots pine too.

However, the commercial pressures on both the Forestry Commission and private landowners resulted in the mass planting of many non-indigenous trees between 1950 and 1985, particularly Sitka and Norway spruce, European and Japanese larch and contorta pine. Hardwoods began to be introduced as an amenity content, often along visible fringes, notably beech, oak, ash, gean (wild cherry), alder and sycamore; few of these are indigenous either.

Since 1985, there has been an increasing awareness of the desirability to introduce indigenous trees from guaranteed native stock. This is encouraged by a number of organisations, including the Scottish Native Woods Campaign, based in Aberfeldy. It is felt that there is a place for amenity and other trees of foreign origin in garden policies and ornamental woodland, but that the wide expanse of Scotland's hillsides should be covered only as they once were, by noble stands of homeland trees.

The Forestry Commission was reorganised in 1991, with Forest Enterprise being responsible in this district for the Tummel Forest Park (now part of the Tay Forest), comprising some 16,000 hectares of forestry within that part of Perthshire north of Dunkeld. The Park includes Faskally Wood to the west of Pitlochry; Allean and Glen Errochty to the north of Loch Tummel; and Frenich, Drumnakyle, Tomphubil, Braes of Foss and Lassintullich to the south of the Loch.

Britain remains proportionately one of the least afforested countries in Europe. The great majority of the country's timber requirements is still met from abroad. The challenge for one and all is to provide more amenity forests for leisure and recreation and more timber for the home market, whilst all the while planning future plantings to fit sensitively into our landscape.

Chapter Two
Early Inhabitants

Wild Animals

After the 'Great' ice age, the land blossomed in the temperate climes which ensued. Dense woodland was quick to establish itself. The first inhabitants of this district were animals. Many of these, quite apart from dinosaurs, no longer exist. Those endemic species extinct or no longer plentiful include:

- elephant (*elephas antiquas*)
- the mammoth (*elephas primigenius*)
- sabre-toothed tiger
- lion
- wolf
- wild horse
- bear
- wild boar
- beaver
- the Irish elk
- reindeer
- the great ox

The great ox, known as *urus* or *bos primigenius,* must at one time have been fairly numerous here. The urus was much larger than the domestic cow, being anything between one and a half to two metres high. Four skulls have been found by local farmers when digging deep for fertilising marl in the Cuilc, a pond to the south of Pitlochry Golf Course. The first skull was found in 1770, measuring sixty-six centimetres in length and over twenty-five centimetres between the eye sockets; it is on display at Blair Castle. The other three were found in 1815, at a depth of over four metres; the largest of these is in the British Museum and one of the others is again at Blair Castle.

Wolves were the natural predator of the Highlands, keeping in balance the numbers of wild deer and other mammals. Even humans felt at risk. It is thought that many of the fortifications erected by early inhabitants of these lands were not against incursions by their enemies, but simply to protect themselves and their livestock against wolves.

In 1427, the Council at Perth enacted that

ilk Baron, within his Barony, ingangand time of the year, shall chase and seek the whelps of the wolves, and gar slay them . . . And when the Barons ordain to hunt and chase the wolf, the tenants shall rise with the Baron, under the pain of a wedder [sheep] *ilk man not rising with the Baron. And that the Barons hunt in their Baronies and chase four times a year, and as often as any wolf be seen within the Barony.*

So it was that from the fifteenth century on wolves were hunted as a matter of policy. In Rannoch, tracts of forest were burnt down in the early part of the sixteenth century to deny the wolf packs their shelter. When Queen Mary came to Blair Castle in the summer of 1564, there was a Great Hunt (or

The urus (or great ox) compared in size with a more modern cow, standing beside William McLauchlan of Balnadrum Farm

"tinchel" in Scots) held in her honour in Glen Tilt, which resulted in a varied bag, including five wolves as well as three hundred and sixty deer.

The last wolf in Perthshire was said to have been killed by Sir Ewen Cameron of Lochiel at the southern entrance to the Pass of Killiecrankie in 1680 and the last wolf in Scotland was said to have been killed at Findhorn in 1743, after it had taken two children. However, both are post-dated by the reported killing of a wolf in 1747 at Mullinavadie ('mill of the wolf', a ruin now between Dunalastair and Trinafour) by the miller's wife wielding a wooden spurtle in protection of her bairn; perhaps this also was the last wolf killed on the mainland.

Palaeolithic Man

Before the last ice age, the climate was relatively warm. This was the Palaeolithic or early Stone Age. Palaeolithic man was large and muscular, in contrast with the smaller Neolithic race which followed. He tended to live on the coastal fringes of the landmass. Inland was relatively impenetrable forest, which he did not clear, but into which he travelled on brief hunting excursions.

His remains have been found in the MacArthur Cave at Oban and in a raised beach on the Hebridean island of Oronsay. He was a wandering cave dweller, endowed with artistic talents as shown in his articulate workings of bone and ivory which depict the animals he hunted. He does not however seem to have domesticated any animals, not even the dog.

Few traces exist, obliterated in part by the slow passage of the last glaciers and in part by subsequent inhabitants. As time wore on, Palaeolithic man wandered less, settling to cultivate the land. It was not until he began to settle that he began to leave sufficient evidence of his existence to last down the centuries for us to ascertain and examine today. He had no bows and arrows, but relied on flints to make sharp javelin points and sharp triangular axes.

Some flint fragments have been found on the shingle banks of the River Tummel, although one prime location, at the ford to the south of Lagreach (from *lag fraoch* meaning 'heathery hollow') on the western outskirts of Pitlochry, has been submerged since 1950 within Loch Faskally. A barbed arrowhead of yellow flint was found at Glenfender, north of Blair Atholl. A small flint scraper was found at Tomcroy in Pitlochry.

Neolithic Man

Probably before the last ice age, a small, dark-haired race came from the European Continent. They are the people of the Neolithic age, literally the 'New' (or later) Stone Age, who were the only inhabitants of Britain for many centuries, from at least 5,500 BC. It has been suggested that more than half of today's Scots can still trace lineage from them. This race was contemporary with the early Egyptians and may indeed themselves have originated from the southern Mediterranean. The Neolithic people in Crete founded the Minoan dynasty and reached a comparatively high level of civilisation; they had ships and excelled in art.

Here, they were of small stature, from 5' to 5'6" in height, with long, narrow heads and no great physical development. They lived in small communities and led an agricultural life, which was principally pastoral in nature. The very countryside of Scotland was well-suited to the grazing of cattle and sheep and from Roman observations it is clear that the hills were well-covered with herds and flocks. The people began to domesticate not only cattle and sheep, but also pigs, goats and dogs. Later, it is believed that they domesticated horses too. They dressed in animal skins and could knit, although it was apparently a long time before they learnt to weave.

The Neolithic people used stone axes, for hunting, for tree-felling and perhaps also for fighting. At Creag nan Caillich above Killin a source of such axes has been found, which is the only known axe-making site in central Scotland. Up a steep slope, a small seam of hard rock was found and, from this, grey-green stones (called 'hornfels') were tapped out. It would take some twelve hours' work to fashion each axe, grinding it on a sandstone boulder, hammering it with a harder stone and finally polishing it with leather.

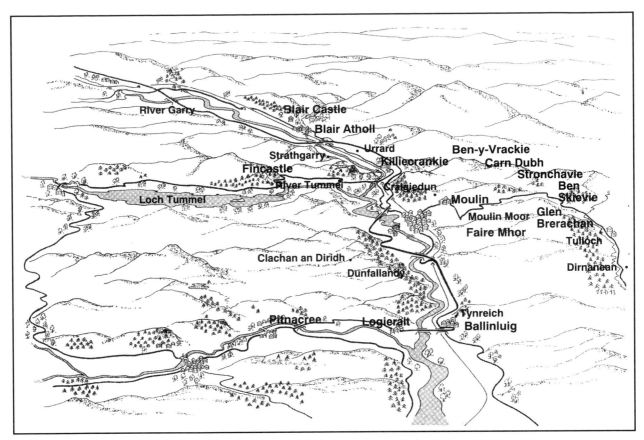

It is extraordinary that they managed to find one of the best seams of rock in Scotland for axe-making, so small is the seam and so steep the hill. Lower down the slope, there are signs of where the fashioning of the axe-heads took place. The use of this site has been dated as being between 2,900 BC and 2,300 BC. Incredibly, for a site where relatively few axes seem to have been manufactured, examples from this source have been found all over Scotland and England, two as far away as Buckinghamshire.

This would indicate that reasonably sophisticated trade routes and other communication links were in operation some five thousand years ago. It also indicates that such items as these axe-heads (and mace heads too) seem to have gained prestige beyond being simple weapons of the hunt.

In this district, two stone axes were found on the beds of the Rivers Garry and Tummel and a small stone axe-hammer was found at Haugh of Tulliemet, to the south of Ballinluig.

It is still possible to come across Stone Age artefacts. Smooth-shaped stones away from any water course may well be worth further examination, as also the curious palm-sized stones which have been fashioned into balls with differing numbers of knobs. These remain an enigma, although it is possible that such unused axe-heads and balls may have been symbols of wealth or power.

Initially, like their predecessors, the Neolithic people may have been cave dwellers. In time, however, they lived in what were probably rudimentary dwellings, made of turf and perhaps strengthened with wood. Later, they developed what are known as 'pit dwellings', consisting of a circular hole dug a metre or more deep and about three and a half to four metres in diameter, with earthen walls, a small entrance and a crude roof of branches and heather. They also built hut circles and settlements, the remains of which are plentiful throughout the area eastwards from Ben-y-Vrackie, into Glen Brerachan and Strathardle, with many notable ones to the north-east of Dirnanean.

Excavation of two of the seven hut circles near Tulloch in Strathardle indicate that these were in occupation around 1,000 BC. Hut circles to the south-west of Carn Dubh, near the eastern end of Moulin moor before it drops into Glen Brerachan, support this dating. The many different types of

Bell barrow on the haugh between Dunfallandy and Dalshian

hut circle, some with single 'walls', some with double outer walls, some even grouped together in twos and threes within one common outer wall, as well as evidence of sequential construction, indicate a lengthy span of habitation.

The Neolithic people have left significant traces of their communal buildings. In about 3,500 BC, these seem to have consisted principally of burial mounds and artificial "barrows". By 2,500 BC, these funerary monuments had given way to more ceremonial sites. In all of these, timber and latterly stone was used. Not only does this mean that these sites are more likely to be discernible today, but they also display both that these were important sites for those who built them and that they were probably built by a whole community. In some cases, sheer size would dictate this. The mound at Bridge of Allan, which was 'discovered' in 1991 as a Neolithic site, is over three hundred and twenty metres long.

One consequence of this relative plethora of funerary and ceremonial sites is that they can take on an undue precedence, whatever the true scale of their importance to the host community. At most, these sites would probably have been to their contemporary communities what religious sites and churches are to our modern communities.

At Pitnacree, just to the south-west of this district, there is a burial mound of the 3,500 BC era. An examination of it may assist our understanding of other mounds within the district. It was constructed in stages over a period of time, to mark a hallowed area, perhaps where corpses were laid until their bones were picked clean by animals and birds prior to burial. Initially, this hallowed area was staked out, literally, by tree trunks; these were surrounded with stones to form a horseshoe shape. Later, more stones were added, built up over time into a mound. Subsequently, this was topped over, with a grave slab placed strategically in the centre of the top, to become what is known as a 'chambered cairn'.

Throughout Scotland, there are many chambered cairns, which can be categorised into different styles. Each style appears to have a reasonably distinct geographical area of influence. The cairns in this district are akin to those found south-west of here, in Argyllshire and Strathclyde, indicating a regular contact with that part of Scotland.

There are a number of burial sites, usually called barrows, within the district, which include:
- one to the north of Killiecrankie at Old Faskally;
- one to the west of Killiecrankie at Clunemore; and
- one to the north of Blair Atholl at Monzie.

These barrows contained short, nearly square stone cists, in which the dead were usually placed with their knees drawn up to the chin.

To the east of the Milton of Fonab Caravan Site, on the outskirts of Pitlochry, lies another of these barrows, in the centre of the haugh between road and river. This is a 'bell barrow', about fifteen metres in diameter and, unusually, it is surrounded by a shallow ditch about two metres wide and half a metre deep. There used to be a row of standing stones encircling the mound, but these were carted away in about 1860 to repair the river embankment. At one time the river may have flowed to the south of the mound, close to the Dunfallandy bank. The ground now on the north side of the river is known as "Dalshian", but it is possible that this burial mound is the *sithean* (pronounced "shian") which, when situated on the north side of the river, gave its name to the whole haugh.

By 2,500 BC, the frequency of these funerary sites become less evident, whilst ceremonial sites become correspondingly more common. These latter include stone circles, other stones ("four posters", pairs and singles), henges (raised enclosures, each with an internal 'ditch') and flat-faced stones which have been marked with cups and rings. These may have marked places of worship, or have been symbols of power either by certain families over their peers or by certain communities over their neighbours.

Cup-marked stones are found not only throughout Britain and Ireland but also in Europe, India and Asia. It is thought that they were the work of the Neolithic people. These cups, with their concentric circles and lines, would seem to be ideograms, but what they symbolise is a secret of the past. Such stones are plentiful in northern Perthshire and include:

(Above) Cup-marked stone near Stronchavie Bridge, in Glen Brerachan

(Left) Standing stone at the bottom of the Balnakeilly drive, Moulin

- one at Badvo, about two hundred metres north of the memorial stone to John Souter (which has twenty-one cups);
- one near Stronchavie Bridge, in Glen Brerachan, on a knoll about one hundred and fifty metres to the west of the former roadman's cottage (twenty-six cups and two incised lines);
- one on the east side of the Cluneskea burn, on the west shoulder of Ben Skievie above Tarvie (sixteen cups); and
- one to the north-west of Tulloch in Strathardle (forty cups).

Some of the stones in the district are likely to be the work of Neolithic man but, equally, some of the pairs and single stones may be the work of later periods, notably the Iron Ages. It is however thought that the "four posters" (four stones in a square) are more likely to belong to the Neolithic period.

There are two single stones close to Moulin, each as it happens standing to the front of the two

(Above) Stone circle above Strathgarry, northwards to the Beinn a Ghlos

mansion houses there. One lies in the field below Baledmund (*baile aodin monadh* meaning 'town on the face of the moor'), which used to be known for some forgotten reason as the 'Dane's Stone', which is unlikely to describe its provenance (as the Danes did not materialise here until about 900 AD, perhaps some two to three thousand years after the stone was raised on its end). The other lies on a wooded knoll immediately beside and to the west of the main gates to Balnakeilly (*baile na coille* meaning 'town by the wood').

Other single stones exist in the district, as at Straloch and on the haugh below House of Urrard where what is now known as Claverhouse's Stone stands (its name deriving from the Battle of Killiecrankie in 1689). There are a number of paired stones, four posters (such as the *na clachan aoraidh* – meaning 'the stones of worship' – to the west of Fincastle and the *faire na paiteag* – meaning 'humpy hill' – to the north-east of Dirnanean) and some sets with less than they originally had (such as a four poster, with only three stones visible but sinking, on the open hill above Strathgarry).

(Below) The stone circle at Tynreich, to the west of Ballinluig

The once celebrated *Clachan an diridh* ('stones of the ascent') lie, now almost forgotten, to the south of Pitlochry near the ridge of Carra Beag ('little rock') and An Suidhe ('the seat'), which together are

popularly known as Fonab Hill. At the beginning of the twentieth century, the *Clachan an diridh* stones would have stood majestically on bare hill and are now half hidden in a clearing within forestry, but there are signs that after the Second World War trees were planted as close as a metre to each stone. Originally a four poster, although only three stones now remain, this site was visited on the first day of May each year, the religious rite being to go round the stones *deiseil* ('sunwise' – that is, clockwise).

There are two sites in the district with a greater number of stones. One is half a mile to the west of Pitlochry, in the garden of a cottage called Greengates, between road and railway. It now has seven stones, although there were originally nine, with a diameter of about five and a half metres, perhaps marking a burial site. The other, with six stones, is still complete and is situated at Tynreich, just to the west of Ballinluig on the north side of the A9 dual carriageway.

Above Moulin, at the top of the Pitlochry Golf Course, lie the ruins of the hamlet of Craigiedun ('fort by the rock'), which must have been of some importance when the old North road passed by it, before General Wade's day. Just to the east of the hamlet, several large stones lie underground, which are the remains of another large stone circle, but how many it contained is not recorded.

(Top) Clachan an Diridh standing stones, as they were in 1925 and (middle) in 1993

(Below) Stone Circle at Greengates

There are in addition a number of stones in this district which have not been given a specific mention in this book, some of which are in poor condition or may not be in their original position. Indeed, it is still possible to encounter stones of which there is no record at all.

Two urns with ashes inside have been found in Ballinluig, dating from the early Bronze Age.

Bronze Age urn found during work on a housing scheme at Buail Bhan, Ballinluig with those who made the find

Celts

The peace which the Neolithics enjoyed came to an end when the Celts invaded Britain, starting perhaps between 1300 and 1000 BC. The first mention of the Celts as such is by the Greek geographer, Hecataeus, in about 500 BC. The Celts in Gaul have been described by Julius Caesar and others as tall, red or fair haired, dark-skinned and warlike. They were spread widely through western and northern Europe, as evidenced by the profusion of Celtic place-names.

The first Celts to arrive had a knowledge only of bronze, but the latter invaders brought with them a knowledge of iron. The Neolithics were not exterminated, but remained as a distinct race, although there would undoubtedly have been intermarriage between them and the Celts.

The Celts called the Neolithics *"sithe"* (pronounced 'she' and meaning 'peaceful people'), which is the same term they gave to fairies. The fact that the Celts bestowed a name upon them at all shows that integration was not complete. It also shows that, by describing them as 'peaceful people', the Celts were accepting tacitly that they were not!

As we have seen, Neolithic barrows became called *"sithean"* (pronounced 'shian' and meaning 'place of the peaceful people'), but called in Gaelic *fairie knowes*. The mystical mountain of the Neolithics was thus called Schiehallion ('mountain of the peaceful people').

There is reason to believe that the Celts, being historically a wandering people, adopted some, perhaps most, of the religious beliefs, ideas and ceremonies of the indigenous Neolithic race they had conquered. Like the Neolithics, the Celts appear to have worshipped stones. Indeed, as late as the Synod of Arles in 452 AD, there was reference to people who *"venerate trees and wells and stones"*. Cup and ring marks seem also to be the unexplained work of these people as the Neolithics before them.

Only two metal artefacts have been discovered in this district from the Bronze Age. One was a flat axe of copper which was found in the grounds of the Atholl Palace Hotel in 1890. It measures four and three-quarter inches by two and a half inches, is roughly trapezoid in shape and has its blade edge longer than at its haft end. Only about ten of the three hundred or so ancient axes found in Scotland are of this same shape. It has been mooted that its ore was Irish in origin. The other was a bronze socketed axe, which was dug up near Pitcastle in 1960.

When Julius Caesar invaded in 55 BC, he found that the Celts had ships superior to those of the Romans, both in size and construction, that they had chariots as good and a gold coinage copied from the Greeks. He reported that they had walled towns, which were probably earthen ramparts strengthened with wood.

The Romans were particularly impressed with the chariots and the dexterity of their charioteers; indeed, perhaps because of this, it has been suggested that the chariot may first have been invented here. Chariots indicate the likelihood that wheeled carts, of a not dissimilar nature, were probably in use for civilian purposes. These chariots and carts also indicate a likelihood of reasonable tracks and roadways, perhaps such as the Queen's Drives locally [mentioned in the next Chapter, as well as the ancient tracks mentioned in Chapter Eleven].

CHAPTER THREE
The First Millennium AD
(From Pictland into Scotland)

The first thousand years after the life of Christ witnessed a time of great turmoil and change in the birth pangs of the new country of Scotland. The indigenous Iron Age races (later referred to collectively as Picts in central and northern Scotland) and the Britons of Strathclyde were confronted by Scots (from Ireland) from the first century onwards, by Romans between the first and fourth centuries, by Angles (from Germany) in the six century, by Vikings (from Norway) in the eighth and ninth centuries and by Danes in the ninth century. The Norman English were the next, but not until the twelfth century.

The Picts, a confederation of Celtic tribes driven together at the beginning of the millennium to face the common foe of the Romans, were successful in retaining the integrity of what is now central Scotland both against the Romans and later against these other comers. By the eighth century, however, the Picts had yielded, ironically to a peaceful revolution, which provided the Scots with dominance of an emerging nation.

The kingdom over which the Scots began to exert control was not the same as Pictland some five centuries earlier. For one thing, its boundaries were much larger, more akin to the country we know today. For another, it was only the Romans who came and went, without leaving anything significantly discernible behind. All the other aggressors – Scots, Angles and Vikings principally – not only came but then stayed, intermingling and influencing language, customs and culture. This is how a nation became melded together from many raw ingredients into the makings of a composite state on the international arena.

Romans

When the Romans under Emperor Gnaeus Julius Agricola invaded Scotland in 79 AD, they advanced at least as far as the River Tay. They met the Caledonian tribes of northern Scotland (later to be named collectively by the Romans as "the Picts") at the Battle of Mons Graupius in 83 AD. Agricola emerged victorious.

This Battle is sometimes referred to incorrectly as 'Mons Grampius', which is the result of one of the very first printing errors, in 1470! That printing error caused the Grampian mountains to be so named although, as it happens, the Battle may not even have taken place anywhere in Grampian Region. Its location remains a mystery still.

However, there are some grounds for believing that the Battle may have taken place at Mause, just to the north-west of Blairgowrie (indeed, *blar* can mean 'battlefield'). The Romans had a major fort at Inchtuthill and another at Meikleour, respectively to the south-west and south of Blairgowrie. Within the *Haer Cairn,* or 'Great Cairn of Maws' (twenty-four metres wide and over a metre high), of which nothing now remains, were found a large quantity of burnt human bones, Roman spears and Roman coins. Victoria, as marked on Ptolomy's map of Britain (and allowing for his ninety degree mis-orientation – see Chapter Four), if it marks the site of this Battle, could well be in the region of Blairgowrie.

After the Battle, the Romans returned to the south of Scotland, believing that they had inflicted a decisive defeat on the Caledonians. As the historian Tacitus (who was Agricola's son-in-law) wrote *perdomita Britannia* (Britain was conquered), but he then went on to admit *statim omissa* (it was immediately lost).

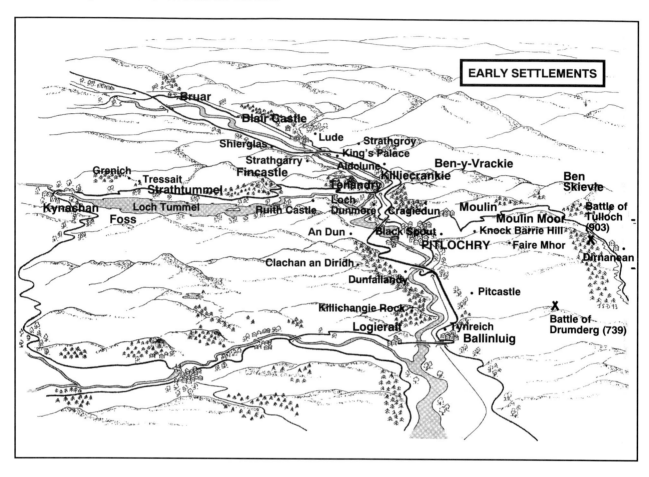

The Romans concentrated on building Hadrian's Wall between about 122 and 138 AD. For the next three centuries, that Wall marked the northern frontier of the Roman Empire within Britain. However, there was the occasional invasion northwards. In about 142 AD, following another advance by Emperor Antoninus Pius the previous year, the Romans began work on the more northerly Antonine Wall, between the Forth and Clyde estuaries, but this was abandoned by the time the Emperor had died in 161 AD.

By about 180 AD, the tables were turning and the aggressors found themselves harried repeatedly by the northern tribes who crossed Hadrian's Wall and inflicted damage on Roman soldiers, Roman camps and Roman pride.

Partly as a result of these incursions, Emperor Septimius Severus began his great invasion in the Spring of 208 AD, crossing the Tay and fighting his way as far north as the Moray Firth. The Roman army was unstoppable in any set piece battle and was indeed one of the most successful armies ever. Where the northern tribes were able to inflict limited damage, usually by undertaking guerrilla-style attacks, for instance on parts of Hadrian's Wall, they were no match for the Romans in any formal conflict on a field of battle.

It is to Severus that must be attributed most of the Roman forts in Perthshire. He set up one of the largest Roman stations at Ardoch, on the northern outskirts of Braco (where substantial earthworks are still visible), occupied Agricola's old fort at Dalginross, Comrie (which commanded the valleys of the Ruchil and Earn), constructed a fort in the Sma' Glen near Glenalmond and one at Gellyburn to the south of Dunkeld.

There is a hill fort called *dun mac tuathal* on Drummond Hill, which is known locally as "the Roman Camp" and it is thought may have been associated, as the similarity of name also suggests, with the fort at Inchtuthil (on the northern banks of the River Tay, about five miles east of Dunkeld), where it is known that the Romans had an extensive camp. It is believed also that the Romans were encamped in Glen Lyon, even if only as a temporary advance station, one of the legends being that Pontius Pilate was born at Fortingall.

It seems that the Romans never came through Dunkeld to Pitlochry and beyond. Yet it has long been said locally that the Romans did come here, in 208 AD (the first year of Severus' campaign), building a camp in the field known as *Dalchampaig* ('field of the camp'). This camp was likely to have been an advance station or staging post, manned for days rather than months. The lines of this camp, whoever built it, were visible at the beginning of the nineteenth century, but were first obliterated by the plough and then, in 1950, flooded beneath the waters of Loch Faskally.

Roman coins and other antiquities have been found in the neighbourhood of Fortingall and Kenmore. A Roman urn was found near Ballinluig. A Roman coin was found near Dunfallandy, which apparently depicted Marcus Ulpius Trajan, who was Roman Emperor between 90 and 117 AD. Of course these items were not necessarily carried there by Romans.

Caracalla led the great Roman invasion once his father Severus fell seriously ill, but after his father's death in 211 AD, lost little time in retreating behind Hadrian's Wall. This was the last time that the Roman army was in the Highlands, although they did not withdraw from Scotland until 410 AD. In their remaining time in the north of Britain, albeit from then on based firmly to the south of Hadrian's Wall, the Romans were required to defend themselves against the Picts (and others) on several occasions.

The Romans conquered Scotland, more or less as they wished, but their failure – and the likely reason why they did not retain Scotland for their Empire – was in not capitalising on their advances. They neither followed up their victories, nor consolidated their territorial gains. They gave the incumbent Picts (and others) time to regroup and retaliate.

The lasting result of the Romans' presence in southern Scotland was that the disparate northern tribes, who had been forced through necessity to amalgamate into a single confederation, remained closely knit after the Roman threat had vanished. That confederation was successful in ensuring that, whilst the Romans passed through the north of Scotland, they did not tarry for long. The strength which came from such unity not only served the Picts well against the Romans, but equally in the coming centuries against the other aggressors on their borders.

Gildas, a Celtic monk, wrote in about 470 AD of the consequences of the Romans' final departure from the Scotland:

> No sooner were the Romans gone than the Picts and Scots, like snakes, which in the heat of mid-day come forth from their holes, hastily land again from their canoes . . . .differing from one another in manners, but inspired with the same avidity for blood, and all the more eager to shroud their villainous faces in bushy hair, than to cover with decent clothing those parts of their bodies which require it . . . .They seized with greater boldness than before on all the country to the north, as far as the Wall.

The Picts

When they first emerge into the light of history, the Picts are found occupying much of Scotland to the north of the Forth. The first mention of a people, called *picti* ('painted people') was in a Latin poem of 297 AD but, apart from this Roman nickname, there is no other evidence that they were a people coming afresh onto the Scottish stage. Nowadays, historians consider them to have been an amalgamation of descendants from indigenous Iron Age tribes, probably of Celtic or earlier origin, who were headed by a warrior nobility.

The Picts may have painted or tattooed themselves when in battle. The Roman poet Claudian wrote in a poem dated about 400 AD that *"the legion . . . reads the marks tattooed upon the bodies of dying Picts."* It is known that the Picts did not speak Gaelic and, although their language has been 'lost', it seems that it may simply have been a dialect of Celtic.

Ptolemy indicated that in about 125 AD there were only ten tribes in the whole expanse of Scotland to the north of the Forth/Clyde valley. The tribe he placed approximately in the Central Highlands he called the *Caledonii*. Two hundred years later, the Roman historian Ammianus Marcellinus divided the Picts into the *Verturiones* and the *Dicalydones*. The former's *Caledonii* and the latter's *Dicalydones* were, as the similarity of name suggests, one and the same, representing further merging of Pictish tribes into larger confederations.

Such confederations were necessary to resist threats from all sides: Romans from the south, then Danes and Angles from the south; Scots from the west (the dividing 'frontier' being Rannoch Moor, referred to historically as *druim alban*); and Vikings from the north. Until their apparent disappearance five hundred years later, in the mid-ninth century, the Picts were successful in retaining their Highland homeland, learning to share Scotland with Scots, Britons and Scandinavians with whom they battled, treatied and intermarried. Indeed, they created a stability which was quite remarkable for such turbulent times.

The Picts carried on rudimentary farming, each family or small community fending for itself and its own needs. They grew wild grey oats and wild barley (known as 'bere' or 'bear'). Most settlements would rely on a few goats particularly, with some cattle and perhaps a number of Highland sheep. These Highland sheep were quite distinct from the tougher Border breeds which began to infiltrate and then proliferate in the eighteenth century, being small, fragile and kept mainly for their milk; their delicate fleeces were spun into 'hard tartan'. Little Highland horses, known as *gearraon* (in Scots, called 'garrons') were kept on most deer forests until the mid-twentieth century, after which deer carcasses began more often to be taken off the hill by mechanical means.

The time of the Picts has been termed a 'Dark Age' in Scotland's history. This is doubtless because little in the way of hard facts remain, other than stones and forts, leaving historians and others to deduce, conjecture and, at times, embroider. Very few examples of the Pictish language exist; most of the Pictish records appear to have been destroyed by the Scots in the late ninth century and what they left intact was probably taken south (and subsequently destroyed by fire) by the Hammer of the Scots in the late thirteenth century. It is clear, however, that the Picts were not worthy of connotations of darkness. Their art, if nothing else, would indicate otherwise.

This district lay near the centre of the Pictish kingdom. Perhaps because of this it is relatively rich in Pictish sites – buildings, crannogs and stones.

Pictish Dwellings, Casteals and Forts

The Picts lived in hut circles, of which there are numerous remains near Pitlochry. These hut circles were formed of sods and stones, built to a height of about a metre or more and a diameter of anything between six and twelve metres. A fire was laid in the centre. The highest concentration of circular enclosures, thought to have been hut circles, is on the wide expanse of Moulin moor, north-east of Pitlochry. They number up to a hundred and cover at least two square miles. Some of the mounds associated with these enclosures are probably burial sites. [These are considered in Chapter Four.]

Although earth houses, or *'weems'*, are of Pictish (or of earlier Celtic) origin, it is doubtful if they were constructed for dwellings. Being built at least partially underground, it is more probable that they were store houses for grain. The only weem or souterrain discovered in this district was to the west of Balnadrum Farm, near Moulin, now covered by houses; it was fifteen metres long, a metre wide and over a metre and a half deep.

As the new millennium progressed, the climate became generally colder. To counter this, the Picts erected small huts, about three to four metres long, roofed with turf divots, An example is above Overton of Fonab, where the remains of one of these huts, with a circular enclosure for cattle, is discernible. On the west slope of Ben Skievie are the remains of three pit dwellings, about three metres in diameter, perhaps one and a half metres below the surface of the ground, evidently having been roofed over when in use.

Reverend Macara, who was minister of Fortingall in the latter part of the eighteenth century, wrote that, when he first arrived in the area, many people in Rannoch were still living in what he called *'scherms'* or low houses, with walls formed of stones and turf about one metre high, roofed with divots, with an entrance hole so small that one had to crawl through to enter.

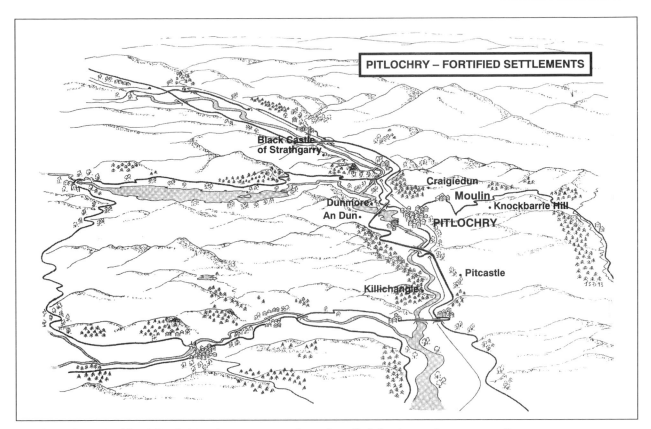

Throughout Highland Perthshire there are a number of small defensive enclosures, usually circular or oval. Their walls were between one and three and a half metres thick, whilst their entrances were narrow and the walls at this point were sometimes thickened to create a passage. Some are prominently positioned, whilst others are on lower ground. These buildings have been included in a chapter about the Picts, but it is important to recognise that some may have been occupied in the Bronze and Iron Ages only, some occupied then and subsequently re-occupied by the Picts and some occupied only in Pictish and early medieval times. Carbon-dating, when applied to a ring fort excavated at Litigan to the west of Aberfeldy, indicated its being occupied up in the ninth century.

These buildings have in the past been labelled as forts, castles (in Gaelic *caisteal* which has perhaps been borrowed from the Latin *castella*) or homesteads. Such labelling would not have been contemporary and just because they were in more recent centuries called 'forts' or 'castles' does not mean that they actually were. The trend nowadays has been to label most of them as defended homesteads, whilst recognising that some sites are more prominent and fort-like than others. Such defence was not necessarily of a military nature, but more of the kind made by natives simply protecting themselves and their livestock against both unwelcome neighbours and animals (such as wolves).

Some of the smaller defended homesteads in the district include:
- one underneath the Castlebeigh Hotel, Knockard Road, Pitlochry, known as Castle Dhubh;
- one near the Black Spout, to the east of Pitlochry, called 'the Black Castle of Edradour' by Thomas Pennant on his tour of Scotland towards the end of the eighteenth century, which is situated about one hundred and fifty metres below the waterfall;
- at least three in Glen Fincastle, including one in the field below Fincastle House, giving the glen its name – *Fonncaisteal* – ('land of the castle');
- two large ones to the north of the eastern end of Loch Tummel, above the Queen's View, one referred to now as the Clachan and the other as the Ring Fort, where an amber bead was found, indicating trade or contact with the continent of Europe, probably Denmark;

- six to the north of mid Loch Tummel, above the farms of Grenich, Borenich and Balnabodach three of which are beside the ancient route between Strathtummel and Struan;
- at least twelve to the south-west of Loch Tummel, at Kynachan, Drumnakyle, Tombreck and Braes of Foss, some of which were on an ancient route between Glen Lyon and Strathtummel, some of which were on an ancient route between Glen Lyon and Loch Rannoch and one of which is close to a stone incised with a cross;
- one called Ruith Castle ('the rushing castle', named after the torrent beside it), located atop the hill to the south-east of the Clunie Dam at the eastern end of Loch Tummel;
- one near Tenandry, at the base of the cliff face known as *sgorr clann Donnachaidh* ('cliff of the Clan of Robertson'); and
- one at Creag Odhar ('dun-coloured rock'), above the Shierglas Quarry, which is very large (with an internal diameter of thirty-five metres by twenty-five metres) and, as an unintentional pun with its name, is classed as a "dun", that is, a defensive homestead;

The ruins of the Black Castle above Strathgarry, now in the midst of a forestry plantation, but at one time affording an excellent outlook to the north-west, north-east and south-east, whilst being on a route to the south-west

Some of the more prominent homesteads in the district, a number of which may have been used as Pictish forts (sometimes called 'duns' or ring forts) include:
- one at Craigiedun where the seventh tee of the Pitlochry Golf Course is situated on top of a knoll which was once a Pictish fort; the fort was circular, about twenty-seven metres in diameter internally, fortified on its north side by stones set with their ends pointed outwards to prevent its being rushed (those stones are no longer there);
- one, visible from the fort on the Golf Course, which is situated atop Knock Barrie hill (1,145'/349m – also known locally as the *faire knowe*) opposite Gatehouse on the edge of Moulin moor; between them, these two forts must have been able to protect the upper Tummel valley, with excellent views in all directions – except due north, which presumably was the least expected direction of any threat;
- one to the west of Pitlochry, to the south of Loch Dunmore ('big fort'), which takes its name from the fortified knoll; this has a sizeable low stone rampart around the summit;
- one in a small walled wood at Pitcastle (indeed giving its name to the area about three miles east of Pitlochry) with excellent views east, south and west; its internal diameter is twenty metres and its walls vary from two and a half to four metres thick;
- one on the south side of the River Tummel, about two miles south-east of Pitlochry on a rocky precipice known as Stac an Eich ('the rock of ice' – 1,181'/360m) above Killiechangie; this is an unusual fortification, consisting of a straight wall, almost two metres high, built across the projecting part of the rock and about a metre and a half thick, with a turf centre and faced on both sides with large stones; in all, it encloses about half an acre and was at was at one time an outpost

of the old castle at Logierait, dating from the fourteenth century, although it is said to have been built atop an older Pictish fort;

- one with earth rampart and intermittent stone retaining walls, called An Dun ('the fort'), situated on a small promontory within Clunie Wood close to *Creag na h-lolaire* ('rock of the eagles') to the south of Cluniemore House; and

- one, known as the Black Castle of Strathgarry, which was a large fortified hut circle with a diameter of about twenty-five metres, now overcome by a plantation above Strathgarry House, beside the ancient route between Blair Atholl and Strathtummel.

The Pictish fort near Craigiedun, now a tee on the Pitlochry Golf Course, with open outlook south-eastwards towards Dunkeld and with the old road from Moulin to Killiecrankie passing to the south of it

More homesteads, relative to the ancient settlement of Moulin, are listed in the next Chapter.

The Picts built the *crannogs* – artificial islands – which were constructed of beams of wood overlaid with stones, usually circular or oval in form. Outside the district, there are several in Loch Tay and one in Loch Rannoch with a tower built upon it. Here, the Black Castle of Moulin was built on a crannog, which was at one time in the centre of a lochan.

Until Loch Tummel was flooded as part of the Hydro-Electric Scheme, there was a crannog opposite Port-an-Eilean (which means 'fort of the island') on which *Donnachaidh Reamhair* – Duncan the Stout – chief of the Clan Donnachaidh (principally comprising the Robertsons) – built a small fortified house and garden. It was Duncan the Stout who was reputed to have found the Chiefs' heirloom on his way to the Battle of Bannockburn; this was the *clach na brataich*, a ball of rock crystal about two inches in diameter, which is reputed to be *"compact of magic"* and can be seen at the Clan Donnachaidh Museum at Bruar. There was also a smaller crannog in Loch Tummel, a little further east, in line with Tressait; its builder is unknown.

Pictish Burial

The Picts had two methods of burial. The first was burning, with the ashes placed in an urn or small stone cist; the second was burial, in a shallow stone cist with a cairn above. When the stone circle at Tynreich, near Ballinluig, was excavated in 1855, several urns containing ashes were found; this does not mean that the stone circle was erected as a burial site, as its use for that could have been by a later people than its builders. In June 1970, beakers of human ashes were discovered at Haugh of Tulliemet, a practice which gave a label to 'the Beaker People'.

Graves are usually in groups of about twenty to fifty in number and from ten to fifteen metres apart. There are several Pictish cemeteries in the district, which include:

- one on Balnakeilly Hill, near the Baledmund march;
- one on the west side of the Kirkmichael road, about six hundred metres above Gatehouse;
- a number on the west side of Fonab moor and on part of Cluniemore, especially one a little to the north-west of the Clachan an diridh stones, with both small hut circles and a circular cattle enclosure nearby;
- a large one near Loch Broom, above Tulliemet;
- a number a few metres north of the Pictish fort at Craigiedun on the Pitlochry Golf Course, which were found towards the end of the nineteenth century, about half a metre below the surface;
- one above Killiecrankie, near Old Faskally House, crowned with the remains of a subsequent church; and
- one near the Golf Course at Bridge of Tilt, where a skeleton dated to 370 AD was discovered in 1985, laid out flat (rather than the more usual sitting position) beneath ten stone slabs.

The traditional method of Pictish execution was by drowning, even for important political prisoners of the royal blood. The victim of one of the executions in 739 AD was recorded as the 'King of Atholl'. This was Talorcan, son of Drosten. Drostren was slain at or shortly after the Battle of Drumderg [mentioned later in this Chapter] by his victor, Oengus mac Fergus, whilst his son Talorcan was put to death by drowning by the same Oengus.

Precisely how the Picts arranged their formal drownings is unclear and these may have differed in detail one from another. There is a Pictish cross-slab stone at Glamis Manse in Angus which depicts a great cauldron hanging from twin supports; the legs of two unfortunate persons stick up in the air, which suggests that they were plunged in head-first and left to drown.

Pictish Stones

The Picts' principal monument is their stonework, of which this district has one impressive example. Given that the youngest of their stones is well over one thousand years old, it is surprising that over two hundred still exist throughout what was Pictland. It is known that over the intervening centuries, many have been moved, broken, incorporated into buildings and memorials, or just simply lost. At one time, there must have been a very significant number standing proud to record whatever it is that their many symbols were carved to mean. These stones, however much spread across the landscape, will have had little to do with the everyday lives of ordinary Picts and much more to do with a wealthy and powerful elite.

Pictish art is graphic in character and no one knows precisely what their designs may mean, although many have recurring themes and recent research has suggested either that they may have been hieroglyphs for the names of chieftains, or that they were public statements of marriage alliances between aristocratic lineages in what many believe to have been a matrilinear society (reckoning descent through the female line). What can be said is that this symbolic stone carving represents an outstanding legacy, incomparable throughout Western Europe.

On the south side of the River Tummel, less than a mile west of the Milton of Fonab Caravan Site at Pitlochry lies Dunfallandy, where there once there was a chapel. The richly sculptured Pictish stone on view there is a hard sandstone. As there is no sandstone within thirty miles of Dunfallandy, it must have been carried quite a distance. It was perhaps conveyed there to be used as a praying stone.

Pictish art was at its acme between 650 AD and 850 AD and, in view of the excellent craftsmanship on the Dunfallandy stone, it was probably executed towards the end of this period. As was relatively common at this later time, the stone depicts the Celtic cross on one side, albeit ornately wrought and flanked by angels and beasts, but not as fine as the Pictish symbols on the other (framed by two serpents and showing seated figures, a cross, a horseman, tools and five Pictish symbols), displaying the harmony which existed between the pagan world of the Picts and the Christian faith which they had more recently embraced. Indeed the two seated figures represent the meeting of the two great monastic saints, St. Anthony and St. Paul.

The King's Palace and the Queen's Drives

The most remarkable site in this district linked to the Picts, apart from the Dunfallandy stone, is situated in a wood to the west of Aldclune and immediately to the south of the exit for Blair Atholl from the A9. Indeed, part of the site was lost to the new road when it was built in 1978 and one might well wonder who could consider planting a forestry block to obliterate the remainder of this unique site, which is probably the largest earthen fortification in the district. It is known as "the King's Palace".

In the centre of the King's Palace, occupying the highest crest, is a square plateau about twenty metres in diameter, with a double ditch or dry moat around it. From the south face of this plateau an earthen rampart extends for about one hundred and forty metres on either side, terminating in a mound at each end, which are the remains of two small watch towers. On the east, the rampart curves northwards, at one time forming a circle containing fully two thousand square metres of ground. In the Statistical

Account of 1793, mention is made of zig-zag stones defending the entrance, but these have all been removed.

Along the south side of the rampart is a levelled terrace, nearly fifty metres wide and standing about ten metres above the field below, which was known as *dail an aonaich* ('field of the galloping horses'), where horse races were held.

About five hundred metres to the north are two *casteals*, nearly round, on the top of a fairly high ridge, having double and in some places triple ditches. There are several obelisks, in a zig-zag position. These were perhaps two outposts.

What is unusual about the Palace is that it was constructed almost entirely of earth, without much in the way of stone. This contrasted with other fortifications of the time, where thick stone ramparts were the norm.

A silver brooch was discovered at the King's Palace during a hastily arranged archaeological dig when the new A9 was being constructed. This is now on display in the National Museum.

(Left) The Aldclune brooch, found at the King's Palace

(Below) The remains of the King's Palace are concealed in the forestry plantation to the bottom left, with the B8079 below it and the A9 above it. The 'sithean' can be seen on the horizon above. This photograph was taken on the Queen's Drive above Strathgarry

From the King's Palace two roads start, still known as "the Queen's Drives". One led east initially, until it forded the Garry opposite Aldclune, after which it circled round to the west, across the face of the hillside where, in spite of the quarry there, it can be discerned yet; on westwards it ran for about four miles until it recrossed the Garry at the ford opposite the old west entrance to Blair Castle, returning to the Palace along the line of the old North Road and across Lude Park, where its line can again be seen as it enters Strathgroy Farm. Its total distance was some twelve miles. The other led northwards towards Loch Moraig and then southwards, a distance of about seven miles. Both roads are between three and a half and five metres wide, so as to be suitable for chariots. Where these roads, which date back to the second or third centuries, have been incorporated into modern roads, their width has scarcely changed to this day.

There is a conspicuous mound on the crest of the hill to the north of the King's Palace, which is about fifty metres in diameter and nine metres high. It has also been called the *sithean* (pronounced "shian"), which indicates a Neolithic provenance. It has been made of a circle of boulders, each weighing on average perhaps

half a ton, with stones and soil heaped inside. Precisely in the centre is a stone burial cist, originally covered with about a metre of soil; it is about one and a half metres in length and one metre wide and is formed of flat stones set on edge, but it has been opened and rifled long ago. On each side of the mound, about fifty metres away, are enclosures of stone and earth suitable for retaining animals. The farm below is called Strathgroy (which derives from *strath druidh*, meaning 'strath of the Druids').

To the north-west of this mound are several small burial mounds, each about two metres high and at one time holding a stone cist in the centre. In each instance, the grave has been opened and its covers thrown aside. On the south face of the hill, in the heather near these mounds, is a curious arrangement of small cairns, one in the centre and five around it in a circle. A short distance to the north are some good examples of hut circles, which are also to be found on the hillside to the east of the burn. This hill is known as *carndeiseil* ('the cairn round which people walk with the sun', that is clockwise, which was the way of 'good luck').

Further north-west again, on the banks of the Fender, stands Tulchan (from *tulachan*, meaning 'little hill'), beside which is another, much larger cairn. In between Strathgroy and Tulchan ran a line of small cairns to the west of Lude House, but these have been ploughed in over the years. To the north of Lude House is the *tom na h'iobart* ('knoll of sacrifice').

Battle of Drumderg 729 AD

Nechtan mac Derilei became King of all the Picts in 706 AD, but his reign was not without its problems and, in 724 AD, there began a period of civil war amongst the Picts. There were no less than four contenders for this over-kingship, namely Nechtan himself and three regional kings, Drosten from Atholl, Oengus mac Fergus from Strathearn and Alpin mac Eachach (originally of Scots descent) from Dalriada.

Oengus was the initial aggressor and this paid off, as he was the ultimate victor. His army defeated an army headed by Alpin at the battle of *monaidh craebi* (thought to be at Moncrieffe, by Bridge of Earn). The next battle brought Nechtan into the conflict; he defeated Alpin at a place called in the Annals of Ulster *caislen credhi*, which is thought to be near Scone.

Like a knock-out competition, the next round was fought between the two previous winners, Oengus and Nechtan. Their armies met at the battle of *monith-carno*, which may have taken place near Tyndrum. Oengus emerged victorious. There followed one more battle, involving Drosten (who, to continue the simile, had a bye in the first round).

This battle took place on 12th August 729 AD, thus the first 'Glorious Twelfth' on the hills of Highland Perthshire. Drosten, styled King of Fodla (Atholl), with his army of northern Picts met Oengus, styled King of Fortriu (Strathearn), with his army of southern Picts. Oengus was again victorious.

These armies met at Drumderg (from *druim dearg*, meaning 'red ridge') which is above Loch Broom, some six miles due east of Pitlochry. The ridge still bears that name. It is an obvious battleground, as the boundary between the northern and southern Picts ran from Dalmally in the west, through Glenlyon and Strathtummel, to Glenshee in the east, passing right beside Loch Broom.

It is stated in the Annals of Ulster that a small tarn on the face of the hill was filled with dead bodies. This small loch or lochan lies about two hundred metres below the crest of the hill and is known as the *lochan dhubh* ('the small black loch'). Locals still regard it with an eerie respect. This lochan is about twenty metres long and three metres wide and is of considerable depth; if drained, its peaty soil may perhaps have preserved some interesting relics of battle.

Drosten was reputedly slain in the battle. Unless his body was carried some sixty miles east, it would appear that Drosten was successful at least in fleeing the field of battle and reaching Arbroath before being overtaken and killed, as the "Drosten" stone at St Vigeans there would seem to mark his grave.

Having despatched his three Pictish rivals, Oengus secured the throne of the Pictish kingdom. Thus unchallenged, he was then able to concentrate on doing battle with the Scots, taking their fortress of Dunadd in Dalriada (Argyllshire) in 736 AD and continuing to keep the upper hand until his death in 760 AD. He obviously encountered a renewal of trouble from Atholl, in the guise of Drosten's son Talorcan, whom he had cause to put to death by drowning in 739 AD.

The Scots

The Scots (also referred to as the Gaels) originated from the north-eastern of Ireland, particularly from County Antrim. Over a number of centuries there was a regular influx of Scots into the western seaboard, from Wales in the south to Ross-shire in the north, notably into Argyll (a name which derives from *earraghàidheal,* meaning 'the coastland of the Gael').

In 297 AD, when the Picts were first mentioned by the Romans, so also were the Scots. Indeed, the mention was of their fighting side by side, further evidence of the confederation of differing people to face a common foe.

However, it was not until about 500 AD that the Scots had sufficiently organised themselves for others to acknowledge their separate kingdom, which was called Dalriada (deriving from one of the Scottish tribes, called the *dal riata*). Their stronghold was at Dunadd, a fort atop a rocky hillock, which was surrounded by marsh and from which ready access could be made to the sea, by the River Add and Loch Crinan.

At its acme, Dalriada was extensive, covering the Hebridean Islands, the West Coast and inland as far as Rannoch Moor – then known as *druim alban* – the frontier with Pictland. The Scots spoke Gaelic, which was related to the native Celtic tongues of both the Britons and the Picts.

Other Irishmen who came east were the early Christians. Perhaps the most famous of these was St. Columba, of Irish royal blood, who founded the monastery on Iona in about 563 AD. In time, Iona's influence extended across the mainland of Scotland and into the north of England.

The Scots began to find themselves hemmed in, by the Picts beyond Rannoch Moor in the north and east, by the Britons to the south and south-east and, more aggressively, by the Vikings to the west and north-west. The Scots were in danger of being elbowed out of their tenuous territory on the fringes of the mainland. They could accept this, or they could themselves try to move further inland, away from their biggest threat.

From Pictland into Scotland

The Picts began to disappear from the national arena during the ninth century, but not as a result of any sudden calamity. Rather, the process of intermingling, inter-trading and intermarriage had increased in tempo, to some extent caused by Norwegian aggression from the north and west, which persuaded the Scots from Dalriada to seek refuge further inland to the east. It was in 794 AD that the Norwegian Vikings plundered the Western Isles and in 802 AD that they burnt the monastery at Iona.

After a further Viking raid in 806 AD, Iona was abandoned in the following year. By 820 AD a new religious centre had been established at Dunkeld, representing a further amalgamation of Scots and Pictish influences. Succession to the Pictish throne fell legitimately through marriage to kings of Scottish blood in the early ninth century. This fact supports the belief that the Picts were matrilinear, tracing descent through the female line, who would of course from time to time marry outsiders.

By 844 AD Kenneth mac Alpin had established Scottish royal, political and cultural supremacy through peaceful means. Some seven centuries earlier the Picts had arisen as a single entity from an amalgamation of Celtic tribes; now it was their turn to be absorbed as an intrinsic part of the emerging nation of Scotland.

Angles

The Angles came originally from Angeln, which is now Schleswig-Holstein in Germany, and established themselves first in northern England. By the sixth century, they held two kingdoms, that of *Bernicia* centred on Bamburgh and that of *Deira* centred on York. It is not known whether the Angles penetrated into this district. Certainly they advanced as far as the Tay, occupying Fife in the early part of the seventh century.

Vikings

The Norwegian Vikings took over the Western Isles during the turn of the eighth and ninth centuries, from which they launched their highly mobile forces to carry out devastating raids almost wherever they chose. As one contemporary commentator wrote: *"Never before has such a terror appeared in Britain as we have now suffered from a pagan race."*

The Vikings followed up their raids by moving in and settling, particularly in Orkney, the Outer Hebrides and, on the mainland, in Caithness. At about this same time they were raiding and settling in Ireland, taking Dublin by force and establishing a base there.

The presence of the Vikings threatened both the Picts and the Scots, provoking the latter to look to Pictland for their future. The religious centre at Dunkeld was ravaged in both 903 and 904 AD, the Vikings doubtless passing through this district on their way to and from Caithness.

Danes

The Danes were aggressors from the east, having travelled up the eastern seaboard from their bases in the north-east of England. Like the Vikings, they specialised in guerrilla-style attacks, intended to paralyse a community. It is known that they came to this district.

The Battle of Tulloch 903 AD

The second recorded battle in the district in fact involved the Danes, who were invading swiftly from the east in about 903 AD. They encountered the defending local Picts at Enochdhu in Strathardle, midway between Moulin and Kirkmichael. The battle is said to have taken place at Tulloch (from *tulach*, meaning 'a knoll'), where there is now a house of that name to the south of the road on a knoll a little to the east of Glenfernate bridge. The Danes were on this occasion repulsed by the Picts.

A grave connected with this battle is in an impressive mound almost six metres long, beside the entrance gate to Dirnanean, with a standing stone (nearly two metres high) at the head and a smaller rounded stone at the foot. One explanation has it that this is the grave of the fallen Danish leader, whose name was unknown, as a result of which the Picts dubbed him *"Ard-fhuil"* ('of noble blood'). It does, however, seem unlikely that the defeated leader would receive such an auspicious grave and such reverence as to name the strath (Strathardle) after him, in preference to its previous name (*strath na muc riabach*, meaning 'strath of the brindled sow').

Perhaps more probable is the suggestion that a Prince Ard-fhuil (or 'Atholl'?), son of King Cruithne, fought in this battle as leader of the Picts and, in pursuing the Danes, was killed where his notable grave now is. It is more likely that the local Picts would name the strath after their own fallen leader, not least because the strath presumably had a previous name which was displaced in deference to this historic event.

Prince Ard-fhuil's grave and its standing stone at Dirnanean, Enochdhu

CHAPTER FOUR
The Origins of Moulin

Moulin: Of Ancient Importance

It was in about 145 AD that Ptolemy, a Greek geographer who worked in Alexandria, published his map of the world, based on information gathered from Roman expeditionary forces returning home. He drew England's coastline reasonably accurately, but he depicted Scotland north of the Tay as running due east instead of due north, a deviation of ninety degrees. Three places (possibly towns) are marked in the centre of Scotland, around the Tay valley.

'Orrea' is thought to be the Roman centre at Abernethy, just to the south of Perth. 'Victoria' is thought to refer to Perth itself, although there has been a not unreasonable suggestion that it might refer to the site of Roman victory at the Battle of Mons Graupius. 'Lindum' is on the north bank of the Tay, about the same distance above Perth as Perth is from the sea. It is not known whether, apart from Victoria, the other names are Latin in origin, or are the best renditions a Roman could make of a local name.

The village of Moulin, as the most ancient settlement of the upper Tay, has a claim to be Lindum. Moulin has three reasons to be considered and, even if all these are discounted, was patently an important settlement for some two thousand years.

The first clue to Moulin's importance is in the name itself, although almost every conceivable spelling of Moulin appears in old records (including Mouline, Muling, Mulleing, Mulzoing, Melyng, Mulone, Mullione, Mowling, Mullen, Mulin, Moline, Muline, Mulyne and Mhaothlinne). There is evidence of some confusion between Moulin and Mullion, the latter of which lies in Logiealmond and was at times referred to of old as Muling; to add to the confusion, the Barony of Mullion seems to have belonged in the fifteenth and sixteenth centuries to the same family of Fergussons who owned Baledmund at Moulin.

The earliest mention is of 'Mulin' in 1276. It is interesting to note the similarity of the two words, <u>Lind</u>um and Mou<u>lin</u>, but that could be a happy coincidence. Lindum means 'fort by the pool', whilst the name of Moulin may come from *magh linne*, meaning 'field by the pool'.

It is clear from all the accounts that there was a pool, or more correctly a lochan, to the south and east of the village. The church was built on a peninsula into the north side of this lochan and a castle was built later on a crannog (artificial island) near its north-eastern corner. It was probably not very deep, perhaps no more than two metres or so. Although there is no high ground to the east which is capable of containing much water, it must be borne in mind that the growth of peat where the lochan was will have been much more rapid than elsewhere, infilling over recent centuries what at one time may have been a deeper lochan than we can envisage now.

The lochan was drained in about 1720, to create more meadow ground, but in fact remained as a marsh for over a century; indeed,

Ptolemy's ancient map

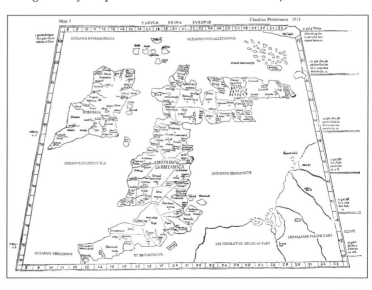

Southern entrance to Moulin village in 1993, looking north. From left to right: Baledmund House on the hillside, Moulin Inn, the wooden Post Office (closed in 1991 – now an antique shop), Blairmount and the Kirk behind

it is still boggy in places. The site of the first Pitlochry High School, a little to the south of this lochan, was called Ballinlochan ('town by the small loch').

Professor Watson considered that the name of Moulin derives from the Gaelic *maoil-inn*, meaning 'a bare rounded hill', but the more likely derivatives could be either *magh linne*, as stated above or, perhaps more obviously, *muileann* meaning 'a mill'. In the sixteenth century, Moulin was sometimes known as 'Balmazie' ('mill town').

The second clue to Moulin's importance is that it is protected by an impressive double ring of fortifications. It is possible that some of these may not be forts at all, but rather defended homesteads instead [as discussed in Chapter Three]; however, they form an impressive link of fortifications, the Gaelic names for which would indicate a defensive purpose. The inner circle comprised four *casteals dhubh*, which were small circular forts made from stone, namely:

- one on the east side of Moulin burn, behind what is now the Moulin Inn;
- one at the seventh tee of the Golf Course, known in recent years as Craigiedun Fort, in view of its proximity to the now ruined hamlet of that name;
- one at Ballinlochan Farm, with a *weem* or souterrain (underground house) discovered nearby which is now under twentieth century houses; and
- one at Edradour, on the west side of the Allt Dour burn and a short distance below the Black Spout.

All trace of these disappeared during the nineteenth century.

The outer ring comprised a number of *casteals*, namely:
- Cnocfaire ('the sentinel's knoll'), on the north side of the railway line, in the grounds of the Pine Trees Hotel near the level crossing at the western end of Pitlochry;
- Cnoc-an-ro-aire ('the knoll of the careful watch'), the wooded knoll to the west of the Local Authority offices near the middle the of Pitlochry;
- Dundarach ('fort in the oaks') four hundred metres further east;
- Cnocfaire (another one) beside the house known as Knockfarrie, near the Atholl Palace Hotel at the east end of Pitlochry;
- Donavourd (*don a fuirt* meaning 'fort by the ford') fully a mile further east;
- the Fourich ('place of watching'), just below Donavourd and above Dalshian, protected by a dry, deep moat twelve metres wide, which is still evident today and is similar in construction and appearance to the Rath at Logierait; and
- Cnoc-an-ro-aire (another one) at East Haugh, a little to the east of Dalshian, to the west of the burn of Allt Roaire.

Whilst such a series of fortifications indicates that Moulin must have been a place of some importance, it shows also that it must have had a considerable population to man so many watching places.

This considerable population is in fact the third clue to Moulin's importance. One of the largest concentrations of Bronze Age and early Iron Age hut circles in Scotland cover the hillside above Moulin, across Moulin moor and extending a couple of miles to the east. This extended settlement is at an altitude which, with a few exceptions, is far higher than chosen since, indicating perhaps a much more favourable climate and better soil than in more recent history.

Some of these settlements were situated on the old road to Strathardle, which until 1830 went from Moulin across Balnakeilly Parks and then up onto the moor (rather than by the current route through Kinnaird). A stone bridge carried the old road over the Kinnaird burn, fully a mile above the

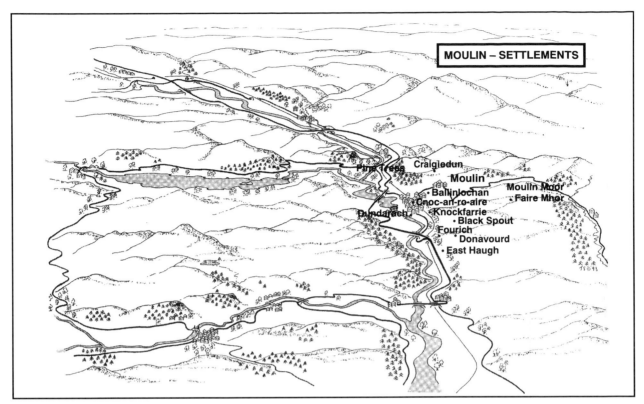

MOULIN – SETTLEMENTS

Pine Trees · Craigiedun
Moulin
· Ballinlochan   Moulin Moor
Cnoc-an-ro-aire   · Faire Mhor
Dundarach   · Knockfarrie
· Black Spout
Fourich
· Donavourd
· East Haugh

hamlet of that name. There is no bridge now, but there are several stones about, many incorporated into nearby dykes on both sides of what must at an even earlier time have been a ford. Beyond this point, the track is clearly visible, running north-east up the slope away from the burn. To the west of this track is a large hut circle, now dissected by a dyke and with an electricity pylon thoughtlessly erected within it. From this point, hut circles can be seen crowning every knoll on both sides of the road for almost three-quarters of a mile.

There are over eighty single and double walled hut circles and homesteads between Moulin and Carn Dubh, whilst more extend in somewhat scattered groups for fully two miles east to Faire Mhor (where the radio masts are) above Ballyoukan as well as south to Dalshian Hill. Most are at least partially stone-built and some had wooden wall-posts and entrance platforms. These hut circles are all discernible today because they lie on moorland which has lain relatively undisturbed since they were last inhabited; who knows how many more were at lower elevations which in succeeding centuries have succumbed to later buildings or to the needs of agriculture.

The evidence suggests more or less continuous occupation of these hut circles between Neolithic times and about the fourteenth century AD. Not all of the hut circles would have been inhabited simultaneously; a group of dwellings may in fact represent the home of one family over several generations, moving a few metres every now and then to create a new abode. As a result of excavations by Jim Rideout between 1987 and 1990, it seems that this area was used as follows (the dates being approximate):

Hut circles on Moulin moor investigated by Jim Rideout of AOC Scotland Ltd. between 1987 and 1990, now surrounded by a forestry plantation

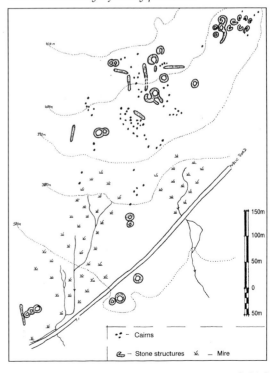

150m
100m
50m
0
50m

·: – Cairns

⌇ – Stone structures   ⭺ – Mire

- from 3250 BC until 1350 BC as pasturage, with some settlement latterly;
- from 1350 BC until 150 BC as widespread grassland, with permanent settlement;
- from 150 BC until 400 AD as grazing for cattle and increasingly for crop production (probably barley, then oats), as shown by field boundaries and numerous cairns;
- from 400 AD until 1350 AD as grazing again, mixed from time to time with some crop production, but with heather cover, promoted by fires, spreading from about 650 AD onwards; and
- from 1350 AD until the present as grazing land, but with little or no settlement (the solitary shepherd's cottage at Badvo now being empty).

During the Bronze and Dark Ages, it seems that this marginal land was home for a comparatively sizeable number of inhabitants.

Moulin Kirk

Moulin Kirk is the oldest in the district, although it is not clear exactly how old it is. In the 'Ancient Church Dedications in Scotland' the kirk is said to have been founded by St. Colm. This accords with the ancient name of the annual market, which was known as *Feill Machalmaig* ('the market of the blessed Colm'). There were, however, some two hundred and thirty saints called Colm, Colmoc, Colman or Columba in the Irish records, so there is real doubt as to which one (or more) of them came to Moulin.

The principal contender is thought to be the St. Colm (originally Colman of Kilroot) who came from Bangor in about 490 AD and was in this district for an unknown time. In due course, he returned to Ireland to become Bishop of Dromore and died there in 510 AD.

The larger of the Crusader graves at Moulin Kirk (with initials 'WMD' inscribed later) in 1925 (right) and detail in 1993 (left) showing recent weathering

The present building dates from 1875, having been rebuilt in 1613, 1704 and 1813. It was used continuously for worship until 1990, when all services were transferred to the West Church (Mount Zion) in Pitlochry, because declining numbers of worshippers could not justify the expense of keeping more than one church in regular use.

The churchyard contains a number of notable gravestones. The two oldest slabs are referred to as "the Crusader graves", because on each is engraved a medieval sword, one being one and a half metres long and the other just over a metre long. Whether these are graves of local Knights of St. John cannot be confirmed, but that is the tradition. On the larger Crusader stone is a crude inscription embracing both sides of the sword which reads:

W M D

1808 Aged 73

These words are nothing other than much later graffiti to the memory of one whose family presumably could not afford its own stone. If these two stones truly mark the graves of crusading knights, they are likely to date back to the reign of the English King Richard 'Coeur de Lion' (when, coincidentally, King William 'the Lion' was on the Scottish throne) towards the end of the twelfth century.

There are many other stones with interesting carvings and inscriptions, some well-worn now. The smallest of the standing gravestones is known as "the Grand Gutcher Stone", the inscription on which reads:

> TIS • MY • LOT
> THIS • DAY • IT • IS
> YOUR • LOT
> TO MOROU
>
> HIER LYES • THO
> MAS • STEUART
> GRAND • GUCH
> ER • TO • IOHNE
> STEUART • LIT
> STER IN DUNK
> ELD • IULI • 1639
> AND • OF AGE 65

"Gucher" (or more often "Gutcher") means 'Grandfather', whilst "litster" (or more often "litstar") was a dyer of cloth.

The Black Castle of Moulin

In the twelfth century, Moulin not surprisingly belonged to the Earls of Atholl. In 1180 AD, Malcolm Earl of Atholl granted the kirk and its glebe lands to the Abbey of Dunfermline. David of Strathbogie afterwards succeeded to the Earldom, but his line had their lands forfeited by Robert the Bruce for taking the side of John de Balliol against him. In 1314, after the Battle of Bannockburn, Robert the Bruce granted all the lands of Atholl to his brother-in-law Sir Neil Campbell of Lochawe, who had been constantly at his side through many years of battle and hardship.

Sir Neil's son, Sir John Campbell, succeeded to the lands of Atholl and was created Earl of Atholl by his cousin King David II. In about 1326, some seven years before his death at the Battle of Hallidon Hill, Sir John built the castle of Moulin on a crannog (man-made island), within the lochan to the east of the village. The landing place for boats was at Balnadrum, where a causeway was uncovered in the mid-nineteenth century. The castle, now a ruin, was nearly a square, twenty-four metres by twenty-three, originally with a round turret at each of its four corners.

The castle was inhabited until 1500, the year of the great plague (*an galar mor*) in Scotland,

The Black Castle at Moulin, in occupation between 1326 and 1500 – a disintegrating edifice: in 1925 (top) and 1993 (bottom)

when it is said that a messenger who had arrived there became suddenly ill and the locals, fearing contamination, waited until all the occupants of the castle had died of the plague before firing on it with cannon, to form a funeral cairn over the victims.

The place has emanated a feeling of awe ever since and has long been known locally as 'the Black Castle'. What little that remains is deteriorating rapidly; there is much less to see now than just fifty years ago.

Moulin: End of an Era

Moulin began to lose its importance when it lost the North Road, which used to pass through the centre of the village. Moulin in effect became one of the first by-passed communities in Scotland when General Wade constructed his Great North Road in 1727. This passed through Pitlochry instead. As the significance of Pitlochry began to grow as a result, so Moulin's position continued to wane.

Moulin has retained particular attractions, because its square is largely unspoilt (including kirk, coaching inn and cottages) and the unity of its colour scheme, like Kenmore's (although not so rigidly enforced as there), provides a glimpse of its former glory.

(Above) Moulin Square in 1993, once an important crossroads
(Below) Moulin Inn, formerly the coaching hotel on the old North Road

CHAPTER FIVE
Centuries of Unrest

Many believed that the world would end at the very end of the millennium, in 999, without regard for the arbitrariness of their reckoning. In 1286, partly because of great and recurrent storms, the word was out that 18th March would be the Day of Judgement. In the bloodshed and during the many hardships in the years which followed, some may well have believed that they were indeed in Hell.

For much of the next seven centuries or so after 1000, Scotland began to be involved increasingly with its neighbour, England. There were English invasions of Scotland and Scottish invasions of England. Some Scots Kings submitted to a recognition of English superiority in order to secure peace. Others were related by marriage to the English royal family and, more than once before 1603, the Crowns were close to becoming united.

Even after James VI of Scotland became James I of England and thus united the two kingdoms, trouble continued, notably when James VII of Scotland was forced to flee to France after three short years as James II of England, in favour of his daughter Mary and his nephew William of Orange (whom his daughter had married some twelve years earlier). This provoked the founding of the Jacobite cause which rumbled on, with notable outbursts in 1689, 1715 and 1745, until its defeat by the Duke of Cumberland after the Battle of Culloden in 1746.

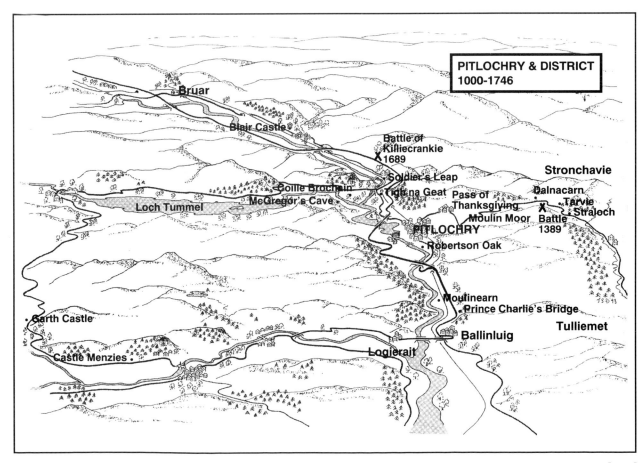

The Hammer of the Scots

For much of his reign in the late thirteenth century, King Edward I of England undertook a relentless, although ultimately unsuccessful, attempt to capture the kingdom of Scotland, which earned him the epitaph of 'Hammer of the Scots', inscribed on his tomb in Westminster Abbey. His army passed through this district on its invasion northwards (when it reached as far as Elgin).

Edward I was involved in the destiny of Scotland in peaceful ways as well. When Queen Margaret, 'the Maid of Norway' as she was known, died at the age of eight in 1290, there were no less than thirteen claimants to the Scottish throne. There were so many because, with the coming to power of the Scots, the Crown began to pass by way of their system of 'tanistry', that is, to the most able person within four generations of male descent of the current incumbent (rather than by primogeniture as followed now, that is, to the eldest male heir or, failing a male, to the eldest female). It was Edward I who was invited by the Scots to arbitrate amongst these claimants and, after due deliberation, he chose John de Balliol, believing correctly that through Balliol he could wield most ongoing influence on the Scottish stage.

One of Edward I's best known acts was his removal of the Stone of Destiny from Scone Abbey (as it was then) to England. This was a provocative theft of the emotive symbol of kingship in Scotland, on which Scottish kings had for long been crowned and on which, from then onwards, all English monarchs have been crowned. He also removed most of the Pictish and early Scots records of government.

It was Edward I's son, Edward II, who took over his father's designs on Scotland, but he was not of the same mettle. His campaign was arrested in 1314, when his army suffered a complete defeat at the Battle of Bannockburn. The victor, King Robert the Bruce, thereby secured Scottish independence.

Robert the Bruce

Remains of Coillebrochain in 1993, with Creag na h'Airigh behind

In 1306, shortly after being crowned King at Scone, Robert the Bruce suffered defeat at the hands of the English forces at the Battle of Methven. He and his survivors travelled all night from the battlefield, crossing the Tay above Dunkeld by what has ever since been called 'the King's Ford' and passing by what was then the main road through Moulin. They approached the Pass of Killiecrankie and then turned west, crossing the ford of the Garry, between its junction with the Tummel and the Pass. Worn out, they rested up in Coille Brochain Wood on the west side of the Garry. The local laird gave them nourishment and drink. A plaque on a ruined gable-end still marks this brief respite.

Tradition has it that Bruce went on from there to fight and win the Battle of Innerhadden near Kinloch Rannoch. His success there, again against the English, who were said to be fortified on that occasion by the Clan MacDougall of Lorn, is commemorated in the names of Innerhadden ('beginning of the battle'), its neighbouring estate to the east called Dalchosnie ('field of victory') and indeed in the name of the glen through which the invaders marched north into Rannoch, namely Glen Sassunn (meaning 'Glen of the English').

During his brief time in the district, Robert the Bruce stayed in a house in Crossmount Wood, to the south of Dunalastair, called *seomar an righ* ('the King's Hall'). That stretch of the River Tummel was known as the Queen's Pool. Some think that the famous Queen's View at the eastern end of Loch Tummel was named after Robert's

Queen, although no road went past the spot until the eighteen thirties.

The Raid of Angus

The 'Raid of Angus' took place at a time of considerable unrest in Scotland. Until more recently it was believed that this took place in 1389, when King Robert II was still on the throne, but 1392 is now the more accepted date, two years after his death. During King Robert II's reign, the country was ruled by his second son (also Robert) Earl of Fife, as his Regent. King Robert II's third son was Alexander, Earl of Buchan and Ross (the notorious 'Wolf of Badenoch'), who delighted in ignoring the Regent's authority in the north of Scotland which, after the symbolic burning of Elgin Cathedral in 1390, he effectively controlled.

Site of Battle at Dalnacarn, near Thomas Telford's bridge at Stonchavie with Dalnacarn Farm and the Pass of Thanksgiving behind

After the death of King Robert II, his first son John duly became King Robert III, but was unfit to carry out the affairs of state, so the Earl of Fife stayed on as Regent, suitably elevated as Duke of Albany. Still the Wolf schemed to undermine the Regent's authority. Away from the Lowland cities, the Wolf (whose appropriate nickname derived in fact from his having a wolf within his crest) ensured that there was continuing unrest.

Early in 1392, the youngest of the Wolf's five illegitimate sons, Duncan Stewart of Garth, who lived at Garth Castle to the west of Aberfeldy, proposed a daring raid into the rich lands of Angus. This gained the Wolf's support, who saw it as an opportunity further to extend his growing influence southwards. Robert de Athole, second chief of the Clan Donnachaidh, also wished to take part because he saw this as his long-awaited opportunity to avenge his wife; she was a daughter of Sir John de Striviling and was due to inherit from her father the estate of Glen Esk in Angus, but this had been given instead to her sister's husband Sir Alexander Lindsay, whose son Sir David fell heir to the estate. The plan thus suited both local and national interests which had been brewing for some time.

So it was that Duncan Stewart and Robert de Athole led perhaps three hundred men or more, who included Atholl men, members of the Clans Donnachaidh, Fergusson and Chattan, as well as other Highlanders, deep into Glen Isla, Glen Esk and other parts of Angus. These districts were harried, their houses were burned and their prized cattle taken off by the Highlanders.

Whilst the stolen cattle were being driven westwards, some of the Angus victims hastily pursued the Highlanders in an attempt to regain their animals. There was an initial skirmish at Glasclune, near Blairgowrie, where the Angus men were beaten back.

Reorganised, reinforced and better armed, the men of Angus, by this time under the leadership of their Sheriff Sir Walter Ogilvie, returned to the fray. The Highlanders were travelling west from Blairgowrie, driving the stolen cattle before them. The Angus men caught up with them at Dalnacarn, near the head of Glen Brerachan, midway between Kirkmichael and Moulin.

There, the Highlanders stood their ground, at the bottom of the Pass to Moulin moor, where the public road now goes. Many of the Angus men were on horseback, clad in armour and carrying lances. They faced determined Highlanders on foot, armed with claymore and targe, on terrain which was difficult for horsemen. Being more numerous as well as more manoeuvrable, the Highlanders soon overwhelmed the men of Angus, killing Sir Walter and many of the other Angus lairds.

By all accounts, it was a ferocious battle. A Highlander, lanced and pinned to the ground by Sir David Lindsay, ignored his mortal wounds and pulled himself up the lance, swinging his claymore one last time, succeeding in almost severing Sir David's foot.

In retreat, the men of Angus made two vain attempts to rally, firstly at Tarvie, where the haugh opposite is still known as *dalchosnie* ('field of victory') and secondly about five hundred metres further east at a gorge known as *claish cath* ('pass of battle').

During the battle, the stolen cattle had slipped over the Pass towards Pitlochry and were soon rounded up by the victorious Highlanders and driven onwards to their homes. As a result, the Pass was called "the Pass of Thanksgiving", a name by which it continued to be known until the beginning of the twentieth century.

Dalnacarn ('haugh of the cairns') is so called because of the numerous recumbent stones marking and protecting the graves of the fallen. Many of these stones were overturned by the plough in the nineteenth century, but a few remain.

As a result of a Council meeting held at Perth, the Highlanders involved were outlawed. Those named included Duncan and Robert Stewart (both sons of the Wolf), Patrick and Thomas Duncanson (of Clan Donnachie [sic]), Robert de Athole, Andrew and Angus Macnayr, John Ayson and the whole Clan Qwhevil (the original name for Clan Chattan – itself a confederation of clans led by Clan Mackintosh). However, the Council was at a loss to determine what other punishment it should mete out.

Some four years later an event took place in Perth which seems at first sight to be unconnected with the Raid. Most recent history books refer to it as 'the Battle of the Clans', with varying degrees of puzzlement as to why this organised battle should take place at all, let alone in the presence of King Robert III. One or two earlier accounts make the connection between this Battle of the Clans as the punishment eventually arranged by the Council for the Raid of Angus four years earlier and this seems to make some sense.

Certainly, it was the same Sir David Lindsay whom the Council charged to arrange for thirty men from Angus "to do battle" on the North Inch at Perth with thirty men from the Highlander clans. Accounts are unclear as to who actually took part, although members of the Clan Chattan are thought to have represented the marauders (which would have been fitting as they were involved in the Raid). Accounts differ as to who the opposing clan was; some say Clan Cameron, others Clan Kay.

Wyntoun, the Prior of St. Serf in Loch Leven, wrote a rhyming Chronicle some twenty-five years after the event and he refers to *"Clahynnhe Qwhewyl"* – 'Qwhevil' being, as we have seen, another name for Chattan – and to *"Clachynyha"* – Clan 'Ha' apparently being closest (at least phonetically) to Clan Kay. Wyntoun, the only contemporary writer, made a connection between the Battle of the Clans and the Raid of Angus four years earlier.

A special enclosure was erected beside the River Tay at Perth for the combatants, paid for by the Exchequer at considerable expense. On 28th September 1396, the King and his entourage were treated to the sight of at least forty-nine of the sixty combatants being killed by the sword. Again accounts vary, but it would appear that the representatives from Angus won that bloody day.

The Wolf of Badenoch did not succeed in his quest for further power and influence. The Wolf's elder brother Robert, continuing as Regent, was sufficient match to the Wolf's ambitions. The reason that there was a Regent was that King Robert III was unfit to carry out the affairs of state, having received a debilitating kick from a horse some years previously.

It is uncanny that King Robert III was crippled by a horse, because his father had suffered similarly. King Robert II's mother was Princess Marjorie (King Robert the Bruce's daughter by his first marriage) who, whilst heavily pregnant, was thrown from her horse and killed on 2nd March 1316. The surgeons were summoned and, carrying out a Caesarean section, delivered a son from her dead body. It was fifty-four years before that son, crippled through life from his injuries, became King Robert II as the first of the Stewart line.

Mary Queen of Scots 1564

In 1564 Queen Mary passed through Moulin on her way to Blair Castle. Some believe that the Queen travelled by the old road around the north side of Ben-y-Vrackie and so on to Blair Castle. However, there is a tale of her visiting the ferryman's house at the southern end of the Pass of Killiecrankie and this she could have done only if she came by Moulin and descended down the old North Road towards the Pass.

It is recounted that, when she reached the ferryman's house, which was then known as Balnafuirt ('house of the ford'), she discovered that a string or two of her harp had broken. The ferryman happened to be a harp player also and offered to repair her instrument. From then on, the house has been known as *'Tigh-na-teud'*, although now said as Tigh-na-Geat ('house of the harp string'). There is no other reason known why the house should be so named.

The house is said to represent the exact centre of Scotland, but is by no means alone in that claim!

The Persecution of the McGregors

The Clan McGregor was persecuted ruthlessly during the sixteenth and seventeenth centuries. Some of the brutal events associated with that suppression took place in this district.

Over the years, the McGregors had clashed with most of their neighbours and, as a result of their oppression of others and their sornings (a good Scots expression for taking 'hospitality' by force), had gained a considerable unpopularity. In spite of their misdeeds, or more likely because of them, they had lost all of their lands. By 1519, they had lost even the power to select their own Chief.

This disinherited Clan – the Children of the Mist as they were called – spread from Glen Orchy into Rannoch where, because of its remoteness, they believed that they could live reasonably unmolested. However, after being there for just four years, the McGregors of Dunan, at the western end of Loch Rannoch, were beginning to feature as troublemakers on a national scale. By the General Band of 1587, King James VI caused landlords to be responsible for their people in attempt to civilise the Highlands. Landlords of the McGregors, such as Sir Robert Menzies in Rannoch, were quite unable to do so.

By the end of the sixteenth century, after further McGregor transgressions, perpetrated in an attempt to win back land and power, the Privy Council drew up a list of one hundred and forty of the Clan who were to be hunted down and brought to trial. The Council charged eighteen Highland lairds with the task of bringing them in, but in this instruction allowed for the named McGregors to be brought in either alive or dead. These lairds acted neither swiftly nor in concert and, as a result, most of the McGregors continued to roam free, defying the King and, perhaps rashly, continuing to cause havoc where they wished.

In 1601 and 1602, McGregors made several raids against the Colquhouns, laying waste to their lands on more than one occasion. In view of this, King James agreed to except the Colquhouns from the terms of an Act of Parliament then in force, which prohibited the carrying of arms. The Colquhouns were thus in a position legitimately to defend themselves from further attack. The McGregors saw this exception as an overt challenge and marched to Loch Lomond on 7th February 1603. There they met the Colquhouns once again in battle, which culminated in what has been known since as the Slaughter of Glenfruin. Notwithstanding the Colquhouns' arms, about one hundred and forty of them were killed by the rampaging McGregors, who returned to Rannoch with all the Colquhoun stock – about eight hundred sheep and goats, six hundred cattle and some two hundred horses.

As a result, the Privy Council proscribed the Clan McGregor on 3rd April 1603, on the day that King James VI set out to London, by which:

> the name MacGregoure suld be altogidder abolisched, and that the haill persounes of that Clan sulde renounce thair name, and tak them some other name, and that thai nor nane of their posteritie sulde call thame selfiss Gregoure or MacGregoure thair efter under paine of deade.

This statute was not finally repealed until 1774, although it was lifted by King Charles II in 1651 in exchange for the McGregors' support at the Battle of Worcester, only to be reimposed by King William III in 1693 for the McGregors' part in the Battle of Killiecrankie. This legislation could also be used against anyone found sheltering a McGregor.

A Perth merchant and his three sons were among the first to abandon this *"unhappie"* ancestral name; they became Johnstons (naming themselves after the former name of their city) and it cost them the significant sum of 2,100 merks to do so, along with a solemn promise never to deal nor to communicate with a McGregor again. Many clansmen adopted the name of Campbell.

It was in fact a Campbell, the Earl of Argyll, who in 1610 took personal charge of wiping out the Clan and spent the next three years doing so. McGregors were hunted down like vermin. No woman of the clan was killed; each was "merely" branded on the cheek and sent with her children to a 'reserve' in the Lowlands.

Not unnaturally, the McGregors of Rannoch went into hiding, but without much success. Some found a cave in which to stay, situated on a rocky outcrop on a lower shoulder of Schiehallion, on the south bank of the river opposite Dunalastair House, which is still known as "McGregors' Cave". They were soon hounded from there, literally flushed out with the aid of bloodhounds, known as *coin dhubh* ('black dogs') and then killed in their forlorn bid to escape across the river.

Others found a cave north-west of the Linn of Tummel, in the face of a sheer cliff-face, to which there was a sole precarious path. Here they were surprised by some of Argyll's men and, after seeing some of their number killed, the rest climbed into a tree which was overhanging the precipice where they clung on grimly to its branches, but the pursuing Campbells simply cut off their arms and sent them hurtling to their deaths at the bottom of the ravine below.

Of the Chief's immediate family, twenty-two were hanged, four were beheaded, three were murdered (two by arrows in the back) and five were *"killed in battle"*. One of the Chief's brothers managed to escape to America – only to be scalped there by Red Indians.

By 1613, the Earl of Argyll could relax from his labours. Shortly afterwards, he converted suddenly to Roman Catholicism, perhaps in an attempt to expiate his actions against the McGregors. Because of his conversion, he lost both his title and his lands, dying as an elderly gentleman of modest means in London.

Some of the Chief's family did survive and perhaps the most famous of these was Rob Roy McGregor. How Rob Roy came to visit this district in 1717 is a strange story. He had fallen out with the Duke of Montrose, with whom he had previously been in partnership. The Duke seized Rob Roy's lands of Craigroyston as recompense for alleged losses. Rob Roy retaliated, on more than one occasion, by reiving the Duke's cattle and by relieving the Duke's factor of the rents he was in the process of collecting.

As a result, Rob Roy became an outlaw. Pursued by Montrose, he took refuge in Atholl, where he began to negotiate with the Duke of Atholl about the terms on which he would be prepared to surrender in exchange for being let free by the Government in Edinburgh. Under a promise of the Duke's protection, Rob Roy was encouraged to surrender at a place called the Boat of Dunkeld. When he arrived, he was surrounded immediately by the Duke's armed men who, on the Duke's command, committed him to his prison at Logierait, delighting to advise both Montrose and the Government of his rich catch,

Whilst the Duke of Atholl was making arrangements to convey Rob Roy to Edinburgh, the prisoner was planning his escape, which he managed to make good when a messenger came to the door of the prison. Some accounts suggest that Rob Roy's ploy was to drink his guards drunk but, whatever, whilst the messenger conversed with the guards, Rob Roy seized his moment, leapt onto the back of the messenger's horse and rode off like the wind, *"o'er the hills and far awa'"*.

The very last of the McGregors of Rannoch, from a family who farmed Ardlarach for generations, was still alive in 1993. There is no other descendant left.

The Battle of Killiecrankie

1689 witnessed the first of three uprisings which were to cause deep divisions between family and friends as well as the most famous battle in this district. According to the doctrine of the Divine Right of Kings, the Stuarts should have continued upon the throne of Great Britain once James VI of

Scotland became James I of England, after his cousin Queen Elizabeth I had died without issue in 1603. However, this was not to be.

When in 1685, James VII of Scotland and II of England succeeded his father Charles I and elder brother Charles II, he showed himself to be an ardent Catholic. The English might have been prepared to tolerate this, especially as they knew that both his daughters, Mary and Anne, were Protestants. What decided them against him though was his overt determination to bring the whole country back to the Roman Catholic faith and the personification of this threat when his son, James Francis Edward, was born to his second wife, the Italian Catholic princess Mary of Modena, in June 1688.

The English retaliated in a bloodless revolution. Principally for that reason, it became known as "the Glorious Revolution", but only in England. In Scotland, nothing about it was considered glorious, nor was it bloodless here. The revolution started with the English Parliament's invitation to King James' elder daughter Mary and her equally Protestant husband William of Orange (who, as a grandson of Charles I, was James' nephew as well as his son-in-law) to come over from the Netherlands. William duly responded by marching on London. One month later, James VII and II fled to France.

John Graham of Claverhouse, "Bonnie Dundee"

The English Parliament proposed that William should act as Regent for the remainder of James' life, on the basis that, although James had been foolish, his misconduct did not warrant dethronement. William curtly informed Parliament that nothing other than the Crown would satisfy him. By a majority of just fifteen votes, the English Parliament agreed by Convention in February to declare the throne vacant. A few days later, William and Mary were crowned King and Queen of England and Wales. The rights of King James and his infant son were thus rudely set aside.

The people of Highland Scotland, many of whom were Catholic and all of whom were proud of the Stuart lineage (which stretched back over three hundred years to 1371), were not content to accept these dynastic changes taking place in London. Meanwhile the people of Central and Lowland Scotland supported the Presbyterians and King William. A Convention in Scotland on 4 April asked William to take over the administration of the country, which led to William and Mary formally accepting the Crown of Scotland on 11th May. The die was cast.

A royalist uprising by the Jacobites (meaning 'of James') ensued within Scotland, the most crucial element of which was the Battle of Killiecrankie. This was fought on 27th July 1689 between the forces of Major-General Hugh MacKay of Scourie, commander-in-chief of the Government troops in Scotland (principally Protestant Covenanters, for King William III) and those Highlanders who followed General John Graham of Claverhouse, Viscount Dundee (principally non-Protestants, many of whom were Catholics, on behalf of the exiled King James).

The Marquis of Atholl had given his allegiance to William (not least because the Marquis was related by marriage to the House of Orange) and was safely out of harm's way in England. However, in his absence, Blair Castle had been seized from him for the Jacobites by Patrick Stewart of Ballechin, who was his Baron Baillie. If this was at the Marquis' behest, it showed a shrewd desire to hedge against either side's winning the day. The order to Stewart had come from Claverhouse himself and, having acted upon it, Stewart wrote to his employer, the Marquis, in these terms:

I crave pardon that I cannot wait upon your Lordship at Pitlochrie for I have received orders from His Majesty's Lieutenant to defend this place [Blair Castle] *for His Majesty's service, which I resolve, God willing, to do.*

Blair Castle today (looking north-east towards Meall Dail Min and Meall Gruaim)

The Marquis was, however, successful in ensuring that, because of his stance, few of the Atholl tenants took part in the Battle on his doorstep.

Claverhouse had been in Lochaber when he heard of MacKay's advance towards Perth. Blair Castle was seen as a significant prize by each commander. Thus when Claverhouse heard that MacKay was moving north he made a hurried march through Drumochter in order to reach Blair Castle first. His swift departure meant that he could not muster all his expected forces; he marched with two thousand three hundred infantry and forty horse. MacKay's forces comprised some four thousand three hundred infantry and one hundred horse.

MacKay, having stayed at Dunkeld on the night of 26th July, marched on to Moulin the next morning, halting his army until sure that the Pass of Killiecrankie was still held open for him by those men of Atholl loyal to King William. He then marched on through the Pass until, at what has since been called 'the Trooper's Well' (near the railway viaduct), first blood was drawn. Iain Macrae, a famous Atholl hunter, who was 'out' with Claverhouse, had been stalking MacKay's advance from the opposite (western) bank of the Garry and, when he saw a cavalry officer tarry by the well, he fired his one shot across the Pass. The officer fell dead by the well.

Early that same morning of 27th July, Claverhouse had convened a lively council of war to consider whether they should tarry for two or three days until the clan muster was complete or whether to go out now, albeit understrength, to confront MacKay. In the end, the council were persuaded to take the latter course by the advice of the respected Sir Ewen Cameron of Lochiel (whose second son incidentally was at MacKay's side, as he held a commission in MacKay's own regiment).

So it was that, by midday, Claverhouse was marching out from Blair, to secure the high ground above the House of Urrard. He arranged for trenches to be dug, which can still be seen today. MacKay came out of the Pass and advanced as far as Aldclune, only to see Claverhouse in a superior position well above him. MacKay formed his lines as best he could on the lower slopes of the hill between Orchilmore and Aldclune. Meanwhile, Claverhouse ordered his troops to march round and round the hill, so as to confuse MacKay about his true strength.

The Highlanders earnestly entreated Claverhouse not to take part in the battle himself because, if he should be killed, they feared that the King's interests would be lost in Scotland. Claverhouse ignored these entreaties (except to remove his scarlet coat) and stood at the head of his troops. There, he was master of position and timing.

The Highlanders waited. In frustration, the Government forces let off their musketry from time to time, to little avail. One spent bullet knocked a Highlander over and, as he regained his feet, he laughed and is reputed to have said: *"Well now! The bodachs* [bad-tempered old men] *are in earnest."*

Still the Highlanders waited. They waited on until early evening, once the sun was no longer in their eyes and then, taking off their heavy plaids, charged in shirts and doublets down the hill, piercing MacKay's line after receiving his third line of fire, in which many Highlanders fell, notably Claverhouse himself. The Highlanders reserved their fire in disciplined fashion, on the instruction of *'Ian Dhubh nan Cath'* ('Black John of the Battles' – as the Highlanders dubbed Claverhouse), until they were close to MacKay's line and, having fired a deadly volley, every bullet finding its mark, threw aside their muskets, ran on with swords raised high, their momentum carrying them into the heart of the enemy.

The Government forces were caught by the onslaught, caught particularly whilst trying to screw

their new bayonets into the barrels of their discharged muskets. Those lost moments cost them dear and they ran headlong, those who could, from the face of such Highland rage.

According to a Jacobite officer, whose narration was not published until 1714, the Highlanders rushed in

with sword, target and pistol and I dare be bold to say there were scarce ever such strokes given in Europe as were given that day by the Highlanders. Many of General MacKay's officers and soldiers were cut down through the skull and neck to the breasts; others had their skulls cut above their ears like night-caps; some soldiers had both their bodies and cross-belts cut through at one blow; pikes and small swords were cut like willows, and whoever doubts of this may consult the witnesses of tragedy.

(Above) The Soldier's Leap, with both railway and road viaducts beyond

One of MacKay's sentries, Donald MacBean, had been posted at the top end of the Pass, but he was soon overrun and pursued by Highlanders down the hill towards the River Garry. He was hit in the shoulder by a bullet, but MacBean kept running and then, faced by the churning chasm of the river, flung himself across at a point where it is about five metres wide. As he himself described it afterwards:

I went above the Pass where I met with another water very deep; it was about eighteen foot over betwixt two rocks. I resolved to jump it, so I laid down my gun and hat and jumped and lost one of my shoes in the jump. Many of our men were lost in that water.

(Below) The Claverhouse Stone, below House of Urrard, with the north end of the Pass of Killecrankie (and A9 bypass) in distance

The spot has ever since been proclaimed as 'the Soldier's Leap'. MacBean lived for many years after and was indeed employed by General Wade some thirty-five years later in the construction of the new road network through the Highlands.

MacKay had lost about two thousand five hundred men as well as his stores, equipment and ammunition, whilst Claverhouse had lost about eight hundred men – all in the space of fifteen minutes. As he himself said:

In the twinkling of an eye, our men as well as the enemy were ought of sight, being gone down pell-mell to the river where our baggage stood.

It was probably MacKay's stores which saved him and the remainder of his force from extinction. His baggage and provisions were piled high by the Pictish stone (known later as the Claverhouse Stone) in the field below the House of Urrard and proved so much of a temptation to the passing Highlanders that they gave up the chase, setting upon the stores and rifling the enemy's baggage. Had they instead followed up MacKay's retreat, then surely hardly an enemy would have been left alive.

MacKay rallied only some four hundred of his men who, after reaching the safety of Castle Menzies, near Aberfeldy, perhaps sang thus of their escape:

I faught at land, I faught at sea,
At hame I faught my auntie, O;
But I met the Devil an Dundee
On the braes of Killiecrankie, O.
An ye had been whare I ha'n been,
Ye wadna been sae cantie*, O;   *[cheerful]
An ye had seen what I hae seen
On the braes of Killiecrankie, O.

The Highlanders came back up the hill to look search for their leader. They found him lying wounded amongst other Highlanders. In the words of Professor Aytoun:

And the evening star was shining
On Schiehallion's distant head,
When we wiped our bloody broadswords
And returned to count our dead.
There we found him gashed and gory,
Stretched upon the cumbered plain,
As he told us where to seek him,
In the thickest of the slain.

Claverhouse asked how the day went and was told *"Well for the King, but I am sorry for your Lordship"* to which Claverhouse replied *"It matters the less for me if the day goes well for the King."* They carried him from the field of battle, wrapped in two plaids. He died shortly afterwards; he was forty-one.

Claverhouse was buried at Old Blair Church. His grave was disturbed inadvertently a century later by a gravedigger, when his armour was unearthed; apparently it was sold to tinkers at first, but was later recovered and the breastplate is now on display at Blair Castle. Many officers fell on both sides and they were buried together near the battlefield. Brigadier-General Balfour, in MacKay's army, is said to have been killed whilst fleeing through the Pass and buried where a large flat stone lies across the path, which is called 'the Balfour Stone'. There is no record of what happened to the ordinary soldiers of either side, dead or wounded.

Victory was duly declared on the side of Claverhouse. When the news spread to Edinburgh (before news of Claverhouse's death) there was panic. The Duke of Hamilton wrote immediately on 28th July to London:

Dundee will now be master of all the other side of the Forth. The King [William] *must send forces to reduce him.*

The following day, the Duke of Hamilton wrote again:

If Dundee takes Stirling he will have all Scotland.

The Duke of Hamilton fretted needlessly; indeed, it was his brother the Marquis of Douglas who received Claverhouse's dispossessed estates.

As his men feared, the death of Claverhouse, once it became known, proved fatal to the prospects of King James. That is why the Battle was so critical; the Jacobites without Claverhouse were not half the threat. His military strategy had been of paramount importance. So long as Claverhouse was in command, Scotland at least, if not England also, was not lost to the Stuart cause; with his demise, the enterprise was doomed. By losing their leader in winning the Battle, the Jacobites effectively lost the war.

A month later, the Battle of Dunkeld took place. The tiny cathedral town had been garrisoned for King William by the newly-formed regiment of the Cameronians (to be known later as the 26th), about seven hundred strong. Flushed with success at Killiecrankie, the Highlanders were determined to take the town, By all accounts, this battle was no less ferociously fought.

The Highlanders, about five thousand strong by now, swept into the outskirts on the morning of 21st August and enjoyed the upper hand at first. Moving forward in the face of stout defensive fire, they began to infiltrate into the cottages of the town. The Cameronians, now short of bullets (even after stripping the lead from the Cathedral roof hurriedly to make more), retaliated desperately by torching the cottages, most of which were thatched. This resulted in the destruction of the town, except for only three houses, and either flushed out the Highlanders from their hiding places or caught them within the conflagration. Within four hours, the Highlanders had had enough and withdrew. This rout of the Highlanders signalled the end of the first Rising.

After the Battle of Dunkeld, General MacKay marched once more through the Pass of Killiecrankie in order to take Blair Castle, this time without any opposition. He placed a garrison of five hundred men there and ensured that the locals surrendered their arms; he required each of them to take an oath of allegiance to King William and Queen Mary.

MacKay learnt from his defeat at the Battle of Killiecrankie. It was he who encouraged the army to adopt a newly designed bayonet which could screw onto the outside of the gun barrel. The fact that until then it had to be pushed actually into the barrel itself, like a plug, had been a crucial failure of equipment, as each of his men was effectively unarmed and undefended in those critical moments between firing his last bullet and affixing his bayonet in order to engage the enemy at closer quarters. MacKay himself died in battle three years after Killiecrankie.

Jacobite Rebellion 1715

In 1694, Queen Mary died without issue. The dethroned James VII and II died in 1701 and, with his death, it seemed that the way was at last clear for his son Prince James to succeed to the throne. However, the Whigs in Parliament were determined that Prince James should not do so. By just *one* vote, the English Parliament passed the Act of Settlement in 1701, confirming that Mary's sister Anne would succeed William III and that, if Anne should die childless, the Crown would pass to the Electress Sophia of Bohemia, a grand-daughter of James VI and I. Thus were the descendants of Charles I set aside.

William III died in 1702, to be succeeded by Anne. By the Act of Union of 1707, the Scots Parliament became bound to the Act of Settlement passed in England six years earlier. In 1714, Queen Anne died, without issue. In terms of the Act of Settlement of 1701, the Crown was duly offered to George the Elector of Hanover (his mother the Electress Sophia having died), who thus became George I. This was insult added to injury for the Jacobites and, indeed, for any adherent to the Divine Right of Kings, who saw the exiled Stuarts as the major claimants.

So it was that in 1715 the Earl of Mar raised some fifteen thousand Jacobite Highlanders at Braemar against King George I. Their intention was none other than to recapture the throne for Prince James (Francis) Edward Stuart – the Old Pretender as he was dubbed by history – the only one of James VII and II's fourteen legitimate children still alive. Once again, families throughout the land were divided. The Duke of Atholl (elevated from Marquis in 1703) found that his support for the Hanovarians was matched only by that of his second son; his other three sons were Jacobites.

The Jacobites marched southwards through Glenshee and westwards up Strathardle. At Kirkmichael they met up with the Marquis of Tullibardine (the Duke of Atholl's eldest son), where their banner was unfurled at the park which to this day is still called the Bannerfield. Five hundred men from Atholl joined the Jacobite cause, in spite of the Duke's support for King George. They marched on to Moulin to rest and refresh themselves.

At Moulinearn, the coaching inn (as it then was) three miles to the east of Pitlochry, the Jacobites were joined by the Earl of Breadalbane's men, who had just returned from invading Argyllshire. The Earl himself had been summoned to Edinburgh, but made his excuses by presenting a note from his physician in Perth and another from the minister of Kenmore each stating that he was too old and infirm to travel; yet the very next day, he did indeed travel, to meet the Earl of Mar at Moulinearn. By the time the Jacobites reached Dunkeld on 26th September 1715, there were about one thousand four hundred Atholl men alone in their ranks.

The Jacobites continued their march south. The army divided. Some, including most from this district, marched into England, where they engaged with General Mackintosh's forces at the Battle of Preston on 14th November 1715, after which many of them were taken prisoner. Finlay Fergusson of Baledmund (Moulin) was imprisoned in Liverpool whilst Archibald Butter of Pitlochry secured a pardon in June 1716. The Rebellion fizzled out, partly because of this Battle, but principally because of poor leadership. The previous day, 13th November, the remainder of the Jacobite army, about four thousand men under the Earl of Mar, had met one thousand men under the command of the Earl of Argyll at Sheriffmuir, which had resulted in an embarrassing stalemate.

Prince James Edward escaped with the Earl of Mar, the Marquis of Tullibardine and the Duke of Atholl's third son, Lord George Murray, to France. The youngest of the Duke's sons, Lord Charles Murray, who had been taken prisoner at the Battle of Preston, was granted a reprieve in 1717 through the good offices of his father, but died three years later.

In 1716, the Duke was successful in petitioning Parliament to vest his titles and estate upon his second son, the loyal Lord James, who succeeded to the Dukedom in 1724.

There was an abortive rebellion in 1719, sometimes referred to as 'the Little Rising', in which both the Marquis of Tullibardine and Lord George Murray were again involved, but no one else of this district appears to have been. This was because the rebellion was confined to its source on the Scottish mainland within Wester Ross. The Marquis was forced to remain in exile but Lord George Murray returned secretly to Scotland in 1724 to visit his dying father and, through his father's tireless work to support his Jacobite sons, gained a pardon in 1725 (just after his father's death as it happened) and took up residence at Tullibardine.

Jacobite Rebellion 1745

On 19th August 1745, Prince James Edward Stuart's son, Charles Edward (Louis John Casimir Silvester Maria, to list all his other Christian names) – Bonnie Prince Charlie, also known as the Young Pretender – raised his red and white silk Stuart standard at Glenfinnan in opposition to King George II, who had been on the throne since 1727. He was then twenty-five years old. Amongst his followers was the Marquis of Tullibardine, who was in fact the one honoured to unfurl the standard.

The Duke of Atholl hastily departed on hearing of Prince Charlie's rapid advance towards Blair Castle, leaving it for his elder brother the Marquis to reclaim after nearly thirty years of exile; the Marqui claimed also his ducal inheritance. Thus for a time there were two Dukes of Atholl!

Lord George Murray, respected Jacobite General

In spite of his pardon in 1725, Lord George Murray also came out again for the Jacobites. As Lieutenant-General, he was responsible for the Jacobite victories. Unfortunately, Bonnie Prince Charlie and Lord George did not see eye to eye. It could be argued that their clashes caused the ultimate and unforgettable defeat of the Jacobites at Culloden. Johnstone was to say:

> Had Prince Charles slept during the whole of the expedition, and allowed Lord George Murray to act for him according to his own judgement, he would have found the Crown of Great Britain on his head when he awoke.

Bonnie Prince Charlie stayed at Blair Castle for two days from 31st August 1745, spending the last night at Lude at a dance in his honour. The tartan jacket he wore that night is on display in the Clan Donnachaidh Museum at Bruar Falls.

On 3rd September, the Prince passed through Pitlochry, stopping for refreshment with the Butter family at the old Mansion House of Pitlochry, which used to jut out into the southern half of the main street, where the BP Garage is now. Thereafter, it was affectionately known as "the Prince Charlie House" until it was demolished almost exactly two hundred years later.

The Prince travelled on eastwards, staying at the Moulinearn Inn, after which he gathered his troops together at one of Wade's bridges on the old road between Moulinearn and Ballinluig, before moving on to Dunkeld and thence to Perth. So it was that Moulinearn featured as a rallying point for the Jacobites in both the '15 and the '45.

The bridge where the Prince stood became known thereafter as "Prince Charlie's Bridge" and continued to carry the Great North Road, until realignments which were made necessary when the railway track was laid in 1862. The bridge is still visible, hidden and forgotten in the woods just to the north of the new A9 dual carriageway between Moulinearn and Tynreich. Its arches are still intact, although the middle has

Prince Charlie's Bridge, now disintegrating within the woods between Moulinearn and Ballinluig

collapsed; in the unkempt undergrowth are traces of the road on either side. It carries an air of history.

Whilst the Jacobite army was in this district, church services at Moulin were suspended for several Sabbaths as the minister was known to entertain hostile feelings towards their cause. The only loss he appears to have sustained as a result was when some of Prince Charles' followers (Camerons, it is said) entered the Manse around 3rd February and relieved him of silver, linen and his dried summer preserves.

From Perth, Bonnie Prince Charlie marched on to Edinburgh, where he waited to raise more men for his intended invasion of England. In the event, his council of war approved the decision to march south by only one vote. Yet, within twenty-one days of entering England, the Prince was at Derby, only one hundred and thirty miles from London. It was Lord George Murray who supported the decision taken on 5th December 1745 to make an orderly retreat homewards. The army had regained Scotland by 20th December and was victorious at the Battle of Falkirk on 17th January 1746.

At the beginning of February, William Augustus, Duke of Cumberland, fourth son of King George II, arrived in Perth, just before his twenty-fourth birthday. As soon as the Highlanders vacated Blair Castle on their way north, Cumberland instructed Sir Andrew Agnew to advance from Dunkeld in order to take the Castle. Agnew's force of five hundred men of the 21st Royal North British Fusiliers, mostly Protestants, passed through Pitlochry and achieved their objective on 8th February.

As soon as the news broke, Lord George Murray returned south from Inverness on 13th March with four hundred men from the Atholl Brigade and three hundred Macphersons. Having carried a successful raid with Cluny Macpherson on barracks and outposts throughout Atholl and Rannoch, Lord George Murray rallied his men at Bruar and travelled on 17th March to Old Blair in order to reclaim the Castle. It was of course Lord George Murray's family home, claimed by both his elder brothers – now it was his turn to try to gain entry!

Early on, Sir Andrew received a surrender offer from Lord George. As none of the Highlanders was prepared to deliver it, it was taken by Molly, the barmaid from the Inn at Old Blair who, before the siege, had been on good terms with Agnew's officers. This offer was peremptorily refused. Lord George threatened to demolish the Castle, although it was his family's home. Indeed, the Marquis had told him to demolish the Castle if necessary, as a "public service".

Lord George's two small cannon fired two hundred and seven shots in all into the Castle. The

The front elevation of Blair Castle, as it was at the time of the siege in 1746, including Comyn's Tower

cannon were too small to cause any significant damage, as he was aware, so he ordered one hundred and eighty-five of the shots to be heated red-hot. On impact into the roof timbers, these were intended to start an inferno. However, the thoughtful defenders rushed diligently around after each salvo, scooping up the 'hot shots' with a large soup ladle and plunging them harmlessly into tubs of cold water, well not water exactly (as this was very scarce within the besieged Castle) but the contents of its chamber pots. Scorched timbers can still be seen in the Castle attics.

Some of his men had a ploy to place a dummy of Sir Andrew in an upper window, dressed up in one of his uniforms and adorned with an eyeglass. This was successful in drawing the Highlanders' fire, but Sir Andrew was not amused and ordered the effigy to be removed.

Sir Andrew's forces were however soon in a desperate plight, as they had finished all the food within the Castle and were reduced to eating horseflesh. Still they held on.

Sir Andrew managed to smuggle out a message to Dunkeld for reinforcements. This was carried by the Duke's gardener, who had been caught up in the siege within the Castle. He stole out in the middle of the night, at first on horseback. On being surprised by some Highlanders, he lost his mount and so made the rest of his way to Dunkeld on foot.

There, Lord Crawford responded by marching north with two hundred and fifty of the St. George's Dragoons and bringing with him the Prince of Hesse leading four battalions (about one thousand one hundred men) of Hessian troops, the last mercenaries to fight in Britain. They camped at Haugh of Dalshian and then travelled north through Pitlochry towards the Castle.

Lord George, with the double news of their imminent arrival and of the Duke of Cumberland's march towards Inverness, raised the siege on 1st April, the last siege in Britain, and withdrew to Inverness. He was perhaps hasty in so doing, because those German mercenaries refused to enter the Pass of Killiecrankie, complaining to their officers for proposing to lead them *"beyond the boundaries of human existence"*. The black memories of 1689 were still strong. James Duke of Atholl was with Lord Crawford and so, had Lord George lingered and fought these troops approaching from the south, brother would have been opposed to brother in battle. Instead, by 3rd April, Lord George and the Atholl Brigade were back in Inverness.

As Lord Crawford drew up at last to the Castle, at lunchtime on 3rd April, he was met by Sir Andrew and his starving officers. Sir Andrew welcomed him thus: *"My Lord, I am very glad to see you, but by ···· you have been very dilatory and we can give you nothing to eat."*

The Duke of Cumberland called in at Blair Castle to commend Sir Andrew for his stout defence of the Castle. Cumberland was on his way south, after his defeat of the Jacobites at the Battle of Culloden, which took place on 16th April 1746.

The Prince's Highlanders did not have their accustomed advantages in this famous Battle, which actually took place on Drumossie Moor to the south-east of Inverness. The ground, being flat and boggy, was more suitable for the enemy's cannon – which was used as a deadly punitive prelude to battle for some twenty-five minutes – than for their usual downhill charge, as at Killiecrankie. The timing was not particularly good, as they were generally weary from the long campaign and had spent most of the previous night in an abortive raid on Cumberland's camp. The conditions were the worse for them, as they found themselves blinded by stinging sleet. Their leadership was poorer than it might have been, as the Prince insisted on taking command himself rather than relying on the greatly experienced Lord George Murray.

Yet, only some three thousand Highlanders (about three-fifths of the Jacobite army) were in the field and only about one thousand of them were killed. The Jacobites' initial conclusion was that the battle had been a defeat but not a decisive one. Lord George Murray had retreated from the battlefield with flying colours and "with the greatest regularity". Indeed, both Lord George Murray and Donald Cameron of Lochiel began planning towards a continued offensive for the summer. What changed an indecisive result into a resounding defeat was Bonnie Prince Charlie's own decision to flee. Without him, the Highlanders were truly lost.

The Atholl Brigade, comprising three battalions, having had no more than three hours' sleep the previous night, found themselves wedged in and pushed forward out of line on the right flank of the Jacobite battleline at Culloden. Having endured enemy cannon fire for too long they were prompted into a military charge in support of the impatient MacIntoshes. They ran forward, although forced to the left by the line of an old turf dyke. Their flank was thus exposed to the firepower of Cumberland's forces, to which they were not really able to respond. Very few of the brave men of the Atholl Brigade returned from that carnage. For example, of the forty-five men from the estate of Kynachan (by Tummel Bridge) who went north to Culloden, only one returned – and he in chains.

Cumberland's reprisals throughout the Highlands, by which he took full advantage of his enemy's flight, were severe, earning him the nickname 'Butcher'. Those recriminations were fiercer than they might have been, given Cumberland's belief that all Highlanders were Jacobites; thus innocents were punished along with the guilty. His soldiers hunted throughout this district for those who had been 'out' with the Prince. In doing so, they carried out punitive raids and harried the locals, many of whom were the ladies to whom now fell the charge of farms and estates until their infant sons were of age. These were hard and harsh times indeed.

George Robertson of Faskally was one of those who had been out in the '45 and, fleeing south after the defeat at Culloden, hid in a farmhouse beside the Aldour burn (from *allt dour* 'burn of the otter'), in those days fully half a mile to the east of Pitlochry. When the Government soldiers came to flush him out, he saw them coming. He sneaked out of the house and escaped by crawling along the burn and climbing into a large oak tree nearby, until the search was over. Afterwards, he made good his escape to France. That tree became known inevitably as "the Robertson Oak" and stands now beside the sewage treatment work at Aldour, on the south-eastern outskirts of Pitlochry, opposite the Blair Athol Distillery. The tree is reckoned to be some four hundred years old. The farmhouse still exists, now part of the Distillery's visitor centre.

Sir Andrew Agnew's greatest moment had been some three years before the siege of Blair Castle, at the Battle of Dettingen against the French, the last battle led by a British King (George II). It fell to Agnew to address the men before battle. He made the curtest of speeches: "*My lads, you see these loons on yon hill there, if ye denny kill them, they'll kill you. Dinna fire till ye see the whites of their een.*"

Earlier in his life, Agnew gained some notoriety when eloping and marrying the fifteen year old daughter of a fellow officer, but the alliance was successful by any accounts, lasting for fifty-seven years and producing eighteen children. It was not just on the field of battle that Sir Andrew performed his duty.

The Robertson Oak at Aldour, Pitlochry – in solitary splendour in 1925 (on left) and accompanied by the town's sewage treatment works in 1993 (on right)

Bonnie Prince Charlie is often portrayed as an ineffectual dandy. Certainly, in the despondency of his later life as an exile abroad, without a cause, he cut less than a regal dash. His faults within his campaign on the Scottish mainland were his inability to realise his shortcomings as a general on the field of battle and his disagreements with the one man, Lord George Murray, who was his ideal battle commander, if only the Prince knew it. Those disagreements coloured the decision to fight at Culloden at all and then the Prince's disastrous decision to flee the country.

That Bonnie Prince Charlie was a doughty campaigner for all that is perhaps best displayed by the extraordinary journey he undertook in his escape from the broken battlefield of Culloden, in the knowledge that there would be a price upon his head. That price was in fact set at £30,000. The Prince's journey lasted five months, including some two hundred and eighty miles on the mainland, difficult sea crossings and further journeys across Skye and through the Outer Hebrides, before his eventual escape to France. His travels were undertaken across open hill, in his normal clothes and with little food. In spite of the sizeable bounty, he was never once betrayed, neither by Flora MacDonald nor by many other equally praiseworthy helpers, some of whom were Hanoverian opponents to the Jacobites, including Flora MacDonald's own stepfather.

The Prince's flight ended in Rome, where he rediscovered his weakness for wine, dying there in 1788. After Culloden, Lord George Murray never saw the Prince again; after hiding up for eight months in Glenartney, he travelled to Holland, where he died in 1760 after extensive travels around Europe.

Chapter Six
The Origins of Pitlochry

What's in a Name?

The name of this essentially Victorian town was thought to be a corruption of *Pit cloich aire* ('place of the sentinel stone'), a name tracing back to 208 AD, when Emperor Septimus Severus led his forces across Scotland. Whilst many commentators do not believe that the Romans penetrated Highland Perthshire, there has been a legend locally that the Romans did have a camp on the north bank of the River Tummel, now submerged under Loch Faskally, on what was the old Recreation Ground and which was called *Dalchampaig* ('field of the camp').

Certainly, there were signs of that camp at Dalchampaig still visible in the nineteenth century. If not occupied by the Romans, as a temporary advance or staging camp on an expedition through this district, then it is difficult to suggest who might have constructed and manned an orderly camp by the River Tummel.

The resident Picts from Moulin were said to have responded to this Roman threat by positioning their own sentinel behind a large boulder stone, situated where Tigh-na-Cloich ('house of the stone') Hotel now is in Larchwood Road, so as to keep watch on the Romans in the camp below. From history's point of view, it is sad to record that this stone was blasted away in more recent times as it was an obstacle in the Hotel grounds.

The Prince Charlie House jutting into Pitlochry's main street until demolished in 1947

Sunnybrae Cottage, Pitlochry's oldest building

There is another sentinel stone a little higher up the hill, in the grounds of Clach-na-faire ('stone of watching'), just to the north of Strathview Terrace, which is probably much smaller now (mainly because of erosion) than it was almost two thousand years ago.

In fact there are many stones littered about the hillsides in the district, either exposed outcrops, or the detritus of bygone glaciers. It is therefore more likely that the town's name derived, albeit less romantically, from the Pictish word *pet* ('place' or 'piece of land') and the Gaelic words *cloich riach* ('stones cutting the surface'). There is some evidence that at least one of the three hamlets was referred to principally as 'Clochrie'. This seems the most likely derivation.

Pitlochry is located at the bottom of a strath; indeed, all roads rise out of the main street. For a town in the Highlands, Pitlochry is surprisingly low, its Post Office being only about 330 feet (100m) above sea level. The Irvine Memorial Hospital is about 455 feet (140m) above. The 1,000 feet (300m) mark is not attained until Gatehouse on the southern edge of Moulin moor. In the Gaelic, *pit* can mean 'a hollow', which would also seem appropriate.

What is certain is that the name of Pitlochry does not have anything to do with its being a place or a hollow beside a loch. Until Loch Faskally was created in 1950, there was no loch beside Pitlochry; the nearest loch, which was in fact a lochan only, was further up the hill, beside Moulin.

Pitlochry was shown on the 1754 Military Survey as 'Pitclochrie', but for long was known as and spelt 'Pitlochrie' until its current spelling first appeared in the Post Office Guide of 1882, which quickly received general acceptance.

Old Pitlochrie

Before Pitlochry was established as a village, it was three small and separate hamlets. The westmost one was in the area where Larchwood Road now is. What is said to be the oldest building in the town, formerly part of this hamlet, is the stone cottage, with red corrugated iron roof, which sits at the bottom of Larchwood Road.

This cottage, now known as Sunnybrae Cottage, was once a public house. Whilst there is nothing unusual in that – there were plenty drinking establishments in the old days, as now – this one was the scene of a murder in about 1855. Two local cousins, Stewart of Bonskeid and Stewart of Shierglas, had looked in on their way back from the Dunkeld Market for some refreshment; unfortunately, they began to quarrel heatedly and Shierglas drew his dirk, stabbing his cousin to death. He fled to Holland, having hidden in the Faskally Wood until after his cousin's funeral. Indeed, there was a saying that if a murderer could see daylight under the coffin of his victim, he himself would escape punishment; so it was with Stewart of Shierglas.

The middle hamlet was situated near what is now the centre of Atholl Road, on both sides of the Moulin burn. In those days the main road used to cross the burn, not as now over a bridge, but by a ford; in fact in those days there was quite a slope eastwards down the hill from Fisher's Hotel to the river; this was even so after it was first bridged. Later, that slope was infilled so that few people are aware that when they pass the southern end of Bonnethill Road they are in fact travelling over a bridge. The middle hamlet was shown as 'Midd Clochrie' on Taylor and Skinner's road book of 1776.

The Mill House, dating from 1701, was situated within this middle hamlet, on the opposite side of Atholl Road from where the Bank of Scotland now is. It became known as the Prince Charlie House [as mentioned in the previous Chapter] after the Prince's brief visit on his way south in 1745. Some accounts indicate that he stayed the night there, but this is not the case; he spent the previous night at Blair Castle, after attending a dance in his honour at Blair Castle, and the next night at the Inn at Moulinearn. After the Moulin burn had been bridged and the level of the main street had been raised, the Prince Charlie House looked very strange; not only did it jut out into the main street, but also its first floor was all that remained visible above street level. Latterly it was both a barber's shop and Thorne's confectionery shop until demolished in May 1947.

The mill did not move a little further north to the present site of the Old Mill until about 1827, the last oatmeal being ground there in 1923.

The middle hamlet also embraced the rising ground immediately to the east of the Moulin burn, which was known as 'Bonnethill', because at one time a 'Pitlochry bonnet' was manufactured there [see Chapter Eight]. There were two rows of cottages and a small square of thatched cottages.

A typical early 18th century cottage, this one at Parkcroy on the eastern edge of Pitlochry

Atholl Road in about 1880, with Gibsons' Stores (now, from left, Panache and J.D. Munro; John Menzies; and the Country Collection) and with Fisher's Hotel beyond

The third hamlet was a little higher up the hill to the north-east of Bonnethill, at Toberargan. It is probably the oldest of the three. When St. Colm founded the church of Moulin, it is said that he had a preaching station at Toberargan, at a well known as *tobar chalmaig* ('St. Colm's Well'), situated to the south of the junction of Toberargan Road with Lower Oakfield, which was covered over a long time ago. There is another well which still exists, at the bottom of Well Brae; indeed the name of Toberargan derives from it (*tobar fheargain* being 'Feargan's Well' and St. Feargain being the fourth Abbot of Iona, who died in 623 AD).

There were in a number of other wells within Pitlochry, which included:
- one on the north bank of the Tummel, near the large rock beside the suspension bridge, which was known as St Bride's Wishing Well, with a reputation of aiding cases of lung disease, but which had to be infilled at the end of the nineteenth century when sewage began to percolate into it from the original sewerage treatment fields nearby (now the Recreation Ground);
- one at Ballinlochan, the site of the High School between 1898 and 1974, where the foundations of its gym were reported to be waterlogged from time to time;
- two in the vicinity of what is now Larchwood Road, one beside the Smithy (*not* the present well which is false and was installed in 1965 simply to collect money for charity!) and one halfway up on the west side of Larchwood Road; and
- one on the north side of the main street, to the west of the present Bank of Scotland building.

A little to the north-east of Toberargan was another hamlet, at Parkcroy, which did not become absorbed into the growing town of Pitlochry until the twentieth century.

The Creation of a Town

Pitlochry's popularity as a centre of Highland hospitality was founded by General Wade's Great North Road of 1727 which was constructed right through the middle of two of the three hamlets from which Pitlochry grew. He sited this road at the bottom of the strath instead of following the previous route at the higher elevation through Moulin. Those three hamlets amalgamated rapidly to form the nucleus of today's town.

The Highland Railway came through in 1863, again at the bottom of the strath. Even at this time, the growing village was little more than a number of houses, a posting inn and some handlooms, although the Statistical Account of 1845 makes mention of persons already holidaying in the district. The railway simply enhanced this, by providing a means of frequent mass transport to the district from the main centres of population.

The development and expansion of Pitlochry, which was created a Burgh on 17th April 1947, is detailed in the next three Chapters.

CHAPTER SEVEN
The Eighteenth Century

Between the thirteenth and eighteenth centuries, much of Scottish life was dominated by the clan system. In exchange for the right to a small homestead, each clan member owed allegiance to his chief; indeed, *clann* simply means 'children'. Pride of kinship, mutual respect and the need for common defence created closely interwoven communities. Many tenants and clan members went so far as to adopt their chief's surname. It has been reckoned that up to half of Scotland's people consciously regarded themselves as members of or related closely to the aristocracy; this is an astonishingly high proportion, far higher than in any other western country, and perhaps accounts for the pride and dignity of the Scots.

Clan chiefs lived amongst their clan members, initially as *primus inter pares* (first among equals) and only latterly as a separate nobility. Those chiefs in turn owed allegiance to their king. That allegiance was given principally by providing fighting men in times of need, which were relatively common within Scotland until the Battle of Culloden and even afterwards for the wars with France in the late eighteenth century. It was therefore vital for each clan chief to attract as many men as possible to his own fiefdom, not only for the protection of his own boundaries, but also to increase his standing at court. The whole way of life was based upon these needs.

Wealth was thus measured in the number of men who could be mustered. As late as 1725, a Highland chief explained to Captain Edmund Burt (who recorded the conversation in his contemporary *Letters from a Gentleman in the North of Scotland*) that he preferred his Highland estate, which was worth about £500 a year, to an English one worth £30,000, simply because of his clan following.

The Robertsons (Clan Donnachaidh), the Murrays (of Atholl), the Campbells (of Breadalbane), the Stewarts, the McGregors and the Menzies were amongst the clans who enjoyed colourful histories and competitive spirits in Highland Perthshire. For centuries, these people lived relatively remote lives in the hills, foraging occasionally for land and perhaps especially for cattle, unaware of and untouched by the significant changes beginning to take shape in the lowlands and cities.

Cattle were then to a successful man what a bank account is now. As Dr. Samuel Johnson declared to his travelling companion James Bothwell on their way through Glen Shiel in 1773, *"The wealth of the mountains is cattle."* Quite literally, any money gleaned in those days was invested in cattle, which not only produced essential dairy products at home but also provided the only viable return for a people who lived from and relied upon the land. There was a doubling of the price of Highland cattle in the second half of the eighteenth century. Cattle were especially convenient in being able to transport themselves over the roadless hills to market. They became in time, when the power of the clans began to subside, the main form of moveable wealth.

The stories of the lengthy droves from the Islands, the West Coast and the far north, lasting for weeks on end and culminating in sales of up to one hundred and fifty thousand head of cattle each year at Crieff and later at Falkirk, indicate how essential this 'export' was. After these sales (or 'trysts' as they were called), many of the drovers went on to escort their cattle to their new owners throughout England, before being able to return to the Highlands. The money obtained from these trysts was used to buy goods and necessaries for the families back at home. Landlords were used to waiting for payment of their rent until the drovers had returned at the back end of the year, around Martinmas.

However valuable cattle were, they were not of course kept in any bank vault. Thus they represented a considerable temptation to a less fortunate neighbour, especially if he was of a different clan. Young men, especially heirs to a chief, would prove their manhood by lifting a *spreidh* ('group of cattle') from a neighbour. Cattle stealing, or *reiving,* was regarded as a somewhat congenial occupation.

In an effort to curb such theft, the Privy Council took bonds from those landowners who controlled the river crossings against their conspiring with the thieves. In this district, a bond was taken in respect of the ferry at Fonab, on the River Tummel (and bonds were also taken for those on the River Tay at both Pitnacree and Aberfeldy).

Whilst for centuries the rhythm of life was set by the cattle which each community raised, kept, protected and exported for sale, some changes began to take place in these rural backwaters, albeit almost imperceptibly. Blacksmiths were less in demand as the desire and need for armour and the claymore dwindled. Shoe-makers were badly affected by increased taxes on leather. Local court officers lost their positions when the Heritable Jurisdictions were abolished in 1746. Weavers suffered during the prohibition of Highland dress in the late eighteenth and early nineteenth centuries.

The Highland Clearances

When change came to the Highlands in the late eighteenth century, it came rapidly, even rudely. In simple terms, people were replaced by sheep. The subsistence smallholdings of earlier times, centred around family clachans, shielings and townships, by which each Highland strath could support significant numbers of inhabitants, were expunged by landlords keen to grasp the commercial opportunities of open estates carrying large numbers of sheep.

Where the number of men had once been critical, then the number of cattle, now it was sheep. Sheep farming was neither a gradual change nor was it a development of the people; it was a complete break with the past. Large tracts of land were required to provide the new 'sheep walks'. As John Knox (a Scottish bookseller living in London) said, it became *the devilish custom of ejecting fifty or a hundred families at a time to make room for a flock of sheep."*

Maybe there is something to be concluded from the fact that, in complete contrast to all other work (from spinning and weaving to kelp farming), the Highlanders' artistic traditions have fallen relatively silent where sheep are concerned. They may look innocent and inoffensive, but sheep have caused more devastation and change throughout the Highlands than any amount of rebellion and battle.

The resultant clearance of people from the Highlands and their reluctant transfer to Glasgow, Edinburgh, the Colonies and the Americas was one of the great enforced movements of people, one of the biggest changes in the way of life and one of the critical tragedies to befall the inhabitants of the Highlands. At that time, the population of Scotland was around one million, with the great majority living in the country. Each glen in Central Scotland boasted a population probably about a quarter of the size of Glasgow, (which had a population then of some twelve thousand) which is impossible to imagine in today's terms. That proportion changed radically with the enforced migration which began then and which, for changing reasons, has continued since. Where over eighty per cent of Scotland's population lived in the countryside at the beginning of the eighteenth century, only forty per cent did so by the end of that century. In national terms, the eighteenth century was the century of urban growth.

The ruins of these settlements and the summer shielings connected with them litter the glens and hillsides of the Grampians. For instance, there are now only a handful of families still living in the sixteen mile length of Glen Tilt, which once supported about fifty families. However, the standard of living of those fifty families then was far below the standard of living of the handful now, probably far below any poverty level since.

Of course, for some, opportunities arose out of such adversity. Scots were in the vanguard of discovery in the New World, were at the frontiers of westward expansion in America and were instrumental in the formation of social structures all over the world. Partly as a result of that mass exodus, there are for instance now more Scots in the United States of America than in Scotland itself.

The rural population was certainly on the increase, given that battles were less frequent and outbreaks of smallpox and typhoid less prevalent. This had been exacerbated by the need to increase the size and strength of each clan by packing as many people as possible onto the land. This need inevitably strained resources to the limit. With primitive methods of agriculture, including the system of runrig (whereby parallel strips, or 'ridges', were worked by different crofting tenants), the land was becoming incapable of sustaining so many people. Some kind of reform was inevitable and overdue.

It was undoubtedly fortunate that, at the very time that this agricultural revolution was taking place throughout the Highlands, an industrial revolution was taking place in the Lowlands. The city ports of Glasgow, Leith and Dundee were beginning to attract significant trade with the Colonies. For the displaced people of this district Dundee, boasting a growing jute trade with India, was the obvious destination, as well as becoming a magnet for others who, whilst not forced to move, yet saw their salvation in the new city.

The estate owners' new-found wealth was spent in travelling abroad and in improving their lands. Formal landscaping began at both Blair Castle and Taymouth Castle at the beginning of the eighteenth century, with other schemes soon following at Dunkeld, the Hermitage, Acharn and Bruar. These were the first attempts to train the bleak nature of the Highlands.

Their sons were educated in France, Italy and the Netherlands in greater numbers than ever before. The French language became well-kent in the upper echelons of society and many families were effectively bi-lingual. The Scots' love affair with French claret, flowing into the port of Leith in particular, was at its acme.

The Privy Council observed that wine *"drawis numberis of* [people] *to miserable necessitie and povertie"* and that when a new shipment arrived *"thay spend bothe dayis and nightis in thair excesse of drinking and seldom do thay leave thair drinking so lang as thair is ony of the wyne restand"*. The Council therefore attempted on many occasions to legislate against the consumption of wine, heavy duties being imposed and the importing of claret even being banned for a short time towards the end of the eighteenth century. It was all to little avail as the wine drinking went on. Wine has aptly been described as the life blood of the Auld Alliance between Scotland and France.

Locally-brewed ale was also readily available and readily drunk. Before the eighteenth century it was perhaps the staple drink of the Highlands. Many clan chiefs were paid the rent due to them not in cash but in kind, usually by receiving quantities of barley. This resulted in their having much more barley than they needed for themselves. It made sense for them to use the excess to brew into ale not only for their own consumption but also for sale locally. Most chief's townships included a brewery from an early date and most chiefs boasted a retained brewer of their own.

However, whilst some lairds prospered, others found themselves heavily in debt, whether from attempting to finance grandiose schemes, or from poor investments abroad or heady gambling at home, or from the costs of competing socially in the capitals of Europe. Such lairds were forced to sell their estates, as often as not to incomers who lacked an innate feel for the local clan members.

When the lairds headed away from the Highlands, for whatever reason and whether or not with success or failure, their absence created a sudden vacuum. Gone were their Gaelic retainers – pipers, fiddlers, poets, sennachies (from *seanachaidh*, meaning 'reciter of family history and of Gaelic heroic tales'), brewers and all – and with their going went also their patronage of many Gaelic traditions and their underpinning of the Gaelic language and its culture.

After the watershed which with hindsight Culloden became, the local power of the chiefs and lairds was eroded in a number of ways. Most notable was the loss, by statute in 1746, of the Heritable Jurisdictions by which their power was particularly manifest.

These changes created further divergence between the lairds, on the one hand, and their tenants, on the other. No longer were the clan chiefs living amongst their own people, centring themselves instead on Edinburgh, even on London, and sometimes undertaking lengthy journeys abroad. The close 'clannish' connection between the chief or laird, on the one hand, and the clan members or tenants, on the other hand, was in serious decline and had almost ceased to exist by the mid-nineteenth century. It was the road and bridge maker, Thomas Telford, who observed in a report of 1802 that

The Lairds have transferred their affections from the people to flocks of sheep and the people have lost their old veneration for the Lairds.

Highland Life

Glimpses of ordinary Highland life in those days can be gleaned from contemporary commentators:
- The Spanish Ambassador, Don Pedro de Ayala, remarked in 1498:

The women are courteous in the extreme. I mention this because they are really honest, though very bold. They are absolute mistresses of their houses and even of their husbands, in all things concerning the administration of their property, income as well as expenditure.
- In the reign of James I of Scotland (1567-1625), Aeneas Sylvius wrote:

The men are small in stature, bold and forward in temper; the women, fair in complexion, comely and pleasing, but not distinguished for their chastity, giving their kisses more readily than Italian women their hands.
- In 1636, Sir John Brereton reported:

The houses [are] accommodated with no more light than the light of the door, no window; the houses covered with clods; the women only neat and handsome about the feet, which comes to pass by their often washing [clothes] with their feet.
- John Ray, writing in 1662, said:

The Scots generally (that is, the poorer sort) wear, the men blue bonnets on their heads . . . the women only white linen, which hangs down their backs as if a napkin were pinned about them . . . They are not very cleanly in their houses . . . The Scots cannot endure to hear their country or countrymen spoken against. . . They lay out most of their worth in clothes.
- Thomas Pennant, wrote in his journal of his tour of the Highlands in 1769:

The houses of the common people in these parts are shocking to humanity, formed of loose stones and covered with clods . . . The men are thin, but strong; idle and lazy, except employed in the chase or anything that looks like amusement; are content with their hard fare . . . The women are more industrious, spin their own husbands' clothes.

These contemporary comments have to be set in context, in that all was not primitive drudgery. The houses might have been simply built and the land basically unproductive (all the more so because of the rudimentary agricultural practices of the day), but the people of the land had an extraordinary pride and dignity. Gaelic culture was impressively intellectual. The *ceilidh* (literally 'a visit') was a chance for a community to sit round a fire, each person participating in entertaining the others by music, song and story-telling as well as entering into fervent discussion on any topic.

Out of the people's simplicity and lack of craving for material possessions sprang an irrepressible *"kind of stateliness in the midst of their poverty"* as Captain Edmund Burt observed, when in the company of Major-General Wade at Inverness in 1725. The Highlanders' artistic talent was well recognised and not merely confined to music. Professor W. J. Watson reckoned that between 1630 and 1830 there were some one hundred and thirty Highland poets whose work was *"really good and some of it outstanding"*.

In the Parish of Moulin

So far as this district is concerned, there were one thousand seven hundred and forty-nine people in the Parish of Moulin in September 1791, fifty-three per cent of them female. There were an average of forty-six births each year, with the average number of children in each family being *"around six"*. As Dr. Webster had reported in 1755 that there were two thousand one hundred and nine people and an annual average of sixty-four births, the population was in decline. The chief reason for this was, as mentioned earlier, the conversion of farms from cornfields, requiring much labour, into sheep grazings, requiring little.

Reverend Alexander Stewart, author of the 1793 Statistical Account for the Parish of Moulin, observed that *"distempers are very rare"* giving early credence to the nineteenth century claims about the healthy air and climate of the district. The men were between five foot five inches and five foot six inches on average, whilst the women were about five foot. The tallest man living in the Parish was six foot four. The oldest man alive was *"about 95 years"*. The people were described as *"humane, very obliging and enough contented"*.

The number of poor who received regular assistance was about sixteen and there were another sixteen or so who were in receipt of occasional assistance. They were paid from legacies, donations and the net amount of the church collections.

Work and Play

In 1791, in Moulin and Pitlochry together there were a total of one hundred and ninety-four farmers, twenty-eight weavers, ten tailors, seven shoemakers, six shop-keepers, five blacksmiths, four flax dressers, four coopers, three sieve makers and one dyer. There were thirty-five servants to look after the forty-six people within the five gentlemen's families.

The Dane's Stone, in the field to the south of Baledmund House, Moulin

Moulin Market

Moulin Market used to be held in late February (and latterly in early March each year), just before the farming year began, as winter's grip was thawing. The market was always located in the field below Baledmund, beside the standing stone (known as 'the Dane's Stone'). It was the custom at the market for a deal to be struck between dealers by their clasping hands at this stone. The market was one of the principal events of the year, in spite of its being notorious for the stormy weather which always seemed to prevail at that time – "Moulin Market weather" it was called. The market began to lose its importance by the end of the nineteenth century and is no longer held.

Many festivities accompanied the market for a people who had just survived the excesses of another Highland winter. Perhaps because of these, there were two unfortunate incidents. The first was in February 1767 which resulted in eighteen people drowning in the River Garry when the overcrowded ferryboat, in which they were returning from the market to Strathtummel, capsized. Hardly anyone could swim in those days and, indeed, the ferryman himself survived only because his quick-witted wife, witnessing the unfolding tragedy from the river bank, was able to reach out to him with a boat hook. Thomas the Rhymer foretold of this disaster.

The second incident was on 3rd March 1887 when John Souter, described in newspaper reports as *"a poor man"*, but who was actually the shepherd at Stronchavie, had set off in the evening of 2nd March to walk the five miles home from the market. Unfortunately, he perished in a blizzard about two-thirds of the way across Moulin moor. There is a memorial stone at the roadside where he was found, just to the south-east of the ruined shepherd's cottage at Badvo.

Memorial Stone to John Souter on Moulin moor

Moulin Market was also the principal market for the sale of linen yarn. The linen came from locally-grown flax (seventy-five acres in 1792), which produced beautiful blue flowers. Once cut, the flax was steeped for a time in water; there were five lint pools for this purpose within Moulin at that time, although no trace of any now exists. The flax was next taken to one of the seven lint mills then in the Parish, to be prepared for spinning and weaving. The only lint mill still existing in the district, albeit a ruin, is at the junction of the Aberfeldy / Tummel Bridge road with the Pitlochry / Foss road, about two miles south of Tummel Bridge.

Most females over the age of eight were involved in spinning the linen during a season of twenty-one weeks, producing a total of some twenty-three thousand spindles. The local Stamp Office for linen was at Logierait. Linen was clearly vital to the local economy, not only for the locals who derived extra income from it but also for the landlords who found that their rents were being paid on account of that extra income. This part-time Scottish craft grew into a major industry, but it was coarse and basic and was inevitably affected in time by the machine-made cotton goods from England.

As the market for making linen declined, so weaving was the next 'cottage industry' which became crucial to the economy. There were about thirty weavers in the district by the end of the eighteenth century. Indeed, there were at one time as many as six looms working in Parkcroy alone, with power taken from the small burn which flows now into the Atholl Palace grounds. There were weavers in Kinnaird, Toberargan and doubtless in most of the other clachans too.

Farming

There were more estates then than now, partly because some have been amalgamated and partly because others have been absorbed into other uses. However, the principal estates then were much as now, including Atholl, Lude, Strathgarry, Urrard, Bonskeid, Faskally, Pitlochry, Baledmund, Balnakeilly, Dunfallandy, Ballyoukan, Edradour, Stronchavie, Cluneskea, Tarvie, Glenfernate, Straloch, Dirnanean and Kindrogan.

Each landowner (or 'laird') would let out part of his estate, usually the more productive parts, in a lease (or 'tack'), to a 'tacksman' in exchange for an annual rent, often paid partly or wholly in kind. The tacksman would then sublet his tack in strips (or 'rigs') to the working crofters who would live in a 'township' on the tack and use their rig or rigs to produce food usually for their own families only, and even then not always sufficiently.

The tacksman at one time held a position of some importance between chief and tenants. In practical terms the whole rural system depended on the abilities of the tacksman, as did the happiness or otherwise of the tenants and sub-tenants below him. His position became precarious once the old systems of runrig and common shielings for cattle were swept out in favour of large-scale sheep grazings.

The houses in each township tended by the eighteenth century to be stone-built, often using the same techniques as used in building the dry-stane dykes. The gaps in the walls would be stuffed with moss or heather. The roof would be covered in crude timbers and topped with heather or, occasionally, in thatch. The fire inside was the only source of heat and, often, the only source of light too. There were usually two rooms, a living room (with small box beds) for the family and a byre for the animals.

The system of *runrig*, the farming of parallel, narrow strips, each one probably farmed by a different tenant, was still being practised extensively. This was to ensure that each tenant received a share of the better and of the worse ground, by the drawing of lots annually. Whilst this ensured a more even distribution of ground, it provided no incentive for any tenant to improve his nominated rigs one year, because they probably would not be his the next. The rig was ploughed into the middle on both sides to produce a fertile ridge, with shallow drainage ditches on each side. Instead of the three (or four) field rotational cropping system favoured in England, the cropping system in Scotland was intensive and continuous, until the land was exhausted. The Highlanders differentiated only between the better, ploughable 'infield' (called *talamh treabhtaidh* generally, but *croit* in Highland Perthshire) and the poorer, less accessible 'outfield' (called *talamh ban* generally, but *roer* here).

Many communities also had access to a 'commonty', where crofters could run their flocks and herds on reasonable summer pasture. In this district there were commonties near Enochdhu and above Kinnaird. There were other common rights too, including the rights to cut peat, to coppice (the cutting of wood – as within the oak wood below Kinnaird), to draw water and to graze. Where those commonties and other common rights were bought out or disbanded by lairds, the local crofters faced inevitable constrictions on their traditional methods of farming.

Farmers grew oats (the wild grey variety, which nowadays is considered nothing more than a troublesome weed), barley (initially the primitive kind, known as 'bere' or 'bear' and only latterly the barley we know now), flax, potatoes, turnips, clover and rye grass. Enclosures were still rare, but were increasing. There were about 1950 acres in cultivation. Oatmeal and cheese were exported from the district.

Locals were almost entirely dependant on what was produced locally. They ate *knockit bear*, that is, oats and barley ground down to porridge, gruel and oatcakes. Game and stock complemented this meagre diet. If the crop failed, the consequences were dire. Only the Church intervened in those days to rescue the poor and starving. Otherwise, they were left to an enforced diet of nettles and mugwort.

With the Disarming Act of 1747, the position of locals was worse than ever. Not only was the possession of any weapon an offence, it was also an offence to trap animals or to fish. The local diet suffered immediately. With fewer men in the neighbourhood, as a result of those killed in the '15 and the '45, the people remaining, mainly women and the elderly, found life almost unbearably hard.

Much time was spent procuring fuel and thus, it was observed, was lost to agriculture. This was no idle comment. It has been reckoned that a hard-working man could cut a thousand peat turfs in a good day and that a family would need about fifteen thousand turfs to heat them through the year. After cutting, the peats were laid out methodically to dry and were then carted, by sack or barrow, from the hill to the hearth. The month or so of work involved in this vital task was indeed a month away from agriculture, especially as it was at the driest time of year, precisely when a farmer should have been working and weeding his ground. The problem was exacerbated when the moorland mosses which yielded the peat, particularly those nearer the villages, became closer to being exhausted.

Trees were also very scarce at this time, forests having been destroyed for a number of reasons, including ship building, the eradication of shelter for wolves and the creation of more agricultural land to sustain a growing population. The distilling of whisky was also partly responsible for the loss of both timber and peat as the process used a considerable quantity of each.

There were in fact two licensed stills of thirty gallons each, one at Kinnaird and the other at Edradour. Licensing and duties were imposed from early in the eighteenth century. There would have been many other illicit stills, dotted all over the place. It is clear that some of these became licensed subsequently, whilst the existence of others is belied by placenames, such as *tomnabrachd* ('knoll of the malting'). Whisky was originally referred to in Latin as *aqua vitae* ('the water of life'), but the Gaelic equivalent – *uisge beatha* – came into common use and from this the Scots word 'whisky' evolved. At that time, whisky was very cheap relative to other commodities but, though whisky was popular, it was drunk less than ale by most locals and less than claret by most of the lairds.

There were as many as twenty-four licensed retailers of ale, beer and liquor. Reverend Stewart remarked:

This seems a high number for such a small population, but there are few reports of people drinking to excess, particularly when it is considered that at the Fair every house, hut and shed in the village is instantly converted into a dram-shop.

Culture

That same Disarming Act of 1747, which followed the defeat of the Jacobites at Culloden the previous year, forbade the wearing of the kilt and tartan and the playing of bagpipes. A direct attack on the culture of the Scots had been made, but by 'mouth music', fiddle music, dancing and word of mouth, the traditions were somehow and marvellously retained through the eighty-four years of prohibition, but it was a time of great austerity.

Those *"gymnastic exercises"*, as the Reverend Stewart described them, which apparently constituted *"the chief pastime of the Highlanders"* had almost entirely disappeared by the end of the eighteenth century. At every fair there used to be contests of wrestling, racing, putting the stone, football and shinty. He reported that, by the end of the century, these had yielded to the *"more elegant, but less manly amusement"* of dancing, which had become very common.

Baron's Court

Until the abolition of Heritable Jurisdictions in 1746, a Baron's Court was held in Moulin. Its jurisdiction extended north-east to Strathardle, but dealt with petty offences only. All serious cases were tried at Logierait.

Punishment meted out included one which locally was called *"chaggs"*; this is thought to have involved the guilty person's being fastened to the old ash tree in the churchyard at Moulin. *"Chaggs"* sounds very like the Scots word 'jougs', the name of a hinged iron collar which was fastened round the neck of an offender and attached by a chain to iron fastenings on a wall or, in Moulin's case, to

The remains of Shierglas House in 1993

a tree. 'Jougs' probably became 'chaggs' in the local dialect; iron fastenings were reportedly visible on the ash tree in the early nineteenth century. There is a current example on the wall of Dowally churchyard, just to the south of this district.

Language

The principal language was Gaelic but, by this time, most people understood sufficient English to be able to transact their business with their 'lowland' neighbours. Gaelic had been declining since perhaps the beginning of the sixteenth century. Its decline was of course exacerbated by the Highland Clearances, which removed the heart of the Gaelic communities. A new Gaelic version of the Scriptures was written by the Reverend James Stuart of Killin and published at Edinburgh in 1767, just one year after Dr. Samuel Johnson had observed that:

> there were lately some who thought it reasonable to refuse them a version of the Holy Scriptures, that they might have no monument in their mother tongue.

This Bible encouraged anew the teaching and studying of Gaelic.

In the parochial school, there were about fifty pupils, of whom seven were taught Latin. There were five other schools in different parts of the Parish, with a total of some one hundred and eighty pupils.

In 1498, the Spanish Ambassador had noted that James IV (1488-1513) spoke many languages, including *"the language of the savages who live in some parts of Scotland and on the islands"*. It is possible that his son, James V (1513-1542), who was in the habit of roaming the Highlands, was the last King to speak Gaelic. Many noble families, notably the Dukes of Atholl, retained and encouraged Gaelic speaking until the twentieth century.

Southern elevation of the Laird's House behind Pitcastle Farm, east of Pitlochry – as it was in 1925 (top) and what was left in 1993 (bottom)

Oldest Buildings

There were four hundred and forty dwellinghouses in Moulin Parish by the end of the eighteenth century. Surprisingly, especially in view of the falling population, none was reported to be uninhabited. On the contrary, there were new houses being built, especially near the highways. At that time Moulin was still the larger settlement, for the last reported time, with thirty-seven families as against thirty in Pitlochry.

There are a number of buildings from that time which still exist today. A dilapidated outbuilding at Pitcastle, about two miles east of Pitlochry, was once a small mansion house, dating from the early sixteenth century, which is perhaps the oldest house in the district. It is seventeen metres long, almost seven metres wide and is on two floors. The front door was studded with nails and had a triangular peep-hole.; it is now on display in Blair Castle. The ground floor had three apartments, with an earth floor and fireplaces, whilst unusually there was both an inside staircase and an outside one leading up to the two bedrooms on the first floor, where it would have been possible to stand only in the middle, the height under the coomb falling to a mere one metre and twenty centimetres. It was in reasonable condition in the early part of the twentieth century, but now only the outer walls and the inner staircase remain, heavily overtaken by vegetation. Further deterioration is inevitable.

The house below the quarry at Shierglas, overlooking Blair Atholl, dates from 1728. Its western gable collapsed in 1992; the remainder still stands, but probably not for much longer. The farm steading behind dates from 1799.

The original sections of both Edradour House and Ballyoukan date back to the end of the seventeenth century or early eighteenth. The original rafters at Ballyoukan were of Scots fir from Mar Forest and though small and bent were hard enough to turn a knife; each rafter had a hole in the end, through which a rope would have been passed to enable it to have been dragged by horse all the way over the old drove road from Braemar.

The west wing of Old Fincastle House probably dates from the early seventeenth century. On its walls are inscriptions which record its owners. Over one window there reads:

```
1640    A G 7
BLISSIT AR THE MERCIFUL
FOR THEY SCHAL OBTAIN MERCE

THE FEIR OF THE LORD
ABHORETH WIKEDNES

IS  ❤  CM
```

This records the marriage of James Stewart (IS) of Fincastle and Cecilia Mercer (CM) of Meikleour. There are other inscriptions of 1702, 1751 and 1754. A concealed underground room was discovered there in the nineteenth century, which permitted escape to the banks of the adjacent burn.

The farmhouses at Pitfourie and Mains of Bonskeid each date from the first half of the eighteenth century. The latter uses as a door lintel a tombstone which came from the old Culdee graveyard at *cladh chille* beside Bonskeid. The cottage at Druid above Killiecrankie was formerly a farmhouse; its lintel stone, probably incorporated from the original building into the present one, reads:

```
16  RR  ◆  MC  51
```

Who RR and MC were is not known, nor why what was doubtless a heart in the centre has been scratched out, but the date is clearly 1651.

Militia Riots 1797

The Militia Act enforced conscription by ballot for men between the ages of eighteen and twenty-three. It was a particularly unpopular measure because men could be sent overseas. Each schoolmaster was given the duty of using his local Parish register to draw up a list of the men in his area to be entered in the ballot.

Riots ensued. Forbes, schoolmaster at Fincastle, had his ear cut off by a scythe in one tussle with objectors. He was left to bleed to death. Robertson, schoolmaster at Moulin, was obstructed and the Parish register in his possession was snatched away. Locals surrounded the house of Mr. Henry Butter, Deputy Lieutenant of Perthshire, and as the report of the time quaintly puts it: *"forced him to come under an engagement not to act"*.

Some Notable Visitors
Nevil Maskelyne

Appointed Astronomer Royal in 1765, a position he was to hold for the next forty-six years, the Reverend Nevil Maskelyne was famous for three things, his founding of the Nautical Almanac, his investigations into determining longitude for navigation and his weighing of the Earth. This last experiment he conducted on the slopes of Schiehallion (3,547'/1,081m), marked on Ptolemy's map of Britain which was published in about 145 AD.

The size of our planet had been estimated reasonably accurately as having a diameter of twenty-four thousand miles as long ago as the third century BC, by Eratosthenes, librarian of a museum in Alexandria. Sir Isaac Newton had estimated the density of the planet as being between five and six times the density of water and Maskelyne wanted to prove the accuracy of this.

Maskelyne knew that a large object, such as a mountain, would in theory attract a plumb-line by a measurable amount from the vertical, owing to the gravitational force of the mountain mass itself. In practice, it was a remarkable experiment to undertake. It involved an astronomical telescope, an astronomical clock and a plumb line suspended on each side of the mountain. All of this was conducted on the exposed flank of the hill, in unpredictable weather.

Schiehallion was chosen because of its unusually regular outline. An observatory was set up and a series of measurements were taken in 1772. The mountain moved the plumb line by just one-six hundredth parts of one degree – a tiny amount. From this, Maskelyne and his scientific colleague Charles Hutton measured the gravitational force of its mass and concluded that the density of the Earth, relative to the density of water, was about five times greater. Subsequent experiments have shown that the true figure is about five and a half times.

Schiehallion in 1924 with Kinloch Rannoch in foreground

When Maskelyne returned to London, he sent north the Yellow London Lady to one of his local assistants, Duncan Robertson of Carie. The Lady was a real beauty, purchased by the Astronomer Royal to replace young Duncan's fiddle, which had been lost when the expedition's supply hut on the shoulder of Schiehallion was burnt down. Young Duncan was so overjoyed that he composed a Gaelic song in honour of his new Cremona violin, which he called "*a bhan lunnaineach bhuidhe*" ('the Yellow London Lady'). The violin was cherished and handed down from generation to generation, suffering from being pawned in Liverpool once, having its neck broken on the way home and undergoing substantial repair many years ago.

Charles Hutton's many calculations used a new notion of drawing lines on his map to show points of equal height, to represent the shape of Schiehallion. His idea was not adopted for some time, but now such 'contour lines' are the basis of every Ordnance Survey map.

Thomas Gray

The famous poet travelled through this district in 1765, on his way to Glen Garry. He was greatly taken with the experience of his travels and, in particular, the juxtaposition between the beauty of the scenery and the danger inherent in untamed nature. He wrote:

Bruar Falls today

I am returned from Scotland charmed with my expedition; it is of the Highlands I speak; the Lowlands are worth seeing once, but the mountains are ecstatic, and ought to be visited in pilgrimage once a year. None but those monstrous creatures of God know how to join so much beauty with so much horror.

Robert Burns

On Friday 31st August 1787, Robert Burns came through Pitlochry, with his friend William Nicol (an Edinburgh High School teacher), on their way to Blair Castle. The day had started at Dunkeld with a meeting in Inver at the house of the famous fiddler Neil Gow. Burns wrote in his diary:

Ride up Tummel River to Blair. Faskally, a beautiful romantic nest with the grandeur of the Pass of Killiecrankie – visit the gallant Lord Dundee stone [he meant the Pictish standing stone at Haugh of Urrard, known as the Claverhouse Stone] *– Blair – sup with Duchess, easy and happy from the manners of that family.*

Burns in fact stayed at Blair Castle over the weekend, with trips over the Atholl Estates and to Loch Tummel. He declared that these were amongst the happiest days of his life.

On his way north, Burns stopped at Bruar, struck by the beauty of the Falls, which were then quite easy to view from afar, being a ravine in an otherwise bare hillside. Burns could imagine their being enhanced by fresh plantings of trees. He penned *The Humble Petition of Bruar Water* in a poetic appeal to the Duke:

Would then my noble master please
To grant my highest wishes
He'll shade my banks wi' towering trees,
And bonnie spreading bushes.
Delighted doubly then, my Lord,
You'll wander on my banks
And listen mony a grateful bird
Return your tuneful thanks.

Let lofty firs and ashes cool,
My lowly banks o'erspread
And view, deep-pending in the pool,
Their shadows' wat'ry-bed!
Let fragrant birks, in woodbines drest,
My craggy cliffs adorn;
And, for the little songster's nest,
The close embow'ring thorn.

Before being published, unsigned, in *The Edinburgh Magazine* in November 1789, the poem was handed to the Duke of Atholl himself, who responded to it, perhaps as a memorial to the bard who died seven years later, by creating the sylvan beauty of that spot today.

CHAPTER EIGHT
The Nineteenth Century

The Growth of a Highland Village

For Pitlochry in particular, the nineteenth century saw a significant shift from a quiet rural backwater, largely unaffected by the outside world, to a village undergoing Victorian gentrification. This process, quickened by the coming of the railway in mid-century, created the heart of the town as it still exists and promoted many of the pastimes which have since become annual traditions. In the space of one century, the population pulled itself up from thatched hovels to stone dwellings, from muddy tracks to civic streets, from homespun neglect to respectfulness.

The nineteenth century was Pitlochry's century, when it took over the mantle from Moulin of being the most important settlement in the district. The events within that hundred year span created the town of Pitlochry largely as we know it today. There was change and progress within almost every sphere of life.

In the Statistical Account of 1845, based on figures from 1839, it was recorded that, whilst the village of Moulin had one hundred and eighty-five inhabitants, Pitlochry's population was larger, with three hundred and twenty-one. Pitlochry's popularity was entrenched in General Wade's new Great North Road, which he constructed in 1727 right through the middle of two of the three hamlets

from which the village of Pitlochry grew. He sited this road at the bottom of the strath instead of following the previous route at the higher elevation through Moulin. As a result, all three hamlets amalgamated rapidly to form the nucleus of today's town.

Pitlochry's next stride was the coming of the Highland Railway in 1863, which was met with considerable resistance at the time, not only from locals but also from such notable visitors as John Ruskin and Sir John Everett Millais. As ever, this was resistance to change, on the basis that it would be for the worse; change took place notwithstanding and, if not lauded universally, was soon taken for granted.

Even by 1865, the growing village was little more than a number of houses, a posting inn (Fisher's) and some handlooms. The mail coach passed through daily at about half past one in the afternoon. Whilst the village itself was of no great distinction, its situation could scarcely be bettered, with expansive panoramas combining the many characteristics of Scottish scenery and, for a backcloth, the bold outline of Ben-y-Vrackie.

Pitlochry had also been blessed by Queen Victoria's personal physician, Sir James Clark who declared its spa waters to be remedial,

(Top) Pitlochry in about 1873 probably by local photographer Paul Cameron, taken from the Pictish fort at An Dun (above Cluniemore) – an astonishing panorama, akin to an aerial view
(Bottom) The same view one hundred and twenty years later (though partly obscured now by afforestation)

Pitlochry's main street in about 1885, looking west from the West Moulin Road junction

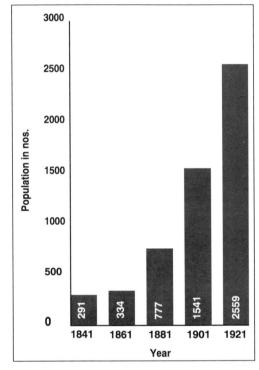

The same view in 1993, with traffic lights and with the old cottages extended upwards

indeed apparently prescribing holidays there to his London patients. This followed the lead created locally by Pitlochry's own Doctor William Stewart Irvine, who was convinced of its splendid climate. It became popular for both the ill and the elderly. All records have indicated an absence of illness and infection locally and a resident population whose members regularly reach an advanced age.

By the time of the Statistical Account of 1845 there were already increasing numbers of persons holidaying in the district. In 1896, it was estimated that seven hundred Dundonians arrived on the last Saturday of July. That estimate may be reasonably accurate because, on the same day in 1897, between just 4pm and 7pm, five special trains arrived at Pitlochry Station, each full of visitors from Dundee.

So it was that Pitlochry's twin achievements as a tourist centre and a retirement town arose from the road, the railway and the purity of its water and air. The development and expansion of Pitlochry is evident from the population numbers returned for the town over a critical period of eighty years [see graph].

Since that ninefold increase, the population of Pitlochry has remained reasonably constant.

In the Parish of Moulin

By 1839, the population of the whole Parish of Moulin had risen to two thousand and thirty-nine, almost equally males and females; three quarters of them resided in the countryside and one quarter in the villages of Moulin and Pitlochry. The yearly average of births had dropped to forty-five. The number of inhabited houses was four hundred and twelve; the average number of persons in each family had reduced to about five. There were two hundred and eighty-one hired servants. There were two dwarfs, two insane persons (both confined in Murray's Asylum in Perth and supported there by the Parish) and one blind person.

Reverend Duncan Campbell, author of the 1845 Statistical Account for the Parish of Moulin, remarked:

> *As a proof that we breathe the wholesome and bracing air of a highly salubrious climate* [there were according to the Census taken in January 1839] *one hundred and twelve*

individuals in the Parish over 70, of whom twenty-nine were over 80 and two over 90. Rheumatism is the most common complaint.

In the severe winter of 1895 a temperature of minus twenty-four degrees centigrade was recorded at Pitlochry on 11th February. Part of the River Tummel was frozen over and a horse and cart were driven over the ice from Dunfallandy. Curling took place that winter on the River Tummel, at Pool Dour (from *poll dobhran* meaning 'pool of the otter') just south of Pitlochry. This remains the lowest recorded temperature in the district, although the most sustained period of cold, of almost the same magnitude, was experienced in the winter of 1984. There were other 'classic' winters too, notably in 1947 and 1962.

Curling in 1895 on the River Tummel, at Pool Dour, below the main road into Pitlochry

According to Reverend Campbell again;

Dwellings are kept in good order. The inhabitants undergo more or less of daily purification. Home made cloths are little worn. It were well however if some of our young people would find their way to the Pitlochry Savings Bank and not throw away their scanty earnings on exterior personal embellishment. Though there are butchers and bakers among us, the style of living is not materially altered from that of our forefathers. Meal, milk and potatoes are the staple articles of diet. Poor indeed is that family which does not rear a pig.

Work and Play

Obtaining fuel was still a great problem in the nineteenth century. Peat, found in the neighbouring hills and procured at great expense, was still the principal fuel. Concern was expressed that it would soon be exhausted. A considerable quantity of wood was cut and burned as fuel. Each household spent a high proportion of its income on fuel. The position was improved by the coming of the Highland Railway, when cheaper coal could more readily be brought into the district.

The men's usual head-dress was a common blue bonnet, worn at church and market,. The women wore the 'curch' (a Scots word deriving from the French *curcheffe*, from which the English word kerchief came), a cap made of linen and tied under the chin. Most of the younger men appeared in public in West of England cloth, hat and stockings. The ladies bedecked themselves in merino and sombre-coloured cotton gowns, with silk or straw bonnets (the latter of which were made locally).

What is believed to be a Pitlochry Bonnet; portrait by Paul Cameron in about 1880

At one time, there was a colony of bonnetmakers, who had come from Glasgow, establishing themselves in a couple of the old thatched cottages which used to exist between Scotland's Hotel and the main street. They made the 'Pitlochry bonnet', of which no known example still exists. It was not unlike a balmoral, being circular, with a band around the forehead, looser felted material tapering outwards above and topped with a bobble. They gave their name to Bonnethill Road – which previously had been known as West Moulin Road and then, when the present West Moulin Road was created, as Mid-Moulin Road – but their product is now long forgotten.

In 1839, there was one medical practitioner, one banker, and one notary public (lawyer), seven excise officers, eighty-eight farmers, eleven shepherds, eighteen weavers, thirteen tailors, thirteen shoe makers, one

(Top left) Pitlochry's main street in 1889, photographed by Francis Smart, looking east from the junction with Bonnethill Road. From left to right: the Prince Charlie House, the Butter Memorial fountain (in front of trees where Alba Place was built in 1897), two storey house (where the Bank of Scotland now is) and two cottages at the bottom of Bonnethill (where the Brook Place buildings now are) (Top Right) The same view in 1993

(Middle left) Junction of Bonnethill Road with Atholl Road in 1889, photographed by Francis Smart, with from left to right: the entrance to a temperance hotel (in what are now the Brook Place shops), bridge (where Connells' shop now is), the East Church up in Lower Oakfield (now flats) in Lower Oakfield, Dyer the jeweller's house beyond (which then became Martins the grocer, now Ian Kemp Electrical) and row of cottages (now Robertsons). For some reason, the three men carry rifles
(Middle right) The same view in 1993 – Brook Place and Commercial Place

(Bottom left) View up Bonnethill Road in about 1890. Martin's the grocer was then a wooden shed on the left (where the TSB Bank now is), in front of his lemonade factory. Thatched cottages on the left (there used to be some on the right too). Mount Zion Church and Scotland's Hotel are at the top of the photo.
(Bottom right) The same view in 1993 – Connells, TSB Bank, Scotland's Hotel, shops

inn-keeper, six retailers of ale, seven blacksmiths, one saddler, seven schoolmasters, one plasterer, three road contractors, two straw bonnet makers, and two midwives.

There were thirty-nine people on the Poor Roll. Of these twenty-one were 'ordinary' and eighteen 'occasional' poor. At that time, the poor were still cared for by Parish funds, which came from Church collections. Reverend Campbell reported on an unseemly upsurge in begging:

Really some measure should be adopted to suppress the system of mendacity, which has lately prevailed to such an annoying extent in the district. To use a homely phrase, we are perfectly ate up with beggars. To supply from 8 to 12 a day is no uncommon call on our benevolence.

Farming

There were 2,719 acres in the Parish either cultivated or occasionally in tillage. There were at least 2,000 acres of woodland, more than half planted in the first half of the nineteenth century.

Farms were no longer let on the *"unpopular"* system of runrig. Instead, they were increasingly enclosed in fields and rotated (at last) in crops. Marl was dug, for instance from the Cuilc, and used by the tenants to fertilise their farms. Some of the old townships on the estates ('fermtouns') were dismantled, to provide stone for new farm buildings and for dykes and to create more parkland for sheep.

In some places, summer shielings were still in use, to provide a summer home for families who travelled to pasture their sheep and goats on land which generally lay above the snowline in winter. Up on the hill above Tenandry is a good example of such a shieling which was in use longer than most, where there is a little street of cottages and byres on a small hidden plateau, reached by a narrow and at times precarious cart track; its existence is celebrated in the names of the crags up there, such as *creag na h'airigh* ('rock of the summer shieling'), *creag an eirionnaich* ('rock of the gelded young goat') and *craig fonvuick* ('rock in the land of pigs').

Some of the estates were given over not only to sheep but also to the newly fashionable moorland sports, that is, deer stalking, grouse shooting and fishing. By 1850, the letting of grouse moors was common practice, their rentals in many cases becoming the principal source of income for the lairds and a welcome boost for local hotels and retail businesses too. Indeed, some hotels took shooting and fishing lets for their guests; for instance, Fisher's Hotel took the fishings on the Tummel from Bonskeid Estate at least between 1859 and 1863.

At Moulin a fair, which previously had been held in February, was by the nineteenth century held on the first Tuesday of March, for the sale of horses and the purchase of seed-corn. At Pitlochry there was a fair on the last Tuesday of April and another on the third Wednesday of October, for the sale of cattle and horses. The October fair, known as *Feill Sraid*, was also a 'feeing market' for farm servants who were lined up to be chosen by their new employers: this practice continued until the First World War. The market was very popular, with stalls lining the length of the main street between West Moulin Road and Bonnethill Road. Atholl Road was very wide then, as Alba Place had yet to be built.

The ruined shieling above Tenandry

During the eighteenth century, there was a Pitlochry Auction Mart, with permanent stalls and pens for animals, on the wooded plateau to the south of the old gasometer site. By 1863 this was rivalled by a new Mart which was established on the area of ground to the west of the Guide Hut at Well Brae (where Pirnie's yard was for most of the twentieth century and where, in 1993, new housing was being mooted). From 1880 this latter business was known as the Atholl Auction Mart. At the beginning of the twentieth century, this relocated to the Lady's Dell, which at that time was on the way to the Recreation Ground, where again there were permanent stalls and pens. The Mart continued to deal in sheep, cattle and horses until after the Second World War. By then the Mart was already dealing in farm and house sales and, from about 1950 onwards has held occasional sales of furniture, household goods and bric-a-brac, usually in the Town Hall.

Culture

The much despised Disarming Act of 1747 was finally repealed in 1831. After an absence of eighty-four long years the tartan and kilt could once more be worn and the haunting sound of the bagpipes could once more be heard. The Highlanders revelled in their old culture, preserved by a number of means during the dark years. Celebrations sprang up, including a revival of the old Highland Games. Pitlochry Highland Games was one of the first to be re-established in Scotland, as evidenced by an ormolu brooch which is inscribed:

> *Presented by Lady Feilden at the First Pitlochrie Highland Games to Mr Charles Duff of Dunavourdie as the Best Player on the Highland Bagpipes, 10th September 1852.*

A Recreation Ground was established to the south of the town, on the north bank of the River Garry. Only the cemetery at Dysart was nearby, otherwise the nearest place was the railway station. It was reached, as the Lady's Dell is now, by Rie-Achan Road and by traversing the Dell. Where now the waters of Loch Faskally lap on a small beach, there was then a vista of the Recreation Ground, with a centrally-located pavilion, a terraced grass bank, the river and, over to the right, a nine hole Golf Course (which predated the Recreation Ground). This was all to be submerged in due course. There was also a path from Ferry Road, to the north of what is now Tummel Crescent and through the wood still shown on maps as *lag na bain tighearna* ('the dell of the laird's lady') to the east end of the Ground.

(Top) Ploughing above Lettoch Farm with Pitfourie in the distance

(Bottom) The original Recreation Ground, now submerged below Loch Faskally, showing its terraced banking (which is now part of the north shore of the Loch)

Schools

The language generally spoken was still Gaelic, but it had lost ground very considerably since the end of the eighteenth century. Indeed, the Education Act 1872, which was useful in producing a system of education designed to suit the whole population of Scotland, had no place for the teaching of Gaelic.

Suddenly, those whose mother tongue was Gaelic found that none was spoken at school. Gaelic was not a subject for which Government grants could be given. Worse than that, Gaelic became actively discouraged; children were punished for speaking their mother tongue at school. At one time, school officers were employed specifically to ensure that no Gaelic was spoken. Soon, it was the parents or grandparents who spoke Gaelic, but not the younger generations.

There were seven schools in the Parish, one being the parochial one. That parochial school, run and financed by the Parish, was considered the most important, the others being privately owned and run (usually in each case by a single teacher). In January 1839, the number of pupils in all the schools in the Parish was three hundred and eighty-eight of whom forty per cent were girls. In the previous century there were many men and most women who could neither read nor write. By the middle of the nineteenth century, almost all men under the age of sixty and most young females could read and write; some could also cast accounts. An attempt was made to establish a circulating library in Moulin, but it did not succeed.

Parochial schools were phased out as a result of the Disruption of 1843, when the Free Church broke away from the Established Church of Scotland and caused the break up of the 'parish state' which had administered schools, poor relief and the like. In national terms, the nineteenth century was a century of religious issues.

Moulin School

Moulin parochial school used to be situated next to the original entrance to the kirk, at its south side, where Blairmount now is. The first schoolmaster mentioned in the Perthshire Register of Sasines was James Ross, former minister of Fortingall, who was appointed in 1649. His appointment would have followed efforts by the Scots Parliament in 1633, 1643 and 1646 to encourage landowners to create schools in every Parish. By 1711, the school building in Moulin was in need of repair; it was still reported as being in a state of disrepair ten years later.

Most pupils attended school in the winter months only. Of a school roll of one hundred and twelve in 1825, only thirty (that is, twenty-seven per cent) attended the summer session. Compulsory attendance was not introduced until 1874 and then only for pupils under the age of thirteen.

In 1851, a new school was built in Moulin (which was subsequently the Laundry and now Moulin Hall). The school closed altogether in 1898 when a new combined school was built at Ballinlochan, at the northern end of Pitlochry, so as to be convenient for both villages.

There was also a Free Church School, established at the hamlet of Kinnaird, above Moulin, in 1844, a year after the Disruption [see Chapter Twelve]. In 1861, its roll was fifty pupils. The school transferred to the church building at Kinnaird, once the new Free Church in Lower Oakfield was opened in 1863, where it remained until closed in 1873, with all pupils being transferred to the new Pitlochrie Public School [see below].

Pitlochry Schools

There were two schools in Pitlochry during most of the nineteenth century. A Boys' School was established under the General Assembly's Educational Scheme . This was situated at the south-eastern corner of the Rie-Achan car park, just to the west of the station level crossing. It started sometime before 1841, but was unlikely to have been in existence before the Scheme itself, which began in 1824. In 1861, its roll was eighty pupils. Its buildings, known as Station Cottages, were demolished in 1966, when the new car park was created.

The 'Pitlochrie Public School' at the bottom of East Moulin Road, which later became the Boy Scout headquarters, until its demolition in 1974

'Pitlochrie Female School' was established by the Society in Scotland for the Propagation of Christian Knowledge (SSPCK) in 1817 at an unknown house and garden which had been gifted by the Butter family. Its roll in 1861 was forty-seven pupils.

Both schools closed in 1873, when the new 'Pitlochrie Public School' was started that same year. The new school was located at the eastern end of the town, on the north side of Atholl Road between the Acarsaid Hotel and the present Scout Hut. Its playing field was where Newholme Avenue now is. When the school moved to Ballinlochan, to be closer to Moulin, this building on Atholl Road became the first Boy Scout building until East Moulin Road was realigned in 1974 and the present Scout Hut was erected nearby.

Once it had been decided to amalgamate the Moulin and Pitlochry schools, the local committee found it very difficult to obtain a feu of land from any of the Baledmund, Balnakeilly or Faskally (now known as Pitlochry) Estate proprietors. The Committee favoured a site at Tomnamoan, but Mr. Fergusson of Baledmund was concerned that it would affect the amenity of the adjoining houses. To this, Mr. James Macnaughton, a member of the Committee, replied: *"We have been knocked about as if it were a fever hospital we propose to erect."* The Committee eventually reached agreement that the new school should be located a little to the north of Tomnamoan, at Ballinlochan. All the while, there had been considerable opposition to any amalgamation of the two schools at all.

(Above) The Pitlochry-Moulin Central School at Ballinlochan, in use between 1897 and 1974 and known as Pitlochry High School from 1935

Work on the new school began in 1897. It was designed by Mr. C. S. Robertson, a Perth architect, from thirty-two competitive designs, at a cost of about £5,000. It was one storey in height and Gothic in style. The new 'Moulin-Pitlochry Central School' was opened at Ballinlochan on 2nd May 1898, as a combined school to replace those in the respective villages. Although the name has since been used for a road a few hundred yards further east, Ballinlochan was then the area just above and to the west of the junction of Tom-na-moan Road with East Moulin Road.

Shops, Offices and Services

The Post Office at Pitlochry started some time after the census of 1811 and before the one of 1821. It appears originally to have been situated on the eastern corner of the junction of West Moulin Road with Atholl Road (where Davidsons the Chemists now are), moving sometime after 1863 to the little lane to the south of the traffic lights (where G. B. Wilson & Son Leatherworkers now are), until the present premises in the centre of Alba Place were opened on 30th May 1898.

The Royal Mail coach began running daily between Perth and Inverness from 6th July 1830. In summer and autumn, Blair Atholl was served by a stage coach twice a day. Three times a week there was a runner to Rannoch.

Gas was introduced by Messrs Connacher in 1830 at the Star Inn (now Scotland's Hotel); it was a novel spectacle in those days. The original town Gas Works were situated between Atholl Road and

Alba Place, opposite Fisher's Hotel, with the Butter Memorial Fountain beside it and gas street light in foreground (below left) and the same view in 1993 (below right)

Opposite
(Top) One of
Mr. Wm. Martin's
'Athol' lemonade
bottles

the north side of the railway line, where the public toilets now are. In 1896 new gasometers were constructed to the south of the railway line, where the Ferry Road car park now is. Because Pitlochry had these gasometers it became a thankful recipient of North Sea Gas in the nineteen seventies.

The tweed mills of A. & J. Macnaughton Ltd. were established in 1835, in those days carrying out the whole process from pure wool to fully-finished cloth all under one roof. The company is still run by the Macnaughton family, one of only a few businesses in Scotland still in the same family after one hundred and fifty years. Weaving had been in the family long before that, the founder's grandfather having been a woollen manufacturer on Loch Tayside at least as early as 1791.

The business came to Pitlochry originally to reap the benefit of being located beside Wade's new Great North Road. The mills (referred to on early plans as the Dye Works) were situated where Penny's supermarket now is, on West Moulin Road. Opposite, where the newer Park Terrace flats and houses are, there used to be the bleaching green, with long rails, like fences, set out in rows. The family built shop premises in the town, close to the railway station, from which they still operate today.

To run their mills, the company required to secure a source of reliable water. This involved their installing a lade across the lower face of Ben-y-Vrackie to take water from a large catchment area into the Moulin burn, then harnessing the Moulin burn itself and adding two mill dams beside West Moulin Road to increase the head of water.

In 1836, branches of both the Central Bank of Scotland and the Commercial Bank were established, the former in the building on the north-east side of the junction between Bonnethill and Toberargan Roads and the latter at Bank House in the centre of the town. A branch of the National Security Savings Bank of Edinburgh began at the end of that same year, its business being conducted by the manager of the Commercial Bank. The Perth Banking Company started in 1853, at what is still known as the Old Bank Buildings opposite the Strathgarry Restaurant, until taken over by the Union Bank of Scotland five years later; the Union Bank then moved to new premises, where the Local Authority offices now are.

J. & H. Mitchell, W.S. was founded in Pitlochry by James Mitchell in 1838. It is one of the oldest country firms of solicitors and estate agents still in existence. James Mitchell was known originally as a 'notary', rather than a solicitor or lawyer, and he practised from one of the Dysart Cottages, at the western edge of town. After he was joined by his son Hugh, the firm moved to the Union Bank of Scotland Buildings (where the Local Authority offices and Library now are, in Atholl Road). The firm's senior partner was also the Bank Agent (effectively the manager), a custom which continued until 1965.

Distilling and Brewing

The Brewery was situated at Birnam Place where what are still sometimes referred to as the Brewery Cottages are; it faced south, to the west of the steps known as 'Jacob's Ladder' leading up to Strathview Terrace. It was erected in 1839 and carried on business until about 1870, but apparently it was never a commercial success. Curiously, the town plan of 1846 listed the Brewery as a 'Distillery'.

There were seven licensed distilleries in Pitlochry, which is why there were that number of excise officers also. These distilleries produced a yearly average of ninety thousand gallons of whisky, most of which was sent to Dundee. There was:

- one sited above Balghulan, close to the first hole on the Pitlochry Golf Course, now in ruins;
- one to the rear of Sunnybrae in Atholl Road, Pitlochry, which ceased production in about 1800;
- one behind the east end of the Pottery at East Haugh (which was known to have been in operation in 1798);
- one at Lettochbeg, Kinnaird (which also was known to have been in operation in 1798) and which continued until burnt down;
- one at Balnakeilly (which was in operation at least between 1817 and 1819);
- one at Balnacraig Farm, which was moved lower down the hill in 1835, to a less suitable site as

it turned out, which caused distilling to cease soon after; and

- one at Aldour, on the south-eastern outskirts of Pitlochry, which is still in operation.

There were other distilleries elsewhere in the district, for instance one at Edradour, which developed as a co-operative of local farmers and is still in operation, and others at Tomnabrachd and Logierait.

There was a soft drinks factory at the bottom of Bonnethill Road, beside the Moulin burn, just behind where the TSB Bank is now. It was known as 'The Atholl Aerated Waterworks' and was in operation from about 1895 to 1906, belonging first to Mr. J.C. Gavin and then to Mr. William Martin. It manufactured lemonade and ginger beer.

To ensure a gas-tight top, there was a constriction within the glass at the neck of the bottle, above which was a small glass ball; when the bottle was full, the ball was forced up against the stopper. A special 'M' shaped wooden plunger was necessary to open each bottle, which would be used to press the ball down, until enough gas had escaped to let the ball fall back down against the constriction. Few specimens remain today, probably because schoolboys were wont to augment their supply of 'bools' by smashing the bottles so as to grasp the glass balls inside!

Hotels and Tourism

With the surge in Pitlochry's popularity as an early tourist destination came the large hotels which provided a noble hospitality to one and all. Predating these was probably only the Moulin Inn which, until the new Great North Road came through Pitlochry in 1727, had been situated on the only important cross-roads in the district and would have provided for travellers mainly between Blair Atholl and Dunkeld.

(Below) Donald Fisher's brochure for his Hotel in about 1880

Scotland's Hotel was originally the Star Inn and is probably the oldest of the larger Pitlochry hotels still in existence, having been started in about 1845. When Mr. John Scotland took over the Hotel in 1880 he not only changed its name but redeveloped the buildings. Over the years, the owners have acquired neighbouring properties on all sides and have further extended the original buildings.

Fisher's Hotel had been built in about 1839, in the centre of town, with ample stables behind for passing coaches. Its renowned gardens, at one time labelled as the finest Hotel Garden in Europe, were created from the old mill dam. The

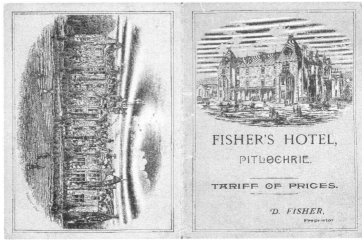

FISHER'S HOTEL,
PITLOCHRIE.

TARIFF OF PRICES.

D. FISHER,
Proprietor

(Top Left) The old Star Inn, which later became Scotland's Hotel, in about 1880 (Top Right) Scotland's Hotel in 1993 (note that the bay window remains)

Hotel was well placed for the Highland Railway's arrival in 1863, being situated next to the new railway station. For years, many of its guests came and went by rail. As its popularity increased, so extensions were added upwards, sideways and behind.

In 1897, the Robertson family (who owned the meal mill and continued running it until 1923) erected Alba Place, comprising shops, offices and flatted dwellinghouses, directly opposite Fisher's Hotel. This replaced their Mill House, which had been located just in front of the Mill (the Mill building itself remaining still, as the Old Mill Restaurant). Because the new Alba Place blocked the Hotel's view of Ben-y-Vrackie, Mr. Fisher built a wing to the west of his Hotel, apparently in retaliation; he was reputed to have said *"If you won't let me see Ben-y-Vrackie, then I won't let you see my gardens."*

Latterly, Fisher's Hotel was owned by a private company, in which a number of local families took shareholdings; thus it remained until the Hotel was sold to the North British Trust chain in 1988. For a time, the Hotel took the tenancy of Lettoch Farm and used its produce in the Hotel.

The Atholl Palace Hydropathic Hotel, designed in a Scottish baronial style by Andrew Heiton of Perth, opened in 1878. It cost in the region of £90,000 which effectively caused the commissioning company's bankruptcy. Its selling price fell to £45,000 and later to only £25,000. It is now owned by Trust House Forte. Its grounds remain extensive, with outdoor ponds, tennis courts, golf course and shooting range. At one time, the four main tennis courts were championship standard, with the Scotland-England-Wales derby being played each September; now those courts host the annual Highland Open.

The Pitlochry Hydropathic Hotel was opened in 1890, in a prominent position above the town, on what was then a treeless moraine. It also was extended to cater for increased demand. Its grounds, developed in the late nineteen eighties for housing, once boasted tennis courts and a nine hole golf course.

Fish

In the Statistical Account of 1793, the local rivers were said to contain trout, eel, par, minnow and salmon, as today, although by all accounts in much greater numbers. Fish were caught for the most part with net and bait, but sometimes with a kind of spear (known as a 'wasp') which had three or four prongs, barbed at each point. Most catches were in those days sent to the London market.

According to the Statistical Account of 1845, Loch Tummel was gradually filling up with alluvial deposits which required to be cleared away annually. At that time, it was much frequented in winter by great numbers and varieties of water fowl, but chiefly swans; there were thirty-six swans in the winter of 1840. The author reported that it abounded with trout and pike, some of the former weighing 14 lbs. while the latter had been known to weigh up to 30 lbs.

Fishing continued as an important source of income for the district, with most of the lochs yielding salmon, trout, pike and perch. Some of the hill lochs began to be stocked with trout.

Moulin Burn

Moulin burn has not been written about in poetry; it has always been a working burn rather than a romantic one. Its heyday was in the latter part of the nineteenth century. Now that it is no longer a source of power, it might perhaps yet gain an air of romance. Although peaceful enough in its passage nowadays, its route has long been dictated by the needs of man.

Above Moulin the small mill dam between Baledmund and Balnakeilly enabled the burn to perform its first duty, that of providing power to the meal mill (probably founded at about the same time as the church) and, latterly, the sawmill at the same location. The burn originally flowed through the village of Moulin to the north-east side of the church, into the lochan to the south-east. This route was blocked up and the burn redirected into its current channel when the mill was removed to Pitlochry.

The next beneficiary was Campbell's monumental sculptor's yard, situated in what is now a field to the south-west of the village, opposite Tigh a Cladaich, with power for a stone polisher between about 1896 and 1915.

When the meal mill was relocated to the centre of Pitlochry, behind the building latterly known as the Prince Charlie House, a new mill dam was located where Fisher's Hotel gardens now are, to gather in the water from the same Moulin burn. Once the mill was moved again, slightly higher up the hill (where the Old Mill Restaurant now is to the rear of Alba Place), this dam proved to be too low.

A new mill dam was therefore created higher up, just within what are now the grounds of the Wellwood Hotel, opposite the Pitlochry Town Hall. Soon this dam was found to be insufficient on its own to meet the needs of both the meal mill and the tweed mills of Messrs A & J Macnaughton, so a second dam was created higher up West Moulin Road, which still exists to the north of Craig Mhor Lodge Hotel. Water was also introduced directly from Ben-y-Vrackie, when a lengthy lade was brought across its lower face, to link in with the burn above Moulin.

(Top) Atholl Palace Hotel
(Middle) Pitlochry Hydro Hotel

Opposite (Middle) Oldest known photograph of the front (north) elevation of Fisher's Hotel as it was originally in the 1840s
(Bottom) Fisher's Hotel after some alterations but before its extension westwards in 1897

The last meal mill remained in operation until 1923. In the nineteen fifties, the building was used for growing mushrooms before being turned into a pub and restaurant. A wheel was refitted later. The tweed mills remained in operation until 1980.

After the burn passed through the mill, it meandered towards the main street of Pitlochry. Just to the north, where the TSB Bank now is, there used to be the lemonade factory, run by the Martin family, which drew its water from the burn. The burn then crossed the main road, originally at a ford and then more recently under a bridge. The surrounding ground is now so built up that most people would not realise that they are travelling across a bridge at the bottom of Bonnethill Road as they turn into Atholl Road.

Finally, opposite the original Gas Works (which used to be situated to the north of the Burnside bridge under the railway line) sluice gates were used to divert the Moulin burn into a lade which ran along the south side of the railway embankment and filled another mill dam, situated where the Ferry Road car park now is. This was for the Pitlochry Sawmill (which was located where Sawmill Cottage now is, on the corner to the south of the Ferry Road bridge under the railway). Just below the Sawmill was the Atholl District Laundry, the last beneficiary of the Moulin burn before it flowed, as it still flows, into the River Tummel just downstream of the suspension bridge to Portnacraig.

(Top) Moulin in about 1900, taken from the top of West Moulin Road, with Campbell's sculpting yard in fenced compound on left

(Bottom) The Old Mill Restaurant in 1993 (site of the last of a succession of three mills in Pitlochry), with Penny's Supermarket behind (site of A. & J. Macnaughton Ltd.'s former tweed mills)

The Coming of the Highland Railway

At first, perhaps as it is with anything new and relatively unknown, there was great resistance to the proposed Highland Railway. Both the critic John Ruskin and the painter Sir John Everett Millais were opponents and entered into a famous correspondence on the subject in *The Times*. Some of the local families were against it too. It was all to no avail. The "steaming monster" came through anyway.

The railway line between Dunkeld and Pitlochry was opened on 1st June 1863 and from Pitlochry to Aviemore on 9th September that year. In fact, it took less than two years to build the one hundred and four miles of track between Dunkeld and Inverness. A line had existed between Perth and Birnam since April 1856, which was operated by the Scottish Midland Junction Company.

Before the railway line came through Pitlochry, the road from Perth came into the village up what is now the drive into Fasganeoin and then the upper part of the drive into Dundarach. The line forced the change to the route we know today.

It was only six days after the new track north of Pitlochry was opened that it was graced on 15th September by Queen Victoria. She was making a detour from her journey to Balmoral in order to visit her friend the sixth Duke of Atholl, who lay dying at Blair Castle. She travelled from Perth in a special train, accompanied by the Chairman and General Manager of the Perth and Inverness Railway Company, as well as several of their engineers, in case of a breakdown or accident.

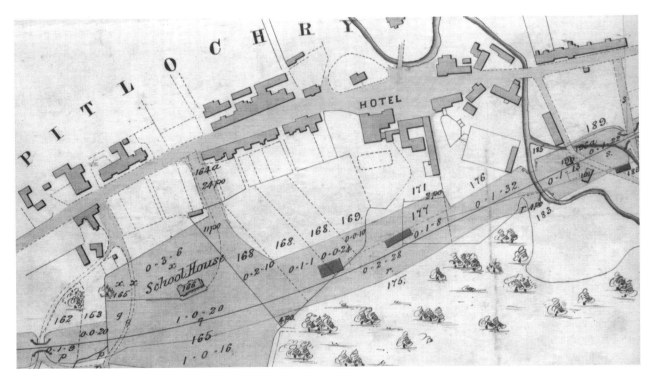

The only recorded accident in the nineteenth century was on 21st October 1865, when the southbound passenger train failed to stop at Pitlochry station and ran past the platform, colliding into the side of an approaching northbound passenger train; nine passengers were injured. As a result, better brakes were fitted on all trains.

From 1865, the line was run by the Highland Railway Company, with carriages resplendent in green and gold livery. Most of its directors and shareholders were Highlanders which perhaps added to its popularity. The Highland Railway was amalgamated into the London, Midland and Scottish Railway in 1922, which then became part of British Railways in 1948. To this day it carries an unusual amount of single track.

Initially four trains left Perth each day, at 6.45am, 9.30am, 1pm and 4.10pm, the journey time to Inverness taking approximately six hours. These times revolutionised travel in the Highlands. It was akin to the progress made by air travel, as against the trains, during the twentieth century. At a stroke, the northern backwaters of North Britain were readily accessible. In 1877, three sleeping carriages were introduced. From 1902, all night trains were fitted with gas lighting.

The impressive viaduct through the Pass of Killiecrankie was completed in 1863, by Joseph Mitchell, the son of Thomas Telford's deputy engineer. He it was who managed to persuade the Duke of Atholl to overcome his initial reluctance and allow the railway through his estate on its way to Inverness. It has ten spans of eleven metres within a length of one hundred and fifty-five metres and stands almost seventeen metres high. It has castellated towers at each end. It is finely curved, the curve being part of a circle with a radius of one quarter of a mile. It cost the princely sum of £5,730. It leads into one of only three short tunnels between Perth and Inverness.

(Above) Plan of Pitlochry, drawn in 1864, showing the route of the new railway line through the centre of town

(Below) Killiecrankie Station in its heyday; it operated between 1863 and 1965

Mitchell was also responsible for the railway bridge over the River Tilt at Blair Atholl. It has two castellated turrets at each end, with arches through which the trains passes; it must have been an impressive sight in the days of steam. These two ends are connected by latticed trusses. It also was built in 1863.

The bridge at Struan was also built in 1863 again by Mitchell, who surmounted the original road bridge with a castellated triple arch bridge for the new Highland Railway. In 1900, another railway bridge was added in parallel, with four arches, when the single track was upgraded to double.

The main station building, on the 'up' platform at Pitlochry, was rebuilt in 1890, on an H plan, with wings at each end, crow-stepped gables and Tudor chimneys. Both platforms were raised by about a third of a metre in 1933, in response to carriages being built with higher steps.

The Aberfeldy branch line, which had been sanctioned since 1846, was opened on 3rd July 1865. It ran for merely nine miles west from Ballinluig, but involved forty-one bridges, including two over the River Tay. Its route is still quite evident and a number of the bridges still stand, the one at Logierait serving as a short cut now for vehicular traffic.

Two Notable Locals

Dr. Alexander Duff – "Fervent in Spirit and Serving the Lord"

Dr. Alexander Duff, the Church of Scotland's first missionary to India, was born at Auchnahyle, between Moulin and Pitlochry, on 25th April 1806. Once, he almost drowned in a nearby burn. When he was thirteen, he and a schoolmate were lost for a time in a snowdrift on Moulin moor.

Having been ordained a minister on 12th August 1829, Duff left Britain in the *Lady Holland* in October 1829. After suffering shipwreck and losing his all, he landed on the shores of India on 30th May 1830, opening the Institution in Calcutta by the end of July that same year. It later became known *(Left) Half bust of* as the Duff Missionary College. His policy was to evangelise by education, sponsoring the English *Dr. Alexander Duff* language as the only effective means of higher education. He was well liked and respected in India. *on the Memorial* He died in 1878.

A fine Iona cross was erected in 1889 to his memory and is situated in the park to the east of Mount *(Right) The* Zion Church in Pitlochry.

unveiling of the Duff
Dr. W. Stewart Irvine – "the guid doctor"
Memorial beside Pitlochry's most famous doctor was Dr. William Stewart Irvine, M.D., F.R.C.S.E. whose father had *Mount Zion Church* been minister at Little Dunkeld and whose brother was minister at Blair Atholl. On his mother's side, *in 1887* he was descended from the Stewarts of Garth. He began his practice in 1833, at the age of twenty.

Dr. William Stewart Irvine

Although centred on Pitlochry, his district stretched from Rannoch and Dalnacardoch in the west, to Glenshee and Strathardle in the east, *"with a score of interesting glens to right and left"*. If that were not arduous enough, much of it was wild moorland without roads.

'The good doctor' (as he was known in the district) travelled on horseback and conducted his duties single-handed. Sometimes he would travel miles to a remote farmhouse to confront a disease which he did not know. At other times, he would no sooner return from a lengthy journey to find that he had been summoned somewhere equally far in another direction.

The locals trusted him completely. One of the most impressive references was to be able to say *"the guid doctor kens me"*. 'The good doctor' died in October 1893. His memorial from a grateful village was the Cottage Hospital which was built in his name.

Some Notable Visitors

Joseph Mallord William Turner

In 1801, at the age of twenty-seven, Turner toured the Highlands. He left Edinburgh on 18th July and travelled to this district via Glasgow, Loch Lomond and Killin. Here, he sketched Tummel Bridge, the Falls of Bruar, the Pass of Killiecrankie and Ben-y-Vrackie in particular, as well as many studies of river and hill. Many critics believe that this expedition represented an influential turning point in Turner's work.

William and Dorothy Wordsworth

On Tuesday 6th September 1803, the famous poet and his sister, who documented their journey, travelled east from Aberfeldy. In leaving, Dorothy described the famous Wade Bridge, which had been designed by none other than William Adam, Scotland's foremost architect, as *"a bridge of ambitious and ugly architecture"*.

They travelled along the River Tay, stopping at the Logierait Inn for a meal. There the young widow, *"very talkative and laboriously civil"*, showed the Wordsworths the ruins of the old Regality Courthouse, which still stood at that time behind the Inn, *"the walls entire and very strong, but the roof broken in"*.

They crossed the River Tummel on the ferry and, turning north, reached Faskally where, with advancing twilight, they decided to rest themselves and their horse, *"besides, the Pass of Killiecrankie was within half a mile, and we were unwilling to go through a place so celebrated in the dark"*. But through they went, because they were unable to find a place on the south side which would take them in, *"so we were obliged to remount our car in the dark, and with a tired horse we moved on, and went through the Pass of Killiecrankie, hearing only the roaring of the river, and seeing a black chasm with jagged-topped black hills towering above"*. They finally found lodging that night at the inn at Old Blair.

The following day, 7th September, the Wordsworths took a three hour promenade in the grounds of Blair Castle, before breakfast. Later in the day, they travelled up to the Falls of Bruar, at the instigation of Burns' famous poem. As Dorothy relates:

> We walked upwards at least three quarters of a mile in the hot sun, with the stream on our right, both sides of which to a considerable height were planted with firs and larches intermingled – children of poor Burns' song; for his sake we wished that they had been the natural trees of Scotland, birches, ashes, mountain ashes, etc., however, sixty or seventy years from now they will be no unworthy monument to his memory.

Felix Mendelssohn

The famous composer stayed at the old Tigh-na-Drochait Inn at Tummel Bridge in 1828. At that time, the new bridge was almost one hundred years old. His visit coincided with a storm, which he sat through by the fire in an otherwise large and bare room.

Queen Victoria

Queen Victoria was the first British monarch to visit the Highlands of Scotland, since King Charles II in 1651, when she came to Dunkeld and Taymouth Castle in September 1842. Throughout her reign she was responsible for creating a general acceptance of and popularity for all things Scottish. It is said that she was at her happiest when at Balmoral, which she acquired in 1853, and in her expeditions around the Highlands.

Queen Victoria visited this district for the first time in 1844 when she took Blair Castle for three weeks' private holiday between 11th September and 1st October. Her visit was billed as an informal one. The royal party was to comprise the Queen, Prince Albert, the Princess Royal, two ladies-in-waiting, four gentlemen and servants. It indeed seemed a small, informal party, until one realises that the servants were about sixty in number, including a full kitchen staff (themselves comprising a roasting cook, a pastry cook, a baker, a confectioner and three other cooks), a butling staff and a stabling staff. The royal party spent time shooting on the Atholl Estates, visiting Glen Tilt (the rugged beauty of which the Queen particularly enjoyed), Bruar Falls, the Falls of Tummel and Faskally.

It was not until 9th October 1861 that the Queen and Prince Albert returned, stopping in at Blair Castle after coming south through the Drumochter Pass. They then continued up the length of Glen Tilt to Bynack Lodge on Mar Estate and thence to Braemar and Balmoral. For the royal party it was an epic day's adventure of about seventy miles, much along rough tracks. The greatest moment was probably their fording the River Tarf just below the Falls of Tarf. The Queen and the Prince were on horseback, but some of the others, notably the Duke of Atholl, John Brown and two Atholl pipers, waded through the water waist high, the pipers continuing to play all the while.

Queen Victoria crosses the River Tarf on 9th October 1861, preceded by two piping Atholl Highlanders, her horse being led by the Sixth Duke of Atholl

In 1863 the Queen, herself recently widowed, returned to Blair Castle for a brief hour on 15th September, specifically to visit the sixth Duke, who was terminally ill (he died four months later). She came and went by train, less than a week after the brand new Blair Atholl station was opened to the public. The Duke, though frail, insisted on getting up to accompany the Queen back to the station.

The Queen next visit was based in the Dowager Duchess of Atholl's house, St. Adamnan Cottage, in Dunkeld, between 9th and 13th October 1865. On their way from Pitcarmick to Dunkeld, after passing Loch Ordie, the royal party were lost for some time in the gloaming and in heavy rain. On the way back to Balmoral, the Queen went by Ballinluig, where she met Pitlochry's famous Doctor Irvine on the road. At Croftinloan, she took the High Drive up the hill through Edradour and over Moulin moor to have lunch at Kindrogan.

The Queen's final visit was in the first week of October the following year, when she stayed again with the Dowager Duchess in Dunkeld. On Wednesday 3rd October, the Queen undertook one of her grand expeditions by Dalguise, Grandtully, Aberfeldy and Kenmore to Fearnan, then turning through Fortingall and Coshieville, up Glen Goulandie to Tummel Bridge and then on to Pitlochry, before returning to Dunkeld. It was a journey of some seventy miles. Even today, it would be an arduous enough outing, but then, on horseback and along poor roads, the journey was a notable achievement. In Strathtummel, the Queen witnessed the autumn colours and, stopping at the 'Queen's View' overlooking Loch Tummel, she noted in her diary that it was *"called after me"* although she had not been there previously; it is in fact believed to be named after King Robert the Bruce's Queen.

Sir John Everett Millais

Co-founder of the famous Pre-Raphaelite Brotherhood in 1848, John Millais met the powerful critic John Ruskin in 1853. He travelled with Ruskin and Ruskin's wife Effie (who originated from Perth) to Scotland later that year. The Ruskins' marriage had not been a success and, when their marriage was annulled two years later, Millais married Mrs Ruskin. The Millais lived near Perth until 1862, when his work required him to be based more often in London.

However, trips to Scotland remained a regular feature, with Dunkeld their most frequent destination. There, apart from undertaking sporting activities, the Millais entertained the likes of Disraeli, Baldwin and Gladstone. They encouraged the Potters, neighbours in London, to take a lease of Dalguise House nearby, and to bring their little daughter Beatrix to sample the Highland scenery.

Many of Millais' famous paintings came from the Perthshire countryside.

William Ewart Gladstone

The Prime Minister visited in both 1864 and 1887, speaking at Fisher's Hotel in Pitlochry on the latter occasion. He was a more regular visitor to Dunkeld.

Reverend Benjamin Jowett

The famous Master of Balliol College, Oxford, holidayed in Pitlochry in 1864 and again in 1867. In later years, he stayed at the peaceful Tigh-na-Drochait Inn at Tummel Bridge, spending several summers working on his book on Plato. He was paraphrased thus:

> *Next come I, Benjamin Jowett.*
> *All there is to know, I know it;*
> *What I don't know isn't knowledge.*
> *I am the Master of Balliol College.*

Robert Browning, Ivan Turgenev and Algernon Swinburne

In August 1871, Robert Browning leased Balavoulin, a small mansionhouse halfway up Glen Fincastle, for the summer season. A stone there commemorates his visit.

When there he met up with the famous Russian novelist Ivan Sergeyevich Turgenev. It was unusual to find a Russian in Scotland in those days. Turgenev was staying with the industrialist Ernest Benzon at Allean (pronounced "Allain") House, now the Queen's View Hotel. He enjoyed the grouse shooting which his host had arranged at Fincastle. After his visit, Turgenev remarked on the Highland air, which he found *"a joy to breathe"*.

Later in the month, Browning met up with both the poet Algernon Swinburne, who was also staying in the Glen, and Benjamin Jowett.

Professor James Stewart Blackie

Professor Blackie was an eminent scholar, principally of Greek (of which he held the Chair at Edinburgh for thirty years). He was passionately involved in the Gaelic language and was primarily responsible for the establishment of a Celtic Chair at Edinburgh University.

Blackie summered at Pitlochry for twenty-five years, between 1869 and 1894, first at Balghulan, above the Cuilc, then at Kinnaird Cottage and latterly at Tom-na-monachan Cottage. He was dynamic; *"he carries a breeze with him"* as Sir James M. Barrie declared.

Robert Louis Stevenson

Robert Louis Stevenson was married in San Francisco on 19th May 1880. The following year, he and his wife arrived in Pitlochry from Edinburgh on 3rd June, staying at Fisher's Hotel, until they were able to move into Kinnaird Cottage on 7th June. In previous summers the Cottage had been taken by Professor Blackie. Stevenson wrote:

> *We have a lovely spot here: a little green glen with a burn, a wonderful burn, gold and green and snow-white, singing loud and low in different steps of its career, now pouring over miniature crags, now fretting itself to death in a maze of rocky stairs and pots; never was so sweet a little river. Behind, great purple moorlands reaching to Ben Vrackie. Hunger lives here, alone with larks and sheep. Sweet spot, sweet spot.*

Whilst there, until 2nd August, 'RLS' wrote three short stories, *Thrawn Janet*, *The Body Snatchers* and *The Merry Men*.

Map of central Pitlochry showing how it had grown by 1867

He travelled on to Braemar, conceiving during the journey the initial storyline which would later become *The Master of Ballantrae*. Whilst at Braemar, he wrote the first nineteen chapters of *Treasure Island* – to keep his thirteen year old stepson amused.

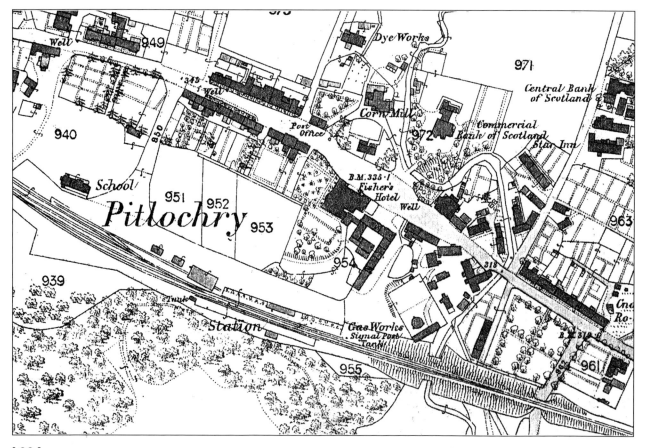

CHAPTER NINE
The Twentieth Century

The celebration of Hogmanay (a Scots term derived from the old French *hoguinane*, which is called *oidhche challuinn* in the Gaelic) is an ancient custom in Scotland, with whisky and the oatcake bannock being the traditional ingredients of 'first footing' to grant good wishes and ensure friendship for the new year. The coming of the twentieth century was greeted not only with whisky and oatcakes but also with fireworks and squibs. Perhaps it would be fitting to celebrate Hogmanay once again with fireworks. New Year's Day 1900 was a holiday, with "only" one delivery of letters.

The principal change in Pitlochry at the end of the Victorian age was a move away from the languor of a circle of gentry and city professionals who had holidayed, or more usually summered here, year after year, bringing with them their servants and gardeners, playing endless tennis and croquet, to a more concentrated bustle and purpose of a resident community of some significance, albeit directed by its continued reliance on tourism.

That tourism was however beginning to be of a different nature. Visitors were less likely to take a house for more than a month, more increasingly for a fortnight or just a week, and they began to arrive by car, rather than omnibus or train, which they would then use to tour about the area. Compared with modern times, visitors still came for reasonably lengthy periods, taking on lease the large Victorian villas within the town, whilst the owners of those villas retired to the purpose-built back cottages from which to administer and look after their paying guests.

More frequently, as the century neared its end, visitors would come, usually by bus or car, merely for a stop during the day, or perhaps for a night or two. Many people visit the town, up to half a million each year, but few stay for any length of time. Visitors include a high percentage of those who have been before, displaying a considerable loyalty. The most popular aspect about a visit has always been the scenery.

In the country at large, the twentieth century witnessed considerable turmoil, some of which touched Highland Perthshire. There were for instance two world wars, the lack of opportunities abroad as a result of the continual shrinking of the British Empire and Scottish soldiers lost as a result of the sectarian strife within Northern Ireland. Nearer to hand, there was occasional violence on city streets and increased crime generally. A country district such as this seemed a welcome sanctuary for young children and the elderly alike.

The magnetism of this district for the elderly in particular has changed its demography markedly. Annual and other frequent visitors have converted their loyalty in making regular holiday visits into choosing to move permanently to this area for their retirement. Others have come for their own reasons, perhaps because of the many recreational pursuits available to fill their spare time and the existence of many clubs and societies geared specifically to senior citizens. Whilst it may be a newer phenomenon that the incomers are older, there has been a regular influx of incomers to the area certainly since the middle of the nineteenth century and, to some extent, the district depends and thrives on it.

New houses have been built at a significant rate throughout the post Second World War period, notably in the late nineteen eighties; most of these have been bought by people over the age of fifty-five. Those not yet retired have bought cottages and houses in the district as second or 'holiday' homes. They have all contributed towards a competition which has ensured that house prices have continued to rise. Local people have found it harder to compete financially and there seems to be few houses left that they can afford to purchase for themselves.

Thus, houses that used to house two parents, five or six children and one or two staff now house one or two people only, except for those which, principally in summer, provide tourist accommodation. So it is that more and more houses have been built to cater for a relatively static local population.

The housing problem has on the one hand been exacerbated by a decline in Local Authority housing (in that council houses have been purchased at discount prices by tenants and the sale proceeds, known as Capital Receipts, have not been allowed by Government to be used for the building of more council houses) and on the other has been tackled by the advent of new-build low-cost housing for purchase and rent, which is provided by Scottish Homes and by various housing associations (who have schemes in Pitlochry at the old school playing field in Ballinlochan and at the former East Church in Pitlochry).

It has become increasingly difficult for the district's young to find satisfactory employment within the area, if they want to stay, let alone their being able to afford the prices of even the lowliest housing. Some commute to jobs in Perth and further afield, whilst others have simply moved away. Even if unemployed, young people often prefer to live elsewhere, thereby adding to another district's unemployment problem. These also are not new phenomena, but continue to influence the peopling of the district.

These issues are by no means unique to this district, but the result is that there are a significant number of children, not many in the twenty to thirty age group, a few more in the thirty to fifty age group and a significant number over fifty. The pressures brought to bear on the district in consequence are beginning to be appreciated.

In the Parish of Moulin
Farming

Local farmers enjoyed perhaps their best era ever during the middle decades of the twentieth century, particularly with all the Government incentives available to encourage the production of food during and after the Second World War. Increased mechanisation – both in the guise of tractors and the like and also better buildings, grain driers and so on – has assisted those who were able and sufficiently progressive to sample the new technology.

However, that technology has been introduced at the expense of people. Agriculture once provided the largest workforce of any industry in the district, but its numbers are now on the decline. Farms where five or six labourers were employed before the Second World War are, with modern systems, sustained by one, perhaps two at the most, by the nineteen nineties. Now tourism is the major industry.

Government incentives, particularly geared towards hill sheep farms, remained available after the War, but became diluted and thus diminished in importance. Many of these were affected adversely by the Common Agricultural Policy of the European Community. Some owner-occupiers tried to diversify from traditional farming, be it into tourism, vegetable growing, venison- and cheese-smoking and silviculture. Tenant farmers were not so able to diversify, if their landlords would not let them, so remaining bound by elderly legislation. The whole question of security of tenure is overdue for change and, although mooted, no change has been made, merely a consolidation in 1991 of the various existing enactments.

Other questions of land use have arisen, caused in part by an urban-based population wanting to exercise its 'right' of free access across the hills, without appreciating properly that those hills are the workplace of others which are vital for local income and employment. Some estate owners have retaliated by trying to restrict access, particularly during the sporting seasons. Some compromise is needed. Mountain bikes and 'all terrain vehicles' cause additional strains on mountain routes, with accompanying erosion of the countryside.

Deer populations have been increasing steadily, causing considerable demands on upland grazings and damage to some crops too. Areas of heather, burnt as part of a muirburn programme, have been grazed by deer and sheep to such an extent that grass, rather than heather, comes back in. Sheep are selective grazers and some areas have become relatively barren of vegetation. Bracken has been marching unchecked up the sides of each strath.

Grouse numbers have declined steadily, perhaps partly because of these factors, as well as an increase in their predators (birds of prey, foxes and hooded crows). A corresponding decline in sporting income has compounded the financial constraints already felt by the estates and hill farmers as a result of a significant fall in the prices of meat (which people are tending to eat less) and wool (which people are tending to wear less).

Pitlochry High School in 1993

Farmers have been unable to afford to invest properly in their environment or to be able to react to the considerable pressures of a global agricultural economy. Farming has been under great stress and, with it, the future management of much of the district's hill ground and moorland lies in some doubt.

Originally the fields on which Pitlochry now sits were part of a number of small farms and crofts. Some of the old farm buildings remain, such as Croftmechaig, which is now a courtyard of three houses just above the Bowling Green. At one time there were no buildings north of Croftmechaig until the croft at Tigh a Cladaich, at the junction of West and East Moulin Roads. The Luggie Restaurant (*luggie* being a Scots word meaning 'milk pail') was once the byre of Dalchampaig, which remained as a working dairy until after the Second World War, the cattle being driven solemnly down the main street each morning, other traffic notwithstanding, to a field at Aldour and back again each evening. A stone limekiln, associated with a former croft at Tomnamoan, still exists within the garden of Crossways.

Culture

Pitlochry has been gaining a healthy reputation for the variety of cultural events of the highest quality which are held in Pitlochry Town Hall, all the Village Halls throughout the district, Blair Castle and the Strathgarry Opera House, quite apart from the world renowned Theatre. Art and Craft Fairs take place at Ballinluig and Pitlochry. In the summer months particularly, but not exclusively, the cultural diary is fairly busy. Indeed, there must be great scope and potential for expanding such activities for the good of locals (both culturally and with employment prospects) and visitors alike.

Schools

The Gaelic Language

In 1951, ninety-three people spoke both Gaelic and English. This was about half the number recorded only twenty years earlier. None spoke Gaelic only, although elsewhere in Perthshire there were six who did. It was the upheaval of the First World War which finally put paid to the Gaelic language.

Gaelic only began to be taught again at the Pitlochry High School from about 1970. There has been a small revival generally at the end of the twentieth century, encouraged by people's search for their heritage, a pride in the nation of Scotland and the beauty of the poetic works of Sorley MacLean, Iain Crichton Smith and others. Since 1979 a National Mod has been held. Gaelic is spoken on the radio, nationally by the BBC and locally by Heartland FM. There are Gaelic evening classes and a new spread of Gaelic dictionaries and language books, the message being that it is never too late to learn.

Pitlochry High School

From 1935, the Moulin-Pitlochry Central School was known as Pitlochry High School. Senior pupils began to be sent to Aberfeldy for their fifth and sixth year studies from 1960. In 1967, consideration was given to the building of a new school; this was rejected simply because the proposed site, beside the Recreation Ground, was thought unsuitable. The school was destroyed by a fire on 8th January 1974. It was not finally demolished until 1990.

After the fire, classes were held in a variety of temporary locations, until the new School was opened in 1975, in the field to the north of the old one. It is well-equipped and, in addition to Primary and Secondary departments, a Nursery department was started in 1988.

There are still primary schools in Ballinluig (although called 'Logierait'), Enochdhu, Struan and Blair Atholl. The one in Killiecrankie closed in 1992.

Croftinloan School

Croftinloan School, one mile to the east of Pitlochry, was founded in 1936 by Hugo Brown, who retired in 1971. At the tender age of twenty-seven, he was backed by his father and other Glasgow businessmen to found a new school. The School, aiming to provide a Christian education, started slowly, with only three pupils in the first year and four in the second. Numbers rose gradually, to fifty by 1950. By 1990, the numbers were steady at about ninety and the School's success was well-known throughout the private educational sector in Scotland. The school was originally boys only but is now co-educational.

Edradour School

Edradour School – founded as the Khiron School in Yorkshire in 1978 – moved to Pitlochry in 1988. It is located in part of what was the Archie Briggs Memorial Home, a children's home at a time when every town had one. The School concentrates on Logic, Computers and other disciplines not readily found in traditional schools.

Sports and Pastimes

Pitlochry Highland Games

The Pitlochry Highland Games were one of the first re-established in Scotland, in 1852. They are still run along similar lines today, on the second Saturday of each September, with Highland dancing, Heavy events, solo piping competitions, running, leaping, cycling and tug o' war.

For a time until 1921, the Games were known as the Pitlochry Athletic Sports. Until the First World War, they were considered one of only a few genuine meetings where world records could be registered; some were achieved.

A pipe band contest was introduced in 1933, which is now limited to those pipe bands in Grade 1. There are about twenty Grade 1 bands worldwide and ten to twelve of these make their last appearance of the season at Pitlochry, playing individually in competition and then, at the prize giving at the end of the day, playing together impressively as a colourful finale of Massed Pipe Bands.

Vale of Atholl Pipe Band

The local Vale of Atholl Pipe Band was formed on 3rd October 1906, under the presidency of Mr J.M. Dixon. The Band has been one of the best promotional symbols of the district. Initially, the Band took part in the weekly Highland Nights laid on by the Tourist Association, but subsequently they started their own. Indeed, it is their own series of Highland Nights, every Monday evening in summer, which is their main fund-raising effort.

The Band decided to enter competitions in 1976, coming sixth (out of thirty-seven) in their first competition (at Hawick). In 1978, they were World Champions in Grade 4. In 1979, they were World Champions in Grade 3. They are now in Grade 1, playing and competing very successfully, being heard by about fifty thousand people each year. A Juvenile Band was formed in 1980 and a Novice Juvenile Band was formed in 1991.

The Band wore the Murray of Atholl tartan for almost ninety years, but has now switched to

Vale of Atholl Pipe Band under Pipe Major Mitchell Pirnie coming up Bonnethill Road, past the old thatched cottages

(Left) Montage of events at Pitlochry Highland Games, clockwise: tug o' war; cycling on grass; the Irish Jig; and the local Vale of Atholl Grade 1 Pipe Band

the 'muted' Macnaughton tartan in recognition of the sponsorship of A. & J. Macnaughton Limited of Pitlochry which began in May 1993.

Curling, Skiing, Shinty and Football

Curling used to be played only outdoors, a popular venue being Loch Kinardochy, on the east side of Schiehallion. Pitlochry Curling Club was founded in 1834 and played on a small lochan, situated to the north-east of Loch Dunmore, now only part of which remains on the northern edge of Faskally Wood, just below the A9 bypass. Many of the stones were said to have been sunk within this lochan during the Second World War. After the Paddling Pool was concreted in 1953, curling and skating took place there in winter until 1956, when play was transferred to a new artificial pond just above the Pitlochry Golf Clubhouse, which is now used only for overflow car parking.

In 1982, the new indoor Atholl Curling Rink was built with significant local investment at Lower Oakfield, in what had been the Pitlochry Festival Theatre. There, some fourteen local curling clubs, all affiliated to the Royal Caledonian Curling Club, play and compete each winter on four sheets of indoor ice. There are a number of open and week-end competitions which involve players from all over Scotland. Atholl players have also distinguished themselves nationally, both at school and at senior levels.

Whilst the district is well placed for reasonable journeys to any of Scotland's ski centres at Glenshee, the Lecht, the Cairngorms, Glencoe and now Aonach Mhor, it offers none close by. In the nineteen sixties, plans were afoot to make snow on Cammoch Hill (from *camadh* meaning 'the bend'

(Bottom Left) The Atholl Curling Rink – once home of 'Scotland's Theatre in the Hills'

(Bottom Right) Curling on the River Tay at Logierait with Cuil-an-daraich in background

– 1,384'/422m), to the west of the Clunie Power Station. This idea faltered when it was realised that there were insufficient nights in winter when the weather was dependably cold enough to convert water from snow cannons into sufficiently stable snow. Perhaps, with real snow becoming less dependable in the winters of the nineteen eighties and nineties, thoughts should turn again to local skiing, on a plastic slope.

Shinty was played locally until about 1885, when it was replaced by football. Nowadays, the nearest shinty is played at Newtonmore.

The Vale of Atholl Football Club was formed in 1885. The Vale, as they are affectionately known, continue to play on the Recreation Ground in Pitlochry, taking part in the local league. Moulin City Football Club was formed in 1922, but no longer exists.

Bowling

Pitlochry Bowling Club was formed in 1887, playing on the green between Bonnethill Road and West Moulin Road, part of the former Croftmechaig Farm. Their first pavilion, a picturesque structure with a thatched roof, was burnt down after an over-enthusiastic attempt to smoke out a bees' bike. The second soon became inadequate and the current pavilion, designed by local architect Mr. John Brander, was opened in May 1933, although it has been considerably extended since.

Moulin Bowling Club was formed in 1893, playing on a green to the north-east of Moulin Square.

Golf

The original Golf Course, consisting of nine holes, was situated to the north-west of the old Recreation Ground (which was later immersed within Loch Faskally). It was reached by the road through the Lady's Dell and by the Recreation Ground, as it lay between the River Garry and the wooded hillock to the south of Dysart Brae and Craigatin.

In 1909, an eighteen hole course was set out on the present site at Drumchorry Farm above the Cuilc by W. Fernie of Troon. As a result of the enthusiasm of the Butter family, whose company still own and run it, the Course was redesigned after the First World War. John Murray was the professional for thirty-three years, his most outstanding local pupil being John Panton. His successor as professional was John Wilson, who retired after forty-two years in 1990. The course is home of the Highland Open and other competitions. It is acknowledged to be quite a challenge if only because of the steep rise up the first three holes; it is said that if one survives that, one is hale and hearty enough!

There is a nine hole Golf Course at Blair Atholl, on the haugh between the railway line and the River Garry. This was originally laid out by James Baird in 1905. It was converted to an eighteen hole course after the First World War, but reverted to the nine holes played now during the Second World War. There used to be a nine hole course on the haugh to the south-east of Ballinluig, but it no longer exists.

In Pitlochry, there is an eighteen hole Putting Course to the south of the railway line and near the Lady's Dell. This is also run by the Pitlochry Golf Course company.

Scouts and Guides

The Pitlochry troop of Boy Scouts, now known as '1st Perthshire' was one of the first to be formed in Scotland, in 1908. Mr. John H. Dixon was the first Scoutmaster and a most enthusiastic one by all accounts. Indeed, he was responsible also for both the Boys Brigade and the Young Men's Society.

The Scouts met in the old school at the bottom of East Moulin Road. When this was demolished, as part of a road improvement scheme to East Moulin Road in about 1970, a new Scout building was erected nearby. This is still used by the Scouts, Cubs and Beavers. It is also used as a headquarters for the Mountain Rescue Service each week-end of the winter.

The 14th Perthshire Girl Guides were formed in 1921 and were soon able to erect a Hut in Well Brae. This is still used by the Guides, Brownies and Rainbows.

Heartland FM

In 1992, Heartland FM, Britain's smallest independent local radio station was formed, their first recording studio being within the Atholl Curling Rink premises. The residents of Highland Perthshire raised over £35,000 towards the launch of this venture. Heartland FM began by broadcasting

at week-ends only, with one full-time administrator and some fifty regular volunteer presenters. By June 1993, weekday evening broadcasting was introduced. The station is partly dependant on local advertising for its revenue, but has to raise the remainder of its funds by many different means, such as a Thrift Shop and arranging successful musical concerts by mostly Scottish musicians.

Societies, Clubs and Associations

As in any village or town, there are a large number of organisations, some old and some newer, to cater for all ages and interests, as well as the Community Council, Probus Club, Rotary Club, Round Table and many others. These wax and wane and change from time to time.

Public and Cultural Buildings

Butter Memorial Fountain

The Drinking Fountain was built in 1887, of Aberdeen granite and in the shape of a gothic spire, in memory of the late Lieutenant-Colonel Archibald Butter who had died in 1880 at the age of forty-four (five years before the death of his father who had been instrumental in the building of Mount Zion Church). It was located in the space between the Royal Bank and the Bank of Scotland. Before the First World War, great concert parties were held beside it in summer. As it was felt to be in the way of traffic, it was removed in the mid nineteen sixties. The memorial plaque has been saved, but the stone has disappeared.

Irvine Memorial Hospital

The idea of a Cottage Hospital for the growing town was promoted by Miss E. Molyneux of

(Middle) The opening of the Butter Memorial Fountain in 1887, between what are now the Royal Bank of Scotland and the Bank of Scotland

(Bottom) The Butter Memorial Fountain beside the old Mill House

Irvine Memorial Hospital: the eastern elevation and front door as originally built (top) and the new therapeutic garden and western elevation of the Atholl Ward in 1993 (bottom)

Tom-na-monachan. She also encouraged the idea that it would be a fitting memorial for the late Dr. William Stewart Irvine (1812-1893), the much-loved and well-respected local medical practitioner.

The idea was realised in 1901, when the foundation stone of the new Irvine Memorial Hospital was laid, at the top of the steep brae between the Hydro Hotel and the School. It was built in a domestic style, from plans prepared gratuitously by Mr. John Leonard, a local architect. The building, costing just under £1,400, was inaugurated in July 1902, but Miss Molyneux was herself unable to attend, ironically "on doctor's orders".

Extensions were added in 1929, 1936 (the X-ray room) and 1980 (the Atholl Ward for long-term geriatric patients). In 1992 a therapeutic garden for the Hospital was established in adjacent ground acquired from the Castlebeigh Hotel.

An ambulance service was started in 1945, their base now situated at Kennedy Place. Given the large geographical area covered and the fact that this includes all traffic accidents on the A9 (attended also by the Pitlochry Doctors who operate a voluntary service), the station, run by the Scottish Ambulance Service, is well-equipped.

Although not a public building, it is worth mentioning the Doctors' Surgery. At the beginning of the century, there was one doctor, then two who had their own surgeries at home. A partnership was created in time, initially with two of the three doctors then in the town; each continued to consult in his own home, relatively independent of the other and with neither nurse nor secretary. In 1969, the partnership combined at last by setting up a new Surgery at the top of Toberargan Road. This Surgery has been expanded on a number of occasions to reflect the growing medical work load, illustrated clearly by the simple facts that the square footage of the buildings has doubled between 1969 and 1993 and that there are now five doctors in the partnership where there were two.

To match the increase in the older echelons of the local population, there has been additional health care for the elderly. An Abbeyfield Home was formed at Sunnybrae, at the west end of Atholl Road. The Church of Scotland started a successful 'eventide' home at Chequers, also in Atholl Road. Donavourd House, a mile to the east of Pitlochry, was turned into a private nursing home, after a brief time as a hotel. The Irvine Memorial Hospital added its own geriatric wing, named the Atholl Ward, opening a therapeutic garden in 1992 beside it.

The Institute

In 1895, the Barbour Institute was built, in memory of the late Reverend Robert Barbour of Bonskeid (who had been a minister of the Free Church). The chosen site was just to the south of the main street, in what previously had been part of a nursery garden. It is a distinctly Scottish building in character, designed by Mr. J. Murray Robertson, an architect from Dundee, at a cost of about £3,000. It housed baths (at a time when few private houses included a bathroom, let alone an indoor toilet), three billiards tables, reading room, smoking room, ladies' room and a meeting room, as well as a caretaker's flat in the basement. It ceased to be used as an Institute after the Second World War, being transformed into a restaurant and café for a time, before becoming offices. The Local Authority Library was housed in a building to the rear until 1981.

Local Authority Offices and Library

In 1965, the Union Bank of Scotland moved from their buildings at 26 Atholl Road. These were then acquired by the Local Authority for use by the Town Council. What had once been a beautiful garden under the care of two men became a central car park, whilst sheltered houses known as Elm Court were built to the rear, where outbuildings had once been.

Following Local Authority reorganisation in 1974, the buildings were from then on occupied as local offices by departments of the Perth & Kinross District Council and, in 1981, their Library was moved there.

Pitlochry Town Hall, Regal Cinema and the Atholl Leisure Centre

Having been talked about for about thirty years, the foundation stone of Pitlochry Public Hall (as it was originally known) was laid in May 1898, by Sir Alexander Muir Mackenzie of Delvine. It was designed in the Scottish Renaissance style by Mr. Alexander Ness, a Dundee architect, who won the competition for designing the building. The Hall itself was opened in 1900 and quickly encouraged many community activities, including concerts, drama and opera.

The first cinema showings took place in the Town Hall in 1919. In 1920, these were transferred to a wooden building (an old army hut) situated on the south side of Atholl Road just to the west of the Strathgarry Restaurant. Then, in 1935, purpose-built premises were opened in West Moulin Road, sponsored by local finance, which had been formed into the Pitlochry Picture House Limited. The Pitlochry Regal Cinema continued in business until about 1985, declining markedly from about 1965 onwards, owing to the coming of television and then videos. By the time of a revival in films in the 1990s, it was too late; the building by then had been transformed into the Atholl Leisure Centre.

The Atholl Leisure Centre was created by Pitlochry Leisure Company Limited in 1990, from the Regal Cinema, to provide an indoor facility for badminton, five-a-side football, indoor hockey, aerobics and much more besides. In 1991 Pitlochry Leisure Centre Limited then took over the management of the Town Hall from the Perth & Kinross District Council. There followed a refurbishment and, with active marketing, the role of the Town Hall as a venue was expanded to include touring plays, musical concerts and children's shows as well as the traditional uses for meetings, local plays, auction sales and the like.

Paddling Pond

What is now known as the Paddling Pond in West Moulin Road was built in 1933, originally intended as a children's sailing pond. Indeed, at the opening ceremony, Mrs. Butter launched a toy yacht. The pond was built by unemployed ex-servicemen. It continues to be used, albeit not much. There is a tennis court beside it, intended to replace the public one which used to be at the Recreation Ground, but sadly it is quite unusable because of an uneven surface and lack of surface drainage.

Pitlochry Festival Theatre

The Pitlochry Festival Theatre started in 1951. Mr. John Stewart, having previously run the Park Theatre in Glasgow, moved to Knockendarroch House in 1944. He had been keen to build a small theatre by extending the house, along the lines of the Opera House at Glyndbourne, but building restrictions at the end of the Second World War made that impossible.

Instead, nothing daunted, Stewart hit on the idea of erecting a tent within a tent, the inner one being the auditorium and the space between the two being the foyer and restaurant. The tents were duly erected in 1951, at Lower Oakfield, but gales wrought havoc to the outer tent, which was replaced by a semi-permanent building in 1953, which could house 500. Mr. Stewart died suddenly in 1957, aged 55, having gifted the Theatre and his house to Pitlochry Festival Society Ltd.

The Theatre was an immense success and, with the Dam and Fish Ladder, has been primarily responsible for sustaining Pitlochry's popularity as a tourist resort since the Second World War. In 1977, it was decided to move the Theatre from its original home in Lower Oakfield to new premises

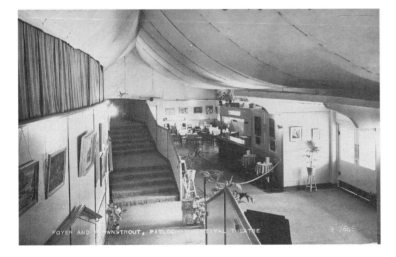

FOYER AND BROWNSTROUT, PITLOCHRY FESTIVAL THEATRE

at Portnacraig, where the new Theatre opened on 19th May 1979, at a cost of some £2 million. Prince Charles, the Prince of Wales, visited the new Theatre in 1980 to mark its official opening.

The Theatre is an astonishing building to find on the outskirts of a small Highland town. In 1992 a refurbishment and development plan began, to repair the roof, provide offices and workshops and to extend the catering facilities.

The Theatre still runs to its original format, between May and October, principally with a repertoire of six or seven plays, a different one being staged every day, as well as concerts, musical evenings, foyer events and art exhibitions. It employs one of the larger repertoire casts and is well respected as a teaching ground for young actors. It has become a national – if not an international – arts venue.

Shops, Offices and Services

The twentieth century saw the main roads through the town covered in tarmacadam, with pavements on both sides of the main street; at last there was no more dust! Many of the side streets had been laid out with insufficient width for pavements and, to this day, there are many busy roads in the town with no pavement, such as Larchwood Road, Lower Oakfield and part of Toberargan Road. As horses yielded to motor cars, the roads became less messy, especially once cattle were no longer driven the length of the main street twice a day. Although many roads had familiar names, there were not named officially until 1954 (and houses were not numbered until 1956).

The Post Office moved to Alba Place (*Alba* meaning 'Scotland'), in the very centre of Pitlochry, in 1898. In spite of the volume of business, especially in the summer months, and even though the sub-Post Office in Moulin closed in 1990, Pitlochry Post Office was itself reduced to a sub-Post Office in 1991. The Sorting Office was moved from Alba Place to new purpose-built premise within the Aldour industrial estate in 1989.

Telephones were introduced in 1912, the original Exchange being located above the Post Office in Alba Place. It then relocated to Tiree House, which is now the Tourist Information Centre, until a new Exchange was constructed behind there in 1956. This is now fully automated.

As early as 1896, the Pitlochry Gas Company commissioned Professor Forbes to assess the viability of introducing electric light into the village, with power derived from the Falls of Tummel. The Professor concluded that the saving over gas lighting could be as much as two-thirds, but the company did not take the idea any further and, indeed, proceeded almost immediately to spend £2,000 on a new gasometer of thirty thousand cubic feet. In the event, electricity was not introduced until 1930 and even after the Second World War there were a number of buildings without it. The Professor's plan was ahead of its time, but the power of water was harnessed eventually for electricity, some fifty years later.

The gasometers at Pitlochry were situated latterly to the south of the railway line, to the west of Ferry Road. Once the town was connected by underground pipe to North Sea Gas, the gasometers were removed. The site was transformed into an enlarged car park in 1992.

The Police Station was originally in Bonnethill Road opposite Scotland's Hotel. At the turn of the twentieth century, there was only one policeman, Sergeant Grant, who apparently *"managed well, except on Market night".* In 1957, the Police Station was moved to its present location at what had been the doctor's house called Newholme on Atholl Road. The former quarters then became the District Nurse's house and clinic. With the advent of increased traffic on the A9 between Inverness and Perth, the Police became increasingly involved at the scene of the many vehicle accidents.

In 1897, complaints were made that, although there was a public fire hose, situated under the Town Hall, there was no organisation for its use. A part-time Fire Brigade was formed. They moved to Newholme with the Police in 1957. The Fire Brigade practice one evening each week and attend fires, floods and (using their cutting equipment) vehicle accidents. All the volunteers are now contacted by personal radio bleepers, but time was when they were summoned to an emergency by an air-raid siren, which boomed across the town, day or night.

The Bobbin Mill, referred to on some maps as the 'turning mill', was situated to the south of the railway between the Armoury and the gasometers. It was operated by Mr. Taylor from 1893 until it was burnt down in 1926. It supplied the bobbins used in the jute trade, hence its name, as well as tent pegs. The wood used was birch of which there was a plentiful supply locally.

There was a Sawmill, to the east of the Ferry Road car park, which was operated by the Marshall family. They provided all types of fuel – wood, peat, charcoal and coal. Their mill was powered originally by the water of the Moulin burn, collected in a mill pond at what is now the eastern half of the car park in Ferry Road. They had a depot by the station, as the coal came by rail.

The first Laundry was established by Thomas Muir in the old school building in Moulin in about 1905. The laundry was collected and delivered in baskets carried on a horse-drawn van. When he wished to expand, Mr. Muir was told that the load-bearing capacity of the building was inadequate; the building was at the edge of the former lochan at Moulin and the soil there was unstable.

So, in 1916, Mr. Muir moved to Pitlochry. He set up the Atholl District Laundry in Ferry Road, where the coaching stables and Smithy run by Adam Doggart used to be. To some extent, his site was as problematic as the Laundry building at Moulin, because this one in Ferry Road, because this was built partly on old sand pits. There the Laundry continued until 1978, coping with a seasonal business which could see the summer turnover eight times higher than the winter, reflecting the very nature of Pitlochry.

The Smithy at the western end of Pitlochry, at the foot of Larchwood Road, was last in use as such in about 1965, at which time the house was

Opposite
Pitlochry's original Festival Theatre at Lower Oakfield in 1952 – (top) the opening of the Theatre; (middle) inside the inner tent: foyer and Brown Trout restaurant; and (bottom) the new Theatre at Portnacraig

The Old Smithy, now a restaurant

still lit by gas, with neither kitchen nor bathroom; it was possibly the last house in the town without these amenities. It was used as a shop for the next twenty years, before being converted into a tearoom and latterly a restaurant.

There was a Smithy at Moulin until the beginning of the twentieth century. Initially this was situated on the east side of Moulin Square and latterly on the west side of the burn, opposite the old Post Office.

A. & J. Macnaughton Ltd's tweed mill in West Moulin Road closed in 1980, when all production was transferred to the company's mills in Aberdeenshire. After standing empty for a time, the mills were sold in 1988 and transformed into Penny's Supermarket. Macnaughtons still own and operate from the original shop premises in Station Road.

To celebrate the company's 125th anniversary, on Saturday 18th June 1960, Macnaughtons broke the record set up in 1811 by the famous Throckmorton Coat, for the time taken between fleecing a sheep and donning the finished coat, on this occasion a kilt jacket. The jacket is still on display. In 1811, it had taken the Berkshire firm thirteen hours and twenty minutes. One hundred and forty-nine years later, Macnaughtons achieved the task in just six hours and ten minutes.

The company's 150th anniversary in 1985 was celebrated by a dinner to which they invited members of other firms and companies throughout Scotland still in the original owner's family for one hundred and fifty years or more. Through its subsidiaries Isle Mills Ltd. and House of Edgar Ltd., the company provides a significant proportion of the fine tartan woollen cloth manufactured in Scotland today.

The Commercial Bank became the Bank of Scotland in 1868 and on amalgamation with the Union Bank, they moved (the former from north of Scotland's Hotel and the latter from what are now the Local Authority offices and Library) to new premises at 76 Atholl Road, near the centre of town. The old Union Bank premises at 26 Atholl Road became the Town Council premises, which on local government reorganisation in 1974 was taken over by the Perth & Kinross District Council. The Perth and County Savings Bank began in 1911, moving in 1953 into new premises in Bonnethill Road, which after amalgamation became the Trustee Savings Bank and now TSB Bank Scotland plc.

The Brown Trout Research Laboratory was set up in 1948, in a row of huts near Faskally House. It quickly earned a reputation for its highly-organised research. In 1960, it became the Freshwater Fisheries Laboratory, to include the study of salmon and sea trout, for which it has become renowned the world over.

Faskally House, situated to the west of Pitlochry, used to be a home of the Butter family and latterly of the Fosters. After the Second World War, it was used by the North of Scotland Hydro-Electric Board as a technical staff training college. In 1953 it became the Forestry Commission's Training School. From 1971, it was owned first by Glasgow District Council and then by Strathclyde Regional Council as a well-equipped outdoor activity centre. Strathclyde decided to close the Centre in 1993 and its future is unknown.

In 1985, the Highland Perthshire Development Company Limited was set up, to act as an Enterprise Trust in support of existing and new local businesses. Its other role is to encourage the young of the district to stay locally, rather than feel forced to leave to find affordable housing and job opportunities elsewhere. It was located initially in Bank House and then moved to Bonnethill Road, where Frank Henderson's famous photographic studios had once been. The company has an impressive record of saving jobs and assisting in the creation of new ones, as well as taking an interest in the affairs of Community Councils and in public projects.

In the late nineteen eighties the site of another sawmill, just beyond Aldour, became a small industrial estate. The Post Office Sorting Office was relocated here on 16th December 1988. About this time, the Local Authority closed the rubbish tip within the Black Spout wood, which was at capacity anyway; it is now fully landscaped. Instead, they provided a Refuse Transfer Station within the industrial estate to cater for different categories of rubbish. Other businesses at the industrial estate include local builders and garage mechanics.

One of the original distilleries remains at Aldour, the Blair Athol Distillery. This was licensed in 1825, although known to be in operation before then. It now forms part of United Distillers, although still under the Bell's Scotch Whisky division, producing the Blair Athol single malt. Its three storage buildings hold the equivalent of some ten million bottles of whisky maturing in oak casks. About two per cent of the liquid volume of each cask evaporates each year – "the angels' share" as it is philosophically known. The walls of the buildings and the trunks of surrounding trees are blackened from these alcoholic vapours. The Distillery has a visitor centre and hospitality rooms incorporated within some of its stone buildings, which include the original farmhouse of Allt Dour.

Towards the end of the twentieth century, there was great concern about the number of shops selling clothing (especially knitwear and woollens) within the centre of Pitlochry. Certainly there were quite a few – up to twenty-two out of a total of fifty-eight shops in or near the centre of town. Whilst that concern was well understood, such numbers being disproportionate anywhere, it is perhaps useful to note that there have previously been trends in the shops of Pitlochry which have not lasted indefinitely; these include:

- five shoe shops, famous for their leather, at the beginning of the twentieth century, where shoes could be custom-made during a visitor's stay; there were two saddlers also;
- four cycle shops in 1903;
- six fishing tackle makers in 1903;
- nine gift shops in the mid-nineteen seventies;
- eleven shops selling principally knitwear at the beginning of the nineteen nineties.

Pitlochry's near 'mono market' in clothing and the unremarkable appearance of its high street are valid causes of concern to local residents and others as the century draws to its close.

First Flight in Britain?

John Dunne had been experimenting with flying machines since 1900. In 1904, just one year after the Wright Brothers' first famous flight at Kittyhawk, North Carolina, Dunne had moved beyond models and built by hand his first aeroplane. The War Office ordered tests of his machine, but these had to be conducted in secret. The hills of Highland Perthshire were considered to be suitable.

The plane was driven by road to be assembled in a field up Glen Tilt in 1907 and tested then and the following year. Dunne flew it himself. It was tail-less, had backward-sloping wings and incorporated aerodynamic ideas from the zannonia leaf (of the cucumber family). It was very stable, at the expense of speed and manoeuvrability, which is why it was not chosen by the War Office for combat purposes. However, it is probable that the first air flight in Britain took place in Atholl!

Apart from being one of the first aeroplane engineers, Dunne wrote four books, *An Experiment with Time*, *The Serial Universe*, *The New Immortality* and *Nothing Dies*. He had a lifelong interest in the meaning of dreams and their ability to foretell the future as well as in a related theory that time is serial, rather than linear.

First World War 1914-1918

Many locals rushed to serve King and Country. Throughout the War young boys fresh from school could not wait to be able to sign up. In all, though, the town lost eighty-one of its sons in the Great War, many on one day at Flanders.

Women stepped in to take over the shops and some of the other businesses, whilst the men were away overseas or at training; thus did most of the local businesses survive. Tourists still came to the area each summer of the War.

Fonab House was used as an Auxiliary Hospital during the War, with many local women training to become nurses there. The Hospital looked after nine hundred and twenty-six patients in all. Bonskeid House was used as a Red Cross Convalescent Home.

The Armoury for the district was situated at Loch View, to the south of the railway line. The small armoury and drill hall still exist. Outside drill practice for the local reserve took place on the paddock between the old Armoury buildings and the Dam.

Hotels were used to house relocated schoolchildren, such as those from Queen Margaret's School of Scarborough who were at the Atholl Palace between 1917 and 1919, or passing troops of soldiers.

Second World War 1939-1945

Although the theatres of war were predominantly overseas, its effects were felt within Highland Perthshire. Many families and schools were evacuated from other parts of the country to the district, billeted on families or housed in hotels and other premises. The Atholl Palace Hotel was taken over between 1940 and 1944 by the Leys School, Cambridge. Ninety pupils from St. Joseph's Roman Catholic School in Glasgow stayed between 1939 and 1942 and continued their lessons together in the Town Hall. Sixty-two private evacuees swelled the High School roll.

Canadian lumberjacks were stationed in the district in order to fell some of the great woods of Highland Perthshire, so that timber was available to feed the war machine. When they left, absorbed into the War themselves in Europe, locals and locally-based prisoners continued the felling and transportation of timber.

The local prisoner-of-war camp was at Pitagowan, near Bruar. The new A9 runs through the site. It was used initially for Italian prisoners, who were reportedly cheerful, musical and resourceful, making all sorts of items from wood, melted-down toothbrushes and any other available material. Later, Germans and some Austrians were housed there, who were apparently more sullen. The prisoners worked on farms in the neighbourhood and were involved in felling Bruar Wood. This was loaded onto trains at Struan Station (to the west of Struan Inn), where up to two trains a day took the lumber away. It is believed that there were no successful escapes.

Sixteen locals died in the War and many were taken prisoner in 1940 at St. Valery. Those who fell were added to the War Memorial in the middle of Pitlochry, which already held the roll of honour of those who had fallen in the First World War.

Essential food supplies, including peanuts and linseed, were stored in garages within Pitlochry. This resulted in a lovely show of the blue flax flowers wherever the linseed had been spilt, at the railway station and along the verges of the main road.

No German bombs were dropped in Pitlochry, but a number fell in the vicinity:
• four high explosives on Fonab moor on 4th August 1940;
• five high explosives at Dalreoch, Enochdhu on 10th May 1941;
• one high explosive on Balnacree Wood, to the east of Pitlochry, on 25th March 1943; and
• one unexploded mine to the east of Edradour on 6th April 1943.

Hydro-Electricity

The Hydro-Electric Scheme undertaken in the aftermath of the Second World War owed much to the Grampian Electricity Supply Company, which had been established in 1922 to promote a small Hydro-Electric scheme at Lochs Ericht and Rannoch.

There is an interesting legend about Loch Ericht, that it was not always a natural loch, but became one in the space of just one night when, as a result of some huge subsidence, the village and Parish of Feadail, with its people and livestock, were engulfed all of a sudden by this stretch of water, never to be seen again.

From 1945, the initial scheme was expanded by the newly-formed North of Scotland Hydro-Electric Board. The Board's Tummel-Garry Hydro-Electric Scheme was designed to harness both the headwater from the River Spey and water from Lochs Eigheach (raised ten metres), Garry, Ericht and Rannoch, to create new reservoirs at Dunalastair Water and at Lochs Errochty, Tummel and Faskally as well as building nine power stations (with a generating capacity of about two hundred and fifty thousand kilowatts) and nine dams.

It is not often realised that water flows north from the Boar of Badenoch towards Dalwhinnie, intended via the Spey for the Moray Firth to the east of Elgin, which is now diverted instead south-

Loch Tummel from the Queen's View before being raised 17 feet in 1950

westwards into Loch Ericht and so into the sea by Dundee. The waters of the Bruar and other upper tributaries of the River Garry are diverted by a twelve mile long pipe into Loch Errochty.

The total catchment area of the Scheme is over seven hundred square miles, with an annual rainfall varying from three hundred and sixty-five centimetres in the uplands to ninety centimetres in the straths.

Not all was plain sailing, however. In March 1945 a Pitlochry Protest Committee was formed, expressing grave concern about the proposed scheme and its effects, which would include:
- Loch Tummel's being raised five metres;
- the reduction in height of the Falls of Tummel;
- the disappearance of the Clunie Bridge; and
- the loss of the Recreation Ground (beneath the artificial Loch Faskally).

A Public Inquiry was held, as a result of which the Scheme was given the go-ahead. There was still great controversy and, initially, the landscape was indeed spoilt on a massive scale, perhaps inevitably, until the raw works of man were allowed to settle in and be subdued by nature.

Many construction firms were involved, including George Wimpey & Co. and Sir Alexander Gibb & Partners, in what was one of the first major projects in Scotland to follow the Second World War. The workmen set up a camp at Cammoch, at the base of Cammoch Hill (really more accurately at the base of Creag Dhubh) on the south side of the River Tummel opposite Faskally House. This encampment was more like a village, which merited its own Post Office, along with many other offices and trades associated with its workings.

A tunnel was constructed from the end of the enlarged Loch Tummel, at the Clunie Dam, through to the Clunie Power Station, near the head of the new Loch Faskally. It involved tunnelling through the hillside for almost two miles, the pipe being horseshoe-shaped and having a diameter of six and three-quarter metres, allowing two thousand seven hundred million gallons of water to flow through every day. The inner arch of the Clunie Monument, about a mile and a half from Pitlochry on the Foss road, is the same size as the pipe; it is a memorial to five men who lost their lives when caught in the tunnel, whilst laying blasting explosives which went off too soon during one of the most violent thunderstorms in local memory.

The foundation stone for the Pitlochry Dam was laid by the Countess of Airlie, wife of the first Chairman of the North of Scotland Hydro-Electric Board, on 25th April 1946, *"a day of sleet and rain"*. The new Loch Faskally was then named, after the mansionhouse and estate which are now situated near the head of the loch.

As the banks of the river were glacial moraines, with the bedrock in places being as much as fifteen metres below the level of the river bed, it was necessary to build retaining walls on both sides. The

one on the south (Fonab) side is over seventy-five metres long, but the one on the north (town) side is over two hundred and seventy-five metres long (that is, almost twice the length of the Dam itself and stretching up to the railway) as well as being one and a half metres thick and up to forty metres deep. To ensure that all leakage would be stopped, the trench for the retaining wall was, astonishingly, over sixty metres deep and the face of the moraine at that depth had to be grouted under pressure. Like an iceberg, the visible parts of the Dam are only a small proportion of the entire construction.

Incorporated within the Dam is a 'Fish Ladder', designed to enable salmon and sea trout principally to surmount this wall of concrete (over sixteen metres high) and reach their spawning grounds beyond. Each year, between April and October an average of five and a half thousand salmon return from their Atlantic feeding grounds to the rivers where they were born in order to lay their eggs in precisely the same spot. The flow of water through the Fish Ladder attracts them into the first pool, which then rises in forty-five centimetre steps up to the level of Loch Faskally above. There are thirty-four pools in all, three of them being resting pools to give the fish a respite from the climb. Each pool is connected to the next by an underwater pipe, through which the fish swim. There is an Observation Chamber within two of the tanks about halfway up the series.

There is also a 'fish pass', as they were originally called, at the Clunie Dam, at the foot of Loch

(Right) Pitlochry Dam and Fish Ladder, with Loch Faskally beyond, shortly after completion in 1950; Fonab Castle on the left, once Scottish home of the Sandeman family, now operating headquarters of Scottish Hydro-Electric plc

Constructing the Pitlochry Dam in 1949, with the cutting on the north bank which meant that Ben-y-Vrackie could be seen from the Dam

Constructing the Clunie Dam in 1948, at the southern end of Loch Tummel

Tummel. This has forty-three pools. Fish ladders also exist at Dunalastair and Kinloch Rannoch .

The Tummel Scheme was the masterpiece of Sir Edward McColl, who wished to harness the power of the Tummel valley to its full potential, whilst preserving or even improving the natural charm. The motto of the Hydro Board was *neart nan gleann* ('strength of the glens'). The results are there to be judged:

- Lochs Faskally, Tummel, Errochty and Eigheach;
- Dunalastair Reservoir, its height carefully maintained to preserve the rich birdlife which is sustained on its wetland;
- the Pitlochry Dam (one hundred and forty-five metres long);
- a new Recreation Ground for Pitlochry, (which had previously been the town's sewage fields until these were moved east to Aldour in 1932), which in layout is very similar to the former Ground, including its natural terrace;
- a road bridge half a mile east of Pitlochry at Aldour which was opened in 1949 to replace the old Clunie Bridge half a mile to the west of the town;
- the Clunie footbridge, situated close to the old Clunie Bridge across the upper part of Loch Faskally, which was opened in 1950 and was the first bridge in Britain to be built of aluminium-alloy; and
- the Fish Ladder at Pitlochry Dam, famous perhaps the world over.

Pitlochry Dam in spate on 17th January 1993 (above) and (below) in January 1974 (showing overflowing fish ladder)

After almost half a century, the consensus is that Sir Edward McColl succeeded remarkably well in achieving both his aims.

There is an Exhibition Centre at the Dam, near the Observation Chamber of the Fish Ladder, which is reached from the town by a walk across the Dam itself. Whilst crossing, one can compare the serenity of Loch Faskally on the top side with the energy of the River Tummel on the lower side.

After heavy rain and particularly after quickly thawing snow, the Dam's drum gates can open automatically (although usually controlled manually), providing a spectacle of raw power, as the bow wave of white spume spreads out down river, the roar of the water being audible in many parts of the town. Occasionally, land downstream can suffer flooding, as can some houses and the road south of Aldour.

There were notable floods in January 1974, February 1990 and January 1993, when the river was almost high enough to touch the walkway of the Suspension Bridge, some seven metres or more above its normal level. To the south, a new and thankfully temporary loch was created between Ballinluig and Dowally, with all the fields of the haughland and the railway line itself (albeit on an embankment) being submerged for a couple of days. At the peak of the January 1993 flood, the flow over the Dam was near maximum capacity, at thirty-four thousand cusecs (cubic feet per second), which is equivalent to about ten and a half double decker buses going over the top of the Dam *every second*. Nearer Perth the flow every second was equivalent to about twenty-four double decker buses, which demonstrates most clearly that the catchment area of the River Tay is the largest in Europe.

Perhaps the only 'blot' on the landscape is the lines of tall electricity pylons marching thoughtlessly through many a vista. This is most evident to the south of Tummel Bridge. These pylons might better be painted in camouflage or the lines they carry placed underground. It seems strange that they have been allowed to escape the careful attention given to other aspects of our natural heritage.

From LMS to ScotRail

From 1922, the Highland Railway became the London, Midland and Scottish (LMS), being absorbed into the national network of British Railways in 1948, which changed its name to British Rail and became regionalised into ScotRail.

At its peak, the line caters for large numbers of passenger and freight trains. Operation of the line is usually trouble-free, except where flood waters intersect the line south of this district. Some accidents have occurred. In October 1914, the postal van on the express train was destroyed by fire, whilst standing at Pitlochry station. Derailments occurred of the Aberfeldy train near Balnaguard Halt on 20th November 1959 and of the southbound sleeper train just south of Pitlochry at 3am on 22nd September 1983, without loss of life.

The impressive expansion of the rail network through Highland Perthshire in the second half of the eighteenth century was followed by retraction one hundred years later. The station at Guay was closed on 3rd August 1959. On 3rd May 1965, the stations at Ballinluig, Killiecrankie and Struan were closed, as was the branch line to Aberfeldy, all as part of 'the Beeching Plan'. With the closure of these small stations went the ability to transport sheep and cattle by train to market in Perth; from then on, they all went by road.

The line between Blair Atholl and Dalwhinnie was increased from single track to double between 1900 and 1901, then reduced from double to single in 1966, only to be doubled again at great expense in 1978. The station at Blair Atholl ceased taking goods after 1966 and was downgraded further in 1989, with fewer passenger trains actually stopping there. Despite its being a major tourist destination, Pitlochry was downgraded by ScotRail in 1993, by being partially demanned. Is this the thin edge of the wedge?

Hotels and Tourism

As we have seen, this district has long been a tourist centre, where people have come to take the air and relax in the Highland scenery. Part of the attraction has been the particular hospitality which is on offer, epitomised by the various 'bed & breakfasts', guest houses and hotels. Every visitor has his or her own favourite.

Some hotels no longer exist as such, including Burnlea (opposite Scotland's Hotel in Bonnethill Road), which was once a temperance hotel, run by Mrs Margaret Paton. The shop there, at Burnlea, was originally a food shop serving hot pies and lemonade; as the licensed premises closed at 9pm in those days, this shop was very popular once the cinema show was over.

Brook Place (now four shops with two flats above, on Atholl Road immediately to the west of Bonnethill Road) used to be a temperance hotel owned by the Russell family. At street level was a row of shops (although neither of the single storey shops at each end was there in those days), with the letting rooms above. A flight of steps led up the western elevation of the tenement to the large entrance hall of the Hotel; this was removed when McPhersons' fish shop was built.

Prospect Place (opposite the Baptist Church in Atholl Road) was originally Doggart's temperance hotel, with Doggart's grocery and sweet shop below. His trade must have dwindled once the school removed from Atholl Road in 1898 up to Ballinlochan. The ground floor later became a garage and motor repair shop. Now there are a shop and an office at street level and flatted dwellinghouses above.

The only original temperance hotels, known as such, which still exist are the Craigower and

MacKay's (originally Reid's Station Hotel), side by side in Atholl Road, although both now serve alcohol. The arcade which extends outside the shops to the east of the entrance to Craigower Hotel once impressively ran further westwards and around the corner into Birnam Place.

In 1990, both the Pitlochry Hydro Hotel and Scotland's Hotel installed indoor swimming pools and leisure centres in order to compete effectively in the tourist market. In the absence of a swimming pool for the town, Pitlochry residents are able to pay an annual subscription to use these hotel facilities.

Some of today's big hotels used to be private houses, with large indoor and gardening staff. The Pine Trees Hotel, when called Tom-na-monachan (now the name of a house to the west of the Hotel, itself a farm originally known simply as 'Tom', as shown on an early plan of 1846), was owned first by Miss Molyneux and then by Yervent Hagof Iskender, a Turk who was President of Citizens of the World. The Green Park Hotel, formerly Lagreach, was where the Misses Cowan lived, but half of its original stately gardens were lost in 1950 beneath Loch Faskally.

More and more houses have become developed to cater for the influx of tourists, as a rule the larger houses becoming hotels, medium-sized houses becoming guest houses and smaller houses becoming 'bed & breakfast' establishments. Even small cottages and flats have been made available to tourists, as self-catering lets. There is a well-equipped Youth Hostel on the corner of Well Brae and Knockard Road. For a small town of some two thousand four hundred inhabitants, Pitlochry can in fact provide paying beds for some seven thousand at any one time. Many local incomes derive directly, and many more indirectly, from tourism.

Caravan sites were established at Milton of Fonab in 1952 and at Faskally in 1954. Both developed strongly with the tourist boom of the late twentieth century. A caravan site was also established and developed within the grounds of Blair Castle and there are others at Bridge of Tilt and Tummel Bridge.

Pitlochry began one of the first Tourist Associations in Scotland, in about 1956. It was originally named the Pitlochry Development Association and provided both a Hotel Bureau and some marketing of the town. Marketing came to play an increasingly important role, notably after the nineteen sixties when the tourist market at home became adversely affected by the growth in the package holiday trade abroad.

The Pitlochry & District Tourist Association (as it became) opened a new Tourist Information Centre at Tiree House, Atholl Road, on 19th May 1979, introducing a Bureau de Change three years later. By agreement, the Association and its Centre were taken over by the Perthshire Tourist Board in 1992.

The opening of a town bypass might in normal circumstances be perceived by many locals with considerable apprehension. This was not so in Pitlochry. Having undertaken considerable research, the Pitlochry & District Tourist Association adopted a positive approach to the opening of the A9 Pitlochry Bypass, on 19th May 1979 (the very same day that the new Theatre, the new Tourist Information Office and the new toilets at the West End car park were all opened!). Their message was that, with the removal at last of the heavy lorries and the fast through-traffic, the time was now right to visit the town and enjoy, peacefully and without rush, the beauty and amenities of the area.

As the century nears its end, it is clear that, as in the case of local agriculture, too little investment has been made in the infrastructure and amenities of the town, for visitors and locals alike. Talk of a swimming pool went on for years, without much progress; meanwhile, Aberfeldy residents were raising almost £1 million, from a variety of ingenious sources, to build a most impressive pool and indoor recreation centre, which was opened in 1983. There is still a lack of wet-weather facilities in Pitlochry.

Since 1958, when all but six shops were locally owned, Pitlochry's main street have been transformed. Most of the change has taken place since 1970 so that, by 1993, locals owned fewer than half of the shops. Many of the incoming purchasers are part of national shop chains, with corporate identities relatively indistinct one from another. As a result, the centre of Pitlochry has lost its own

Victorian character and looks from the outside like any other bland high street. The very similarity of goods for sale inside most of the shops has further devalued the demeanour of the town. At a time when quality is the key, Pitlochry is looking ordinary.

From old photographs, it is clear that the main street of Pitlochry was full of character at the end of the nineteenth century, with rows of cottages, many with small trees along their frontages, with wrought-iron arcades (not only where the last survivor still is, albeit multi-painted now) and with many tall glass-paned gas lamps. Almost all of this character has been lost or smothered in the name of post war 'development'.

There seems to be no single organisation available to grasp the nettle of reform. In days gone by the local lairds ("Superiors" in legal terms) were responsible for the management of their estates and the feus created from it, but their control has waned. The Town Council provided a strong local voice, but was replaced both by a Local Authority, based outwith the area, and by a Community Council which, whilst local, has no teeth. The Local Authority has acted as a planning authority, assessing each application on its own merits, perhaps without sufficient regard for the overall character of the locality. Latterly, however, the Local Authority has shown a willingness to be more pro-active. The Atholl Mercantile Association had been the real power at the time when most of the shops were owner-occupied, but few of the incoming shop chains are represented in the Association, which as

Victorian Pitlochry: (Top) Westwards from Fisher's Hotel – ornamental arcades, gas lights, turrets and spires (Bottom) The same view in 1993

a result has a lesser voice. The local Tourist Association succeeded 'the Mercantile' as the most effective local forum, but in turn lost some of its voice once it was amalgamated with the Perthshire Tourist Board in 1992; the Board considers tourism for the whole of Perthshire and is less concerned with local issues, even if these do have an impact on tourism.

At a time when Pitlochry most needs an overall management strategy to deliver quality and to inject pride, there seems to be no one there to play the essential co-ordinating role. Without it, it is difficult to see how the town can sustain its ranking as one of Scotland's premier tourist destinations, in a global tourism market which at one and the same time both is contracting and becoming more discerning.

(Top) View eastwards from the Old Smithy in about 1890. Old Bank Buildings on left, untarred main road, trees where Macnaughtons now is

(Bottom) Same view in 1993 – the West End

*(Top) Westwards
from Atholl
Highlander before the
Institute was built in
1895 where the trees
are on the left
(Bottom) The same
view in 1993*

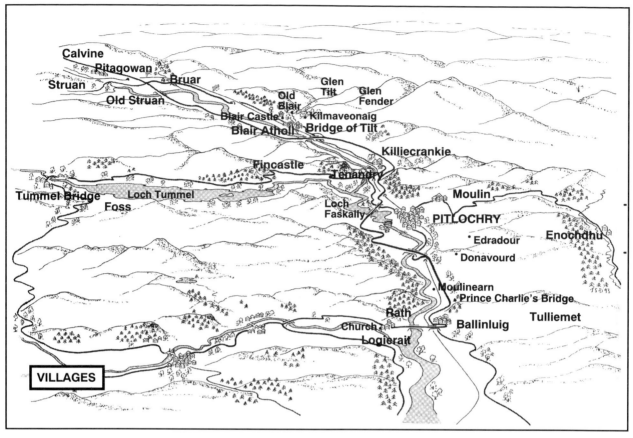

Calvine
Pitagowan
Struan
Bruar
Old Struan
Old Blair
Glen Tilt
Glen Fender
Blair Castle
Kilmaveonaig
Blair Atholl
Bridge of Tilt
Killiecrankie
Fincastle
Tenandry
Moulin
Tummel Bridge
Loch Tummel
Foss
Loch Faskally
PITLOCHRY
Edradour
Enochdhu
Donavourd
Moulinearn
Prince Charlie's Bridge
Rath
Tulliemet
Church
Ballinluig
Logierait

VILLAGES

(Right) The Rath –
site of Pictish fort,
Royal Hunting
Palace and now
Atholl Memorial –
showing ancient
ditch and roadway

(Below) The three
mort-safes at
Logierait

CHAPTER TEN
The Smaller Villages

Pitlochry is at the centre of a ring of villages and hamlets, some of which were strategically important in days gone by. Now, because of the Theatre, the railway station and the many shops and services, Pitlochry has become the effective centre of Highland Perthshire. Nevertheless, the history and continuing influence of these neighbouring settlements remain important not only in an understanding of the district and its people but also in the way the rural life of Highland Perthshire actually operates. A brief tour of these settlements follows, from Logierait in the south through to Foss in the north-west.

Logierait and Ballinluig

About five miles east of Pitlochry, the ancient settlement of Logierait is situated in a hollow, at the junction of the Rivers Tay and Tummel. In days gone by, before road and rail passed through Ballinluig, it held a position of strategic importance, with ferries over both rivers which provided the only means of communication to and from Strathtay and further west.

The name of Logierait comes from two Gaelic words *laggan* ('a hollow place') and *rath* ('fortress' or 'royal seat'). Ballinluig, situated across the Tummel from Logierait, derives from *baile luig* ('village of the hollow').

Logierait Church was founded in about 650 AD by St Cedd, whose brother St Chad founded those at Grandtully and Foss at about the same time. The two brothers were passing through the district on their way home to Lindisfarne from instruction in Iona. They worked under the enlightened patronage of Oswald, King of Northumbria. Logierait was originally known as Lagmachedd *('the hollow of St Cedd')*. The present church was built in 1805.

The churchyard contains many items of interest, including some beautifully wrought memorial stones. One of the oldest appears to be in memory of Patrick Douglas, who died at the age of 21 in 1680. There are some 'Adam and Eve' stones and a much older Pictish stone, which has an interlaced design on one side and Pictish symbols on the other.

In a small walled enclosure just beside the church are three iron mortsafes, each with shaped bars more than an inch thick. These were used in the early part of the eighteenth century to place over the coffin of a recently deceased person, in order to guard against a raid by grave robbers. Two are full sized and the third is smaller, infant and child mortality being much more prevalent then than now.

Less than half a mile north-east of Logierait is a glacial knoll known locally as 'the Rath', which derives from the Gaelic *rath* [referred to above], near where the ferry formerly crossed the Tummel. The Rath was first the site of an ancient Pictish fort, the defensive ditch of which is still noticeable, particularly on the west and north sides.

The Rath later became a royal castle or hunting-seat, which is said to have been the residence of Robert II (after he gave up the administration of the country to his brother the Duke of Albany, as Regent), and of his son Robert III. James III (1448-1460) is supposed to have been its last royal resident. It has been a ruin for many centuries and now only a very few traces of old masonry remain. The King's Stables were situated about eight hundred metres to the west of the ruined castle. The old earthworks of the King's Stables have been partly obliterated by more recent forestry tracks.

After the royal castle was no longer used, the Rath became the Gallows' Knoll (*tom na croich*) of the Regality Court of Athole.

The jurisdiction of the Earls of Atholl was extensive at one time, from the twelfth century until the abolition of such Heritable Jurisdictions in 1746. Originally, their Regality Court was located at

An old photograph of the main door of Logierait prison, through which Rob Roy McGregor made good his escape

Tulliemet, (from *tulloch mod* meaning 'hill of judgement') until it was transferred to Logierait, but there are no records of its proceedings at either place or when the transfer took place. Below the Rath was *clas an deoir* ('the valley of tears'), where the family of condemned criminals were wont to sit and weep.

The Courthouse at Logierait was apparently of such fine proportions that it was considered to be the noblest apartment in Perthshire at the time. It was about twenty-one metres long, with galleries at each end. The building was still well remembered at the beginning of the nineteenth century, albeit in ruins by then. The main part had been demolished in 1818 as it was in a dangerous state. It was located behind what is now the Logierait Hotel. Indeed, one of the outbuildings still there is said to be a part of the old prison, which was attached to the Courthouse; it has a sunken cellar, which may have been a dungeon.

In 1717, Rob Roy McGregor was imprisoned there, but only for a single day, as he was able swiftly to make good his escape! One not so fortunate was Allan McRory, famous Chief of Clanranald, who was tried and beheaded for *reiving* ('thieving cattle') in the neighbourhood.

Owing to its size, the Courthouse was chosen by Bonnie Prince Charlie to hold a considerable number of prisoners (accounts vary between eighty and six hundred!) after the Battle of Prestonpans, which took place on 21st September 1745, until their fate could be decided.

One of the last persons to be hanged on the Gallows' Knoll was reputed to be Donald Dhubh, convicted on the charge of reiving, of which he protested his innocence. Ironically, he was involved in a search for lost cattle just before his demise. The day of his execution was hot and humid. Nearby were some cattle being looked after by a local woman. In their restlessness from the heat, the cattle made off. The woman's searchings for them brought her up onto the Gallows' Knoll – just at the time that Donald was being strung up high. Looking up at him, she yelled to him: *"Hey man, ye that are up sae heich, gie a look roun' and see if ye can see ony o' my kye [cows] roun' aboot."* Needless to say, poor Donald did not appreciate this final request and told her so in doubtless unrepeatable terms.

Most recently, a large Celtic cross was erected on the Rath in 1866 by the tenants of the Atholl Estates to the memory of George Augustus Frederick John Murray, the sixth Duke of Atholl, who had died on 16th January 1864, at the age of forty-nine. The cross was designed by an Edinburgh architect, Roland Anderson. Initially, it stood alone on the hilltop but is now all but engulfed in tall trees.

The famous philosopher Adam Fergusson, whose father was minister at Logierait for many years, was born in the Manse in 1724. He held successively the Chairs of Natural Philosophy and Moral Philosophy at Edinburgh University. The first Liberal Prime Minister of Canada, the Honourable Alexander Mackenzie, was born in 1822 at Clais-an-deoir [as it is now spelt] on the north side of the village.

Logierait's importance declined from the beginning of the nineteenth century and, by the end of that century, its school, Post Office, Smithy and shop were all located on the opposite (north) bank of the River Tummel, at Ballinluig. Ballinluig was preferred because it was located at the railway junction between the main Inverness/London line and the branch line which went to Aberfeldy. This branch line became a victim of the Beeching cuts in 1965.

Logierait retained the Church, the hotel (although a coaching inn was built at Ballinluig) and the former poor house. The poor house was at Cuil-an-Daraich, catering for up to one hundred inmates. In due course the building became an old people's home, until its replacement, Dalweem Home in Aberfeldy, was opened in 1985.

There are two Garden Centres at Ballinluig, one at Tynreich (beside the stone circle) and one on the former football pitch by the Hall. When the village was by-passed in 1977, much of the pitch was lost to the new road and so was relocated to a site between the railway line and the river. The Mid-Atholl Hall is run by a board of trustees for the benefit of the community. Although separated by the Tummel, as always, the residents of Ballinluig and Logierait consider themselves to be one community.

(Top) The Rath – now crowned by the Atholl Memorial

Tulliemet

Tulliemet is a sprawling hamlet situated along an idyllic plateau some one hundred metres higher than the haugh on which Ballinluig sits, with a backcloth of moorland and a panoramic outlook south to the upper Tay strath and west towards the Pass of Killiecrankie.

The Dukes of Atholl were said to have had a house at Tulliemet at the time when their Court was also located there. Ruins were evident in the mid-nineteenth century, but no trace now remains.

Tulliemet House, although now part of the Atholl Estates, was not built by the family, but by Dr William Dick in the early years of the nineteenth century, after he returned with the fortune he had acquired through the East India Company. The Dicks were Roman Catholics and built a beautiful church in 1855 at a place called Chapelton, to the south of the house. This was probably the site of an earlier church, although there are no old stones to be seen. Services were conducted there for about forty years, until the Dick family died out and the church became derelict. It was subsequently demolished, although there are grave stones still evident.

Tighrioch, near Dalcapon, was originally built as the MacDuff Institute, established under the Will Trust of the late Archibald Campbell MacDuff, to be a Boys' Home. Thus it remained until the 1960s, after which it was altered to a guest house.

Tulliemet was once a busy place, as evidenced by the fact that in 1844 almost twenty per cent of all the Baptists in Tayside were residents of that small community. At one time it boasted a Post Office, a shoe maker and a village shop, but these were all lost to Ballinluig as the people emigrated from the little plateau.

(Bottom) Moulinearn hamlet, where the north road was once carried over the bridge, but which now lies to the south of road and railway

Moulinearn

Moulinearn is situated midway between Ballinluig and Pitlochry, nestling on the north bank of the River Tummel.

Wade's road passed through this once important hamlet, which centred around its coaching inn. The inn played host to the Earl of Mar in the Jacobite Rebellion of 1715, to Bonnie Prince Charlie on the night of 3rd September 1745 and to Queen Victoria, who during her brief visit on 11th September 1844 tasted 'Atholl Brose' (a drink combining whisky, honey, oatmeal and sometimes cream).

About half a mile east, in the wood just to the north of the A9 dual carriageway, is the ruin of what once was a picturesque bridge, built as part of General Wade's Great North Road. The bridge was affectionately known as 'Prince Charlie's Bridge' because it was there that he mustered his growing forces on the morning of 4th September 1745, before marching on to Dunkeld and Perth [see Chapter Five].

When the Highland Railway came through, the Great North Road was diverted to the north of Moulinearn, so as to avoid the main road having to cross the railway. Now it is the residents who have to cross the railway to reach their ancient hamlet. The ruins of the bridge which once carried the Great North Road through the hamlet still remain beside 'the street' of cottages which lie to the east of the former inn.

Edradour

Edradour is a small hamlet situated to the north-east of Pitlochry, between Moulin and Donavourd. Before Wade's Great North Road came along the bottom of the strath, Edradour was on the main road between Dunkeld and Blair Atholl, via Moulin. When Wade's road came through, along the bottom of the strath, the old main road became known as 'the High Drive' and is still sometimes so called.

Edradour was known originally as Balnauld (from *baile-n-allt* meaning 'town by the burn', whilst Edradour, by which it became known in time, derives from *eadar dobhar* meaning 'between the waters'). Before simply being called Edradour, the hamlet was for a time known as Milton of Edradour.

Here there is a famous distillery of some antiquity. It was legally established in 1825, but there were illicit distilleries in the vicinity long before then. Much of its existing plant has been in operation since the distillery was developed in 1825. The wooden paddles which provided power from the burn were replaced by electricity only in 1947. In about 1980 it was used as the set for a television serial.

It is the smallest distillery in Scotland. With only a handful of distillers in its employment, Edradour Distillery has more than once won the Queen's Award for Export. Its main brands are sold as 'Clan Campbell', 'Clan Campbell Legendary', 'King's Ransom' (which, as part of its maturing process used to be sent in cask by sea to Australia and back) and 'House of Lords'. 'King's Ransom' was part of the cargo of the ill-fated *S.S. Politician* which was wrecked off the Island of Eriskay in 1941, as immortalised by Sir Compton Mackenzie in his book *Whisky Galore*. There is a visitor centre at the Distillery.

Edradour Distillery –
Scotland's smallest

It may look a sleepy hamlet now, but the non-parochial school, which was founded in 1822 by Sir John Hay of Edradour, had by 1837 as many as ninety-one pupils, not many fewer than the one hundred and twelve in the Parish school of Moulin at the same time. However, the school had a relatively short life, as it closed when the Free Church School was built in 1844 (a year after the Disruption). It had but two schoolmasters, John Menzies and Alexander MacDonald. The old school building, now a house, still exists, close to the Distillery.

There is now another Edradour School, started in 1988, situated at the top of the village. It runs along the lines of an 'international school', with a curriculum embracing logic and computer studies as well as some of the more traditional subjects. In 1992, it had a roll of twenty-five pupils.

Enochdhu

Enochdhu is a small hamlet situated in Strathardle. It is about nine miles north-east of Pitlochry and two miles short of Kirkmichael. The strath looks to Blairgowrie, although some fourteen miles distant, for shopping, secondary schooling, doctors and the like. Enochdhu has a village shop, whilst nearby at Straloch are a small Primary School and the Church.

The strath comprises large sporting estates, such as Tarvie, Straloch, Glenfernate and Dirnanean, some small hill farms and the Forestry Commission's plantations at Kindrogan which rise up to the summit of Kindrogan Hill (1,625'/495m)

The former country house of Kindrogan is now run successfully as a Field Centre by the Scottish Field Studies Association.

Killiecrankie

Killiecrankie (which derives from *coille critheann*, meaning 'wood of aspen') is situated just to the west of the famous Pass, midway between Pitlochry and Blair Atholl. It sits on a narrow ledge, with a tree-clad hillside behind (still with many aspens) and the fast-flowing water of the River Garry below.

The village of Killiecrankie was originally known as 'Allt Girnaig' after the name of the Allt Girnaig burn which flows south-west from Carn Liath ('the grey-headed mountain' – 3,199'/975m) and Beinn a' Ghlo ('mountain of the veil [of clouds and snow]' – 3,678'/1,211m) into the River Garry just beside the village. In fact Pitlochry's public water supply derives from this source, pumped and piped the three miles east.

The village used to have its own railway station, but no longer does so, though the main London/Inverness line still passes through. There used to be a garage, now the site of two houses, and a Post Office and shop, which closed in 1990. All fell victim to the significant drop in passing trade after the village was bypassed by the new A9 road in 1982. There used to be a School, but this closed in 1992, after the school roll had fallen to four, most parents of eligible children preferring to send them to the High School in Pitlochry.

The village hall, pride of the community, was by 1990 considered to have exhausted its lifespan. At a time when the village services were closing, the community rallied round to support its last centre and, as a result, raised sufficient by 1993 to ensure the building of a new hall, as the essential focus for this well-spread community in years to come.

There is a small sanctuary belonging to the Royal Society for the Protection of Birds to the south of Killiecrankie, which is well placed as so many species of birds use the Pass as their north-south communications corridor, just as humans do.

The village has been made famous by its Battle on 27th July 1689 and the great leap for safety made by Donald MacBean that day. Songs have followed, such as *The Braes of Killiecrankie* and *Weep Ye Weel By Atholl*. The area to the north of the Soldier's Leap belongs to the National Trust for Scotland who, in 1993, opened an extended visitor centre, with displays, a sheltered balcony and the opportunity to test oneself against MacBean's leap, albeit on flat ground rather than between sharp and slippery rocks.

Blair Atholl and Bridge of Tilt

The name Blair comes from the Gaelic *blar* ('a plain') but as such plains were invariably chosen as fields of battle, *blar* came at length to signify 'a battle'. As there is no record of any battle at Blair Atholl, the name probably accords with its original meaning, so that Blair Atholl, situated at the foot of the Grampians, means "the plain of Atholl". Atholl may derive from *ath fod lag* ('ford at the sandy hollow'), or *fod lag* ('sandy hollow'), or from the name of an ancient noble, Prince Ard-fhuil (or 'Fodla'), a son of King Cruithne, who governed this central district of Pictland and who may also have given his name to nearby Strathardle.

Blair Atholl, situated seven miles west of Pitlochry, is actually an amalgamation of two small villages. The more westerly is Blair Atholl itself, created by successive Dukes of Atholl around the

The village of Blair Atholl with the Golf Course in the foreground and the Beinn a' Ghlos behind

great gates of their home at Blair Castle (which was originally known as Atholl House). The more easterly is Bridge of Tilt, so called less often now, which was part of Lude Estate. Lude comes from *leoid* or *leathad* ('a slope', "where" – according to the 1793 Statistical Account – "a plough could bring a furrow only one way"). The technical division between the villages of Blair Atholl and Bridge of Tilt is the march between Lude Estate and the Atholl Estates, along the River Tilt.

Originally, Bridge of Tilt was itself two small hamlets. There was one small hamlet called Ballentoul, really little more than a farm in Wade's time, where the two rows of Ballentoul Cottages now sit at the eastern entrance to the village. Originally, Ballentoul was a little distance to the south of the Great North Road, not situated beside it as latterly.

When Wade built his Great North Road, he took it further north, across Lude Park, passing right in front of Kilmaveonaig Church and then on north-westwards across the River Tilt and into Old Blair to pass behind Blair Castle. Just to the west of the Church, the road passed through the small hamlet of Kilmaveonaig, which in its heyday comprised an inn, a school, a smithy and half a dozen cottages. The name of Kilmaveonaig comes from *cille mo eonaig* ('the chapel dedicated to the blessed Eonan [or 'Adamnan']'). Now the drive of Lude house crosses the site of this lost hamlet, of which no trace remains.

In earlier times, there was an older village, known now as Old Blair (but originally as Blair Town), which was situated a little further north, towards Glenfender and Glen Tilt, behind Blair Castle. Not to be outdone, there is also an Old Bridge of Tilt, a small hamlet where once the Black Bridge stood. The current bridge replaces the one built by Wade to take the Great North Road across the River Tilt on its way to pass behind the Castle.

At one time the village of Old Blair, astride the Great North Road as it was, held some importance. It centred on the Tigh Glas Inn, which was mentioned, as *"Le Ale House with Croft in le kirktoun of Blare"* in a Charter of 1504. The stables built to accompany the Inn in 1756 (replacing earlier ones) could take twenty-six horses, which gives an indication of the amount of passing trade.

Nowadays, the combined village of Blair Atholl is largely dependant on the outstanding tourism success of Blair Castle, which is the most visited private house in Scotland. The Castle hosts a spectacular display of family and historical mementoes, almost too many to absorb in one visit. Its Ballroom witnesses many a fine evening of entertainment, whilst use of the grounds includes the Blair Atholl Highland Games, parades by the Atholl Highlanders (the only private army in Britain, founded in 1777) and a three day equestrian event.

Opposite the main Castle gates is the Atholl Country Collection, a small museum of agricultural implements and displays of post office, schoolroom and the like from the past locally.

The main local employers are Atholl Estates, the two Hotels (the Atholl Arms and the Tilt, now under the same ownership) and Lind's lime quarry at Shierglas.

Struan, Calvine, Pitagowan and Bruar

Struan, or "Strowan" as it was originally written, is a small village some five miles north of Blair Atholl, its name being derived from *struthain* ('streams', given the confluence of the Garry and Errochty there). There is a dramatic waterfall which passes under the three bridges which carry the road and two separate lines of railway. The three bridges are all seemingly interlinked. The original road bridge was built in about 1765, but has been altered since. In 1863, Joseph Mitchell surmounted this with a castellated triple arch bridge for the new Highland Railway. In 1899, another railway bridge was added in parallel, with four arches, when the single track was upgraded to double.

Old Struan is situated a little to the south-east, beside another stone bridge, this one spanning the Errochty Water. This also was built in about 1765 by public subscription, to replace the previous wooden one.

Struan represents the heartland of the Clan Donnachaidh, whose lands at one time stretched far into Rannoch. At Struan, their stronghold was at *tom an tigh mor* ('knoll of the great house'), an artificial mound strategically positioned just at the confluence. The mound, or motte, still exists and is about ten metres high and some twenty metres wide across its top surface, with a moat around three sides. Struan Church stands a little to the east.

There is an inn at Struan, near the three bridges, on the road towards the now abandoned station. In the old days, the local inn was situated beside the church at what is now Struan Farm. In its heyday as an inn it was known as 'Succours' and was situated beside a route still visible, which runs from Struan, by the west of Loch Bhac, to the inn at Strathtummel.

Struan and Old Struan are situated to the south of the River Garry, whereas Calvine is situated opposite on the north bank. The Great North Road used to pass through Calvine, but the new A9 was built to the north-east of the village in 1978. In fact, the line of General Wade's original road is even further north-east, above the new A9.

The Drochaid na h'uinneige Wade bridge to the north-west of Calvine

In a wood about a mile to the west of Calvine can be seen one of Wade's bridges, without parapets, which has been restored by the Association for the Preservation of Rural Scotland. It has a romantic name, *Drochaid na h'uinneige* ('bridge of the window'); the burn known as Allt a' Chrombaidh cascades through its singular arch. One can follow the old military road across the open hill to the north.

In about 1650, the four small parishes of St. Bride's (in Old Blair), Kilmaveonaig (in the village of that name), Kirkton of Lude (in Glenfender) and Struan were united. The manse was built in open country at Baluain (near the West Lodge to Blair Castle), on the simple logic that there it would be equidistant for the minister between his two churches at Old Struan and Old Blair.

Just to the east of Calvine lies the hamlet of Pitagowan, which has never been a large settlement, stretching at its height in 1823 to a population of thirty-seven, which included two weavers. On the south side of the Great North Road, now partly obliterated by the line of the A9, was the site of a prisoner-of-war camp which was set up during the Second World War for Italian, German and Austrian prisoners.

A little further east is Bruar, gateway to the famous Falls. At one time the water drove both a meal mill and a lint mill, but neither exists now. Bruar is now home to the small Clan Donnachaidh Museum, which stands in proud testimony of the Clan. The Museum houses many Clan relics, some of which are referable to this district, where the Clan wielded influence for generations.

The Falls of Bruar were made famous by Burns' *Humble Petition* to the fourth Duke of Atholl [see Chapter Seven], who responded by planting a 'wild garden' and laying out paths, bridges, viewpoints and 'view houses' as a memorial after the great bard's death. Though the several Falls retain their splendour, their glory must have been all the more before much of their water was redirected into the Tummel-Garry Hydro-Electric Scheme.

The old farm at Bruar, which no longer exists, enjoyed a chequered career. Having been a farm for years, it became an inn in about 1836 to serve travellers on the Great North Road. When the railway came through in 1863, it ceased to be an inn, presumably because the trains siphoned so many potential customers away. It reverted to a farm once again until 1963 when, history repeating itself, it became a hotel. This closed in 1991 and was demolished in 1993, to be replaced by an ambitious tourist development, comprising restaurant, shops and garden centre, once again aimed serving travellers on the new road to the north.

Opposite Bruar is *clach na h'iobairt*, the stone of sacrifice, which is described in the Statistical Account of 1793 as being a 'four poster', but which even by then had only one stone still standing, although the others were lying around in a circle. There is now no sign of any of these.

Fincastle

Glen Fincastle is situated roughly halfway between the Garry Bridge, spanning the southern end of the Pass of Killiecrankie, and the Queen's View, at the eastern end of Loch Tummel. The Glen is served now by a single track road, leading to a handful of houses and a couple of farms, which peters out after less than two miles.

Yet, in its heyday, the Glen was the confluence of two major roads and witnessed much through traffic. One road came from the ferry over the River Garry (near where the Garry Bridge is now), passed Bonskied House and then turned north-west up the Glen, to the south of Balnald. The other came south from Blair Atholl, across the ford below the Mill, up the long brae and through Tomanraid and Edintian (which derives from *aodann an t-sithean*, meaning 'face of the fairy hill'). These two roads met just to the south-west of Edintian to travel westwards together as the road, passing by *na clachan aoraidh* ('the stones of worship') and Loch Bhac to Tummel Bridge, to Rannoch and eventually to the Isles. Until the eighteen thirties there was no road to Strathtummel by Clunie and the Queen's View.

The Glen used to be home to many farmers and crofters, but the number declined throughout the nineteenth century, from two hundred and thirty five in 1841 to sixty-five in 1901. In that period, over forty per cent of the buildings fell into disuse and swiftly fell into ruin. In 1841 there were thirty-six farmers and farm workers and nineteen tradesmen (including a blacksmith, three shoemakers, three tailors and four handloom weavers), but by 1901 there were only fourteen farmers and farm workers and no tradesmen at all.

There was a school in the Glen until 1945, which was started sometime between 1707 and 1777. The schoolmaster in post during the Militia Riots in 1797, Forbes by name, bled to death after his ear was cut off by a scythe.

Tummel Bridge

Tummel Bridge is situated about a mile to the west of the western end of Loch Tummel. Here the Aberfeldy and Pitlochry roads join on their way westwards to Kinloch Rannoch and beyond – the old Road to the Isles. Before the days of Wade's bridge, there was only the Tigh-na-Drochait inn.

Tummel Bridge is situated in a hollow and is on the divide between the weather which is attracted to the western half of Scotland and the weather attracted to the eastern. Perhaps because of this, it used to carry the distinction of being both the hottest and coldest place in the British Isles. Now other places carry these distinctions independently, but Tummel Bridge still features regularly in the statistics.

The original Tummel Bridge, built in 1733 by John Stewart of Kynachan for General Wade, still stands, although no longer used for vehicles. Known locally as "Kynachan Bridge" after its creator, it could probably still be pressed into service quite safely, although its rather acute hump-back, with a slight bend in it, did cause a problem or two; there were occasions still remembered when a longer vehicle, such as a Bentley or a lorry, 'bottomed' on the top of the bridge, with wheels in the air fore and aft! John Stewart was paid £200 for his labours, with a duty imposed upon him to repair the bridge for the first twenty years. The contract still survives, in Wade's words requiring a stone bridge *"strengthen'd with a double arch over the River of Tumble . . ."*!

(Below, opposite) The front of the Tigh-na-Drochait Inn

A modern metal bridge was installed in the nineteen seventies, which unfortunately obscures the view of the more noble Kynachan Bridge. The original bridge must have been a notable sight in its heyday, standing proud in a rocky and treeless landscape, with but the humble inn for company.

The famous Tigh-na-Drochait inn immediately to the south of Tummel Bridge is no more; it was transformed into three houses for Hydro- Electric workers. Now the village is dominated by the two post-war Power Stations (one of which was still in its wartime camouflage paint until the nineteen eighties) and a Caravan Park.

Local employment is provided by Scottish Hydro-Electric plc, the Caravan Park and the Forestry Commission.

Foss

Before Loch Tummel was enlarged by the Hydro-Electric Scheme in 1950, Foss (which derives from the Gaelic *fasaidh*, meaning 'a dwelling place') was a thriving lochside community. Apart from its Church, there was a Manse, a School, a Post Office, the Registrar and a Smithy. Now only the Church remains in use and most of the houses are used as second or holiday homes.

The mansion house of Foss, multi-windowed and not particularly attractive, was one of only three buildings lost beneath the waters of the enlarged Loch. Its foundations are visible still, just off the shore beside the Loch Tummel Sailing Club.

The Sailing Club was founded in 1963, its first Commodore being Donald Liddell. The original club hut, which still stands although now significantly enlarged, was the gym from Killin School. Initially, there was some local resistance to the expected eyesore of sails upon the Loch, but this was soon forgotten. Racing takes place around buoys at the western end of the Loch, with a race each year to the Dun Island and back for the Port-an-Filean Trophy (gifted by Colonel Oscar Dixon). Now the Club is very successful, drawing in members from far afield and boasting well over one hundred boats for its annual regatta.

Looking north-west from the south bank of the River Tummel towards the Wade Bridge at Tummel Bridge, built in 1733 beside the Tigh-na-Drochait Inn, long before power stations, caravan parks and houses

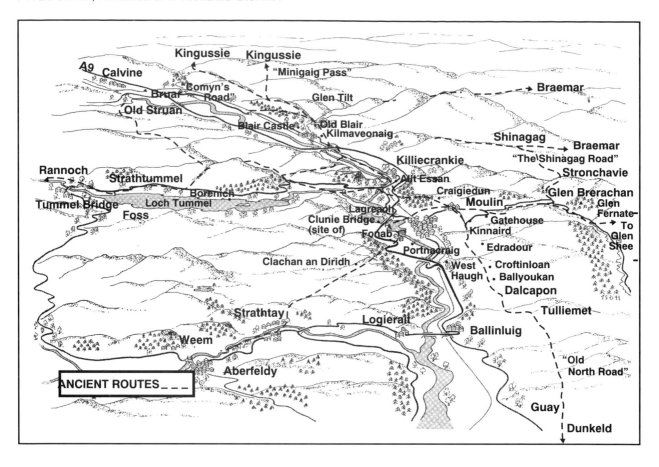

Killiecrankie Bridge, showing storm water circular opening on right

CHAPTER ELEVEN
Roads, Ferries and Bridges

Ancient Roadways

Before the engineering feats of General Wade changed the landscape in the late seventeen twenties, there were two ancient roads which intersected at Moulin. 'Roads' is perhaps too grand a term, as they would have been little more than worn tracks through the countryside, used by pedestrians, horses and, in parts, by animals driven to pasture and, more particularly, to market. Such roads were used of necessity, not for pleasure.

The first such roadway was the old 'North Road', which was higher up the north side of the strath than now. Leaving Dunkeld, the road started to climb at Guay up to the Braes of Tulliemet, along to Dalcapon and behind Ballyoukan and Croftinloan, where its line is still evident. There, between Balnacree and Donavourd, it joined the "High Drive" (as it is still known) passing through Edradour and descending by Kinnaird into Moulin itself.

From the village, it continued westwards by Pitfourie, Drumchorry and the hamlet of Craigiedun (now ruined but once comprising at least eight dwellings), over the shoulder of the hill at *craig na ciche* ('the nipple rock') before descending to the southern end of the Pass of Killiecrankie, close to where the current Garry Bridge is. There, it divided, either travelling west across the Garry ferry towards Fincastle and Strathtummel, or north through the Pass towards Kilmaveonaig and Old Blair.

From Old Blair two ancient roads traversed the Grampians northwards to Ruthven at Kingussie, the more westerly one known as Comyn's Road (made in the thirteenth century) and the other (which was its replacement from about the sixteenth century) known as the Minigaig Pass. Both these old routes were shorter, by some fifteen miles, than the present route of the A9 through the Drumochter Pass and via Dalwhinnie and Newtonmore. However, these old routes traverse the Grampians at an elevation some 1,000 feet (300m) higher than the Drumochter Pass, which would make them wholly unsuitable for vehicular traffic in winter; passage through the Pass can be bad enough in inclement weather as it is.

There is an interesting tale as to how Comyn's Road came to be. The Comyns (or Cummings) were lairds of Ruthven in Badenoch. John the Red, who died in 1274, was passing through Atholl and rested up at the inn at the hamlet of Kilmaveonaig, just to the east of Old Blair. Here, he sampled the local ale, which he liked so much that he determined to have a ready supply at Ruthven. Incredibly, given conditions at that time, he decided then and there to build a road twenty-seven miles long which would connect Blair with Ruthven. The roadway was made so as to be passable by carts loaded with ale and was accordingly called *rad na pheny* (deriving from *rathad na fionnad*, meaning 'road of the wagon').

The Red Comyn, as he was called, helped himself to the Earl of Atholl's property whilst the Earl was away fighting on the Crusades and started building Blair Castle, the oldest part of which is still known as Comyn's Tower. This Tower was once four storeys high, but was lowered when the Castle was gentrified in the aftermath of the '45.

Also from Old Blair were two other roads. One travelled north-east up the length of Glen Tilt and over the watershed to Braemar. The other travelled south-westwards up to Glen Fincastle, (meeting there the road from the Garry ferry at the southern end of the Pass of Killiecrankie) crossing the ridge at an elevation of almost 1,100 feet (335m), before dropping down to the present road line at about the Strathtummel Hotel. The present line of the road, by Allean and the Queen's View, was not made until about 1830. From Strathtummel, by then known as the Road to the Isles, it went on westwards by Loch Tummel and Loch Rannoch.

The second road through Moulin was the hill road which came over Carra Beag (Fonab Hill) from Strathtay, passing the Clachan an diridh stones near the ridge. Much of that road at the top of the hill is still clearly discernible, with an impressive turf wall along its eastern flank; it can be followed down the northern side, towards Pitlochry, as it now forms the pedestrian path between two sections of forestry track. Nearer Pitlochry, this ancient road collected on its way both the roadway westwards from Foss (and the south side of Loch Tummel) and the roadway eastwards from Logierait, Dunfallandy and Fonab. The road then crossed the River Tummel at the ford by the old Pitlochry Recreation Ground (now beneath the waters of Loch Faskally) on up through Lagreach, across the level crossing (where the old Moulin Gates used to be located on Wade's Great North Road) up Cuilc Brae, passing both the Cuilc itself and Lettoch Farm, up to the road end by Pitfourie, where it turned eastwards onto the old North Road into Moulin. This road left Moulin northwards to cross the Balnakeilly Parks (rather than through Kinnaird as now), on up to Moulin moor, passing behind Badvo, before dropping down into Strathardle.

From Strathardle, this road split. One spur went north-east, by Glenfernate, towards Mar and the Linn of Dee. The other – known as the Shinagag Road – went north-west from Cluneskea, across the face of Stronchavie and followed the course of the Brerachan to Shinagag (hence its name), then on to Glenfender and Old Blair, where it connected with the Minigaig Pass into the Spey valley. The distance between Stronchavie and Shinagag is ten miles, whereas the same journey on today's roads, via Pitlochry and Killiecrankie, is almost fifteen.

It was on the Shinagag Road that King Edward III travelled to Blair Castle in 1336, just as King Edward I had probably taken the same route on his way via Comyn's Road to Inverness in 1295. At the beginning of the nineteenth century, a small hoard of coins was discovered near Stronchavie, which perhaps belonged to one of his soldiers; it consisted of coins of Edward I and III and a few coins of Alexander III.

There were probably a number of earlier tracks and roadways through the Highlands which date from an earlier time and which have since been superseded or obliterated by later routes. As we have seen, the Celts and Picts enjoyed the use of chariots and it is likely that these were employed for both military and civilian use. Thus, existing tracks, such as the Queen's Drives which date from the second or third centuries, were likely to be capable in the main of taking a chariot, pulled by one or even two horses.

The old road from Fonab over the hill towards Strathtay, with turf retaining wall still evident in 1993

Wade's Roads

After the Jacobite Rebellion of 1715, English troops were stationed at Bernera, Ruthven, Killichuimen (later renamed Fort Augustus) and Inverlochy (later renamed Fort William). They quickly discovered that it was well nigh impossible to maintain the King's authority in the Highlands, partly because they knew no Gaelic, but principally because of the difficulties of communication across large tracts of land without tracks, let alone roads.

Major-General George Wade was appointed to carry out a survey of military requirements within the Highlands. His report included recommendations that forts be established at Killichuimen, Inverlochy and Inverness and stressed that *"the Highlands of Scotland are still more impracticable from the want of roads and bridges."* Wade was a professional soldier, as his father before him, rising from Ensign to Major-General in twenty-four years. He was also a Member of Parliament, initially for Hinton in Wiltshire and latterly for Bath.

Bath was much in sympathy with the Jacobite cause, in common with other parts of the south-west of England. It was during the '15 that Wade was first confronted with rebellion, at least its potential, when he was stationed at Bath to prevent any risings there.

When Wade arrived in Scotland in the summer of 1725, he knew what he needed to do. The forts were built and then Wade turned his attention to the roads which would enable his armies to march, swiftly, wherever they were needed.

In all Wade was responsible for some two hundred and fifty miles of military roads and twenty-eight bridges. The roads progressed across uncharted territory at the expected rate of one and a half yards (one metre and forty centimetres) per worker per day. He built one road from Crieff, by Aberfeldy, Weem, Tummel Bridge and Trinafour to Dalnacardoch and another from Dunkeld by Pitlochry and Blair Atholl and Dalnacardoch to Inverness. The line of those two roads is still broadly followed today, in many places precisely. A number of the bridges have been replaced, being too narrow an hump-backed for modern vehicles, although fine enough for horses. Today the best examples of those bridges can be found at Aberfeldy and Tummel Bridge.

There was a well-kent saying:

Had you seen these roads before they were made
You would lift up your hands and bless General Wade.

It was said that, before the days of the Great North Road, it used to take the Duke of Atholl some twelve or thirteen hours to travel by sedan chair along the nineteen miles between his home in Dunkeld and Blair Castle, an average speed of one and a half miles an hour (not allowing for stoppages). This may be difficult to believe, but roadways then would have been rudimentary, even boggy, with burns often difficult to ford. When John Knox, a Scottish bookseller living in London, travelled through Scotland in 1786, he said of roads other than Wade's that

it is hardly agreed upon by travellers which is the line of the road, everyone making one for himself. Even
sheep follow better routes, understanding levels better and selecting better gradients.

Knox reckoned that the average rate of travel was about one mile an hour.

When the stage coach began to run at the beginning of the nineteenth century, it took three days to cover the one hundred and fifteen miles between Perth and Inverness; allowing for overnight stops, this probably represented an average speed of about three and a half to four miles an hour.

In 1727, Wade's new Great North Road was constructed through the centre of two of the hamlets which were to become Pitlochry. His new road ran parallel to the River Tummel at the bottom of the strath. This single fact marked the end of Moulin's importance, which it had enjoyed for perhaps more than 2,000 years. At a stroke, there was no longer a crossroads at Moulin. There was instead a new road which brought about the beginnings of Pitlochry as a cohesive village, rather than a disparate collection of hamlets and farms. A major north-south route was established for the first time, linking Dunkeld with Inverness; it changed the fate of the Highlands.

The remains of Wade's original military road above Calvine

It is still possible to trace Wade's 'military road' (as it is referred to on the Ordnance Survey maps) through much of the district. From Ballinluig, travelling north, it is evident firstly as a minor public road which passes through East Haugh, Ballyoukan and Dalshian, then as the main street through Pitlochry and the road which passes by Faskally Wood, the Garry Bridge, Killiecrankie and Aldclune into Blair Atholl and, finally, as the long straight between the old west gate of Blair Castle and Bruar Falls.

All roads need regular maintenance, to repair the wear of travel and the extremes of a Scottish climate. Wade's roads were no exception. After 1770, Government funds for maintenance were reduced, in the expectation that local landowners would share in their upkeep, as they benefited so directly. This was a neat solution in more populous parts of Scotland, but held little relevance in the northern parts of Perthshire, which were so thinly populated. As a result, those once fine roads fell into disrepair. By 1820, the roads were virtually impassable and some of the bridges were falling down.

Thomas Telford was instructed in 1830 to carry out a road building programme for the Government. This was stage-managed in London by John Rickman, Clerk Assistant to the House of Commons, and John Hope, who was an Edinburgh-based lawyer. In all, they were involved in the construction of some nine hundred and twenty miles of road and the incredible number of one thousand two hundred bridges, including the famous Tay Bridge between Dunkeld and Birnam. Telford built the road as we know it from Pitlochry (passing through Kinnaird rather than across the Balnakeilly Parks) via Enochdhu and Kirkmichael to Bridge of Cally in 1830, which accounted for twenty-two bridges alone.

Turnpikes

In the Statistical Account of 1793, Reverend Alexander Stewart noted that, apart from Wade's "Great Road", as he termed it, there were few cross roads and, he somewhat proudly remarked, no turnpikes. However, by the time that Reverend Duncan Campbell was writing his entry in 1839 for the Statistical Account of 1845, the Great North Road had been converted into a turnpike; there was a toll-bar in the middle of the Pass of Killiecrankie where the old toll house at Allt Essan still stands, perched between rockface and road.

Two other toll-bars had appeared, dating perhaps from about the same time, one on the Great North Road at West Haugh about a mile south of Pitlochry and the other on the Kirkmichael road, at Gatehouse just on the southern edge of Moulin moor. Another was formed at Bruar, in 1822, which collected £84 in 1826, but its revenue declined thereafter; its busiest months were September and October, because this was the droving season, when large numbers of cattle and sheep were driven to the trysts in Crieff and, later, Falkirk.

Toll-bars were formally abolished in 1869. The toll houses at Killiecrankie and Gatehouse are now dwellinghouses, the one at West Haugh is uninhabited and the one at Bruar, having been a Post Office between 1886 and 1914, is now part of the Clan Donnachaidh Museum.

Coaches

The first stage coach service from Perth to Inverness began in 1800, but the service was withdrawn after only a few months. The state of the road and the dangerous condition of some of the bridges, which had not been maintained properly since Wade's day, meant that the service was too unreliable.

By 1806, the Caledonian Coach Company had been established, with a twice weekly service, reducing to once weekly during the winter months. The journey took three days. From 1811, the journey time had been reduced to two days and the service was run daily. Coaching inns sprang up along the route, which were usually existing inns with hastily improved stabling, so that they could provide fresh horses for the coaches. In 1836, the mail began to be carried and, by that time, the journey time between Dunkeld and Inverness was reduced to about fourteen hours.

The service provided by these stage coaches was adversely affected by the coming of the Highland Railway in 1863, particularly in winter when the road was often impassable for weeks at a time, when the railway usually managed to remain open.

Ferries

Before the days of bridges, the rivers and their tributaries in this district caused notable obstacles, often being too deep to ford. This is where the ferryman came into his own. There was a ferry on the Garry opposite Tenandry, one on what was then the River Tummel at Borenich, one on the River Tummel at Pitlochry and two at Logierait, one for the River Tummel and the other for the River Tay.

The ferry at Pitlochry was situated at Portnacraig. It was established in the twelfth century by the monks of Coupar Angus who had been gifted the lands of Fonab (*fonn ab* meaning 'abbot's land'). This enabled them to cross from their lands, on the south side of the river, to Moulin, on the north side. To ensure a safe crossing, a coin or brass pin would be dropped into the St. Bride's Wishing Well, which was situated on the north bank until closed up for safety reasons at the end of the nineteenth century.

Latterly, a long chain was fixed from the ferry boat to a rock in the centre of the river. The ferry conveyed horses and carts as well as passengers. After the Clunie Bridge was opened for road traffic in 1834, the ferry continued to be used, by passengers only from then on. At the beginning of the twentieth century, one could cross the river and return for one old penny. It plied across the river for the final time on Empire Day 1913, the day that the Suspension Bridge almost directly above it was opened.

At Logierait, the ferry on the Tummel was designed by the artist and inventor James Fraser, millwright at Dowally, specifically to cope with the swift-running character of the river. It consisted of two boats placed side by side, connected amidships by a platform, moveable on pivots placed over the centre of each boat and, by a connecting moveable rod, fastened to the stern of each. The ferry was slipped across on a long chain, driven by a handle revolving a wheel on the boat. The main improvement over the common ferry boat was that, by setting the twin boats in an oblique position to the swift flow of the river, they were better able to resist the force of the current and so move more gently across the river.

This chain boat was capable of carrying two loaded carts, or three empty ones, with the horses still yoked to them. Although a long way ahead of the old oared boat, it was far from sufficient for the volume of traffic it was required to deal with, even in the mid-eighteenth century. However, not a single life was lost during the time the chain boat was in use, from about 1820 to about 1880, when the first bridge was built. However, the ferry boat was swept downstream many times in spate and on one occasion, it was stranded beyond Perth.

There was another time when a passenger, in too much of a hurry to wait for the ferryman, stepped onto the ferry, slipped the mooring and began to turn the wheel on board in order to draw himself across to the other side. It was only then that he realised that the chain had been removed for repair and that the ferry boat was no longer connected to either bank. The hasty passenger had to sit back and enjoy – or perhaps endure – an unscheduled journey down the Tay.

There were ferries elsewhere of course, such as the three across the Garry, one beside Tigh-na-Geat, one beside the Mill at Garryside in Blair Atholl (where also there was a ford, once crossed by Queen Victoria on horseback) and one beside Woodend, near the West Lodge of Blair Castle (where there was another ford) and one across the Bruar beside the Clan Donnachaidh Museum.

(Top) the old Garry Bridge at the southern end of the Pass of Killiecrankie, (now demolished) built in 1833, with circular storm water opening on right hand side; (Bottom) the new Garry Bridge

Bridges

At the end of the eighteenth century the only bridge of note was over the River Garry, at the southern end of the Pass of Killiecrankie. There was formerly a ferry there, about two hundred yards above the junction of the Garry with the Tummel but, as Thomas the Rhymer had foretold, it capsized because of overcrowding late on the evening of the Fair in February 1767 resulting in eighteen people drowned including four married couples. Only the ferryman survived, as he was rescued by his wife, who was able to reach out to

(Top) Cunie Bridge west of Pitlochry (now submerged beneath upper Loch Faskally); (Bottom) The old Clunie Bridge (just before it was dismantled in 1950) beside the new aluminium pedestrian bridge built in 1949

him with a boat hook. Little wonder that, after such a momentous local disaster, a bridge was in place less than three years later, paid for by public subscription.

The 1770 bridge was in due course replaced in 1833 by a new bridge over the Garry, which was interesting in that it had one large arch spanning the river and, to one side, a circular opening to relieve the pressure of a very high flood. At the turn of the twentieth century, a coach and pair approached this bridge from the Strathtummel direction, coming too fast down the hill, and failed to turn the tight corner onto the bridge, plunging to their deaths over the parapet. The 1833 bridge was in turn replaced by a metal Bailey bridge, which carried the traffic between 1955 and 1968, when the present span was built a little south of the earlier ones.

In 1833, another bridge was built, again by subscription, across the River Garry, at the northern end of the Pass, in the middle of Killiecrankie itself. Like the 1833 Garry Bridge, this one has an arch and a circular opening to one side, which can still be seen because, unlike the Garry Bridge, this one has not been replaced.

In 1832 the substantial Clunie Bridge of two large spans was built, by private subscription, across the River Tummel, nearly a mile west of Pitlochry. This bridge caused a stir at the time because many locals considered that it should have been built further south, at the ferry crossing of Portnacraig *"a spot which seems formed by nature for that purpose"*. Now the pedestrian Suspension Bridge spans that point at Portnacraig, built at a cost of £850 (funded partly by public subscription and partly by a grant from the Highland District Committee), which was opened on Empire Day 1913.

As for the 1832 Clunie Bridge, this lasted until 1950, when it became a casualty of the Hydro-Electricity Scheme. Its stone was used to form the viewpoint looking west over the upper part of Loch Faskally. Remains of the road it carried can be seen on both banks.

The New A9

Wade's Great North Road became classified as the A9 when all Britain's roads were classified as A, B or C, with attendant numbers in a clockwise radius. In the late nineteen seventies a new A9 trunk road was built, with some stretches of dual carriageway. It retains much of Wade's line, but where he took eighteen months to connect Dunkeld with Inverness, the modern road builders have taken over four years to cover the same one hundred miles. Admittedly, some difficult bridges have been built, most notably the raised viaduct above the Pass of Killiecrankie, and it should also be remembered that they had to ensure that the main road remained open to heavy traffic throughout the construction process.

The new A9 has opened out new vistas which previously were not visible from the old road. Four in this district are particularly worthy of mention. From the south, the first is a mile north of the Jubilee Bridge (itself spanning the Tay two miles north of Dunkeld) where the whole panorama of Ben-y-Vrackie is seen for the first time. The second is on the bypass at Pitlochry, where now the whole town (or village as the locals still prefer to call it) is on show. The third is at Blair Atholl, looking from the bypass due north up Glen Tilt and to the Beinn a' Ghlos. The fourth is from the north, having passed Bruar, when the western elevation of Blair Castle comes into view, especially when floodlit of an evening.

The road provides a welcome to Highland Perthshire although, when stuck behind many a lorry or caravan (or both), there is many a local who would wish for dual carriageway all the way between Perth and Inverness.

The Killiecrankie viaduct for the A9, looking south from Urrard

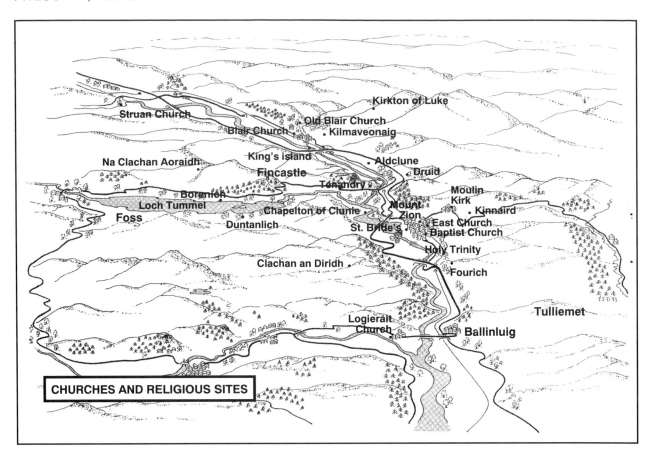

CHURCHES AND RELIGIOUS SITES

Kirkton of Luke
Struan Church
Old Blair Church
Blair Church
Kilmaveonaig
Na Clachan Aoraidh
King's island
Aldclune
Fincastle
Druid
Tenandry
Moulin Kirk
Borenich
Chapelton of Clunie
Mount Zion
Kinnaird
Loch Tummel
Foss
East Church
Duntanlich
Baptist Church
St. Bride's
Holy Trinity
Clachan an Diridh
Fourich
Tulliemet
Logierait Church
Ballinluig

Moulin Kirk, with the Inn behind

CHAPTER TWELVE
Religious Sites in the District

The Religious Establishments of Scotland

When English visitors come to Scotland and see churches here which date from the seventeenth or eighteenth centuries, they compare them, perhaps unfavourably, with their own church at home. Their own village church, dating perhaps from the thirteenth or fourteenth century, may in parts still be the original building and so looks much older than our own church and kirk buildings here.

What many may not realise is that the religious establishments here pre-date those in England not by a whisker but fully by some five or six hundred years. If religion is a sign of civilisation, then the natives here were surely not as uncivilised as some would have us believe. The simple reason that none of our original church buildings remains is that they were built so very long ago, of materials that were not best suited for longevity.

Some of our old church buildings fell down, whilst others burnt down. Where the buildings were made of wood, this was not uncommon. The winters were inclement at the best of times, in earlier centuries more severely so than now. In order to warm up these relatively large church buildings for the Sunday faithful, a fire would be lit in the grate on the Saturday afternoon and then banked up so as to last through the night. Any over-enthusiasm in this exercise could cause a complete conflagration. So it was, for instance, with Moulin Kirk, not once but twice in the same century.

In fact, the Christian religion was firmly established in Ireland by the fifth century, from which over the next two hundred years and more there flowed a veritable stream of missionaries who established monasteries (most notably on Iona) and churches wherever they went, We know that their travels were extensive, not only throughout Scotland, but also to Whitby and Lindisfarne in the north-east of England. Their influence in this district is no less than elsewhere, to the extent that St. Columba, who founded the monastery on Iona in 563 AD, is reputed to have visited the religious settlement at Dunkeld, which at one time was the most important on the mainland and in time succeeded to Iona itself after the destruction of the monastery there by the Vikings in 802 AD.

However, before the coming of Christianity to these islands, there was an earlier religion still. Vestiges remain here, principally in some of the place names – such as Druid itself above Killiecrankie and Strathgroy (from *strath druidh*, meaning 'strath of the Druids') above Aldclune – and also in many of the superstitions and so-called 'pagan' elements of our culture (including the veneration of mistletoe and the choice of 25th December, the major Druidical feast day of *Jul*, for Christmas).

There is little clear light to shed on the subject of the Druid religion. The facts, such as they are, are vested in the many places where it is known that worship of some kind took place (such as Stonehenge in England and the many cup-marked stones here, none of which has yielded its mysteries), in depictions on coins (which show religious practice and apparent human sacrifice) and in the writings of contemporary historians (such as Julius Caesar, but with the cautionary note that he and the others were neither scientific in their observations nor comprehending of what they observed).

It seems clear that the Christians took deliberate steps to obliterate the former religion. As mentioned, they hijacked the Druidical *Jul* feast as their own Christmas Day, they chose sites of Druidical worship as sites for their own Christian churches (as at Druid above Killiecrankie), even called their churches "kirks" (which comes from the Gaelic word *cearcall* meaning a circle and was the name used to describe the circular Druidical temples) and some, such as St. Columba, were said to have burnt Druidical books.

Churches in Pitlochry
Moulin Kirk

The church at Moulin is the oldest in Atholl. It was founded by St. Colm, but it is not certain which one. There were many missionaries called Columba, or its derivative Colm. The market held since time immemorial at Moulin was commonly known as *Feill Machalmaig* ('the market of the blessed Colm'). It was usual for markets to be held on the name day of the Saint to whom or by whom the local church was dedicated. Moulin Market was held in February, the 18th being the name day of not one but two St. Colmans!

One was St. Colm (or Colman of Kilroot) who was in this district sometime between his departure from Bangor in about 490 AD and his death (as Bishop of Dromore) in 510 AD. The other was St. Colman, who was Bishop of Lindisfarne and attended the Synod of Whitby in 664 AD; he was in this district before his death in 676 AD.

In between, the great St. Columba, who founded Iona, was said to have visited Dunkeld. It is quite possible, almost inevitable, that he might at the same time have travelled the twelve miles north to what was, by all accounts, a busy and important Pictish community at the time.

In 1275, Pope Gregory X sent his nuncio Boiamund de Vicci to collect a tithe (literally a tenth of all church revenues) from each parish of the Scottish church to finance the Crusades. The Vatican holds a record of Boiamund's *Taxatio Beneficiorum,* where there is mention in 1276 of *"Ecclesia de Mulin".*

In the case of Moulin, it would appear that the church was founded in about 490 AD or 670 AD and so, whichever is the right saint, it is an ancient foundation. The church itself was rebuilt in 1613, as is indicated by a stone bearing this date which is incorporated into the existing kirk building. In 1704, substantial improvements and enlargements were made. The kirk was rebuilt again in 1813, after a fire, but it lasted a tender sixty years until it was gutted by fire again on a Communion Sunday in November 1873. At that time there was strong pressure to relocate the church more centrally for both Moulin and the growing village of Pitlochry. After great deliberations, it was however decided by the Kirk Session to rebuild on the same site at Moulin, so a new kirk was dedicated there in 1875, with seating for four hundred and ninety.

Moulin Kirk was given electric lighting, instead of oil lamps, as a mark of the jubilee of Mount Zion (West Church) in Pitlochry in 1934. It stopped being used for religious purposes in 1989 when, having shared the Parish since Mount Zion Church was built in Pitlochry in 1884, it was decided that there was insufficient demand to cover the very considerable overheads of maintaining two churches for a smaller congregation.

Until 1896, Moulin churchyard was the only local burial ground. In that year the burial ground at Dysart was established. It could not be extended, so a new burial ground was provided at Fonab in 1958.

Mount Zion Church

Only nine years after the new kirk was built at Moulin, it was decided that a new more central church was needed after all, not least to cater for the growing number of summer visitors to Pitlochry. For a time previously, some summer services had been held in the Pitlochrie Public School, at the east end of town.

So it was that a new church was built in 1884, with the inspiration and support of Archibald Butter, on a knoll donated by him near the centre of the village. Because of its prominent position, it became known affectionately as Mount Zion. After the church in Lower Oakfield was brought into the Union of the Church of Scotland, it was known as the East Church and Mount Zion as the West Church.

Mount Zion was designed by Mr. C.L. Ower, an architect in Dundee, who incorporated a novel mixture of Victorian Gothic, Romanesque and Byzantine, with two rose windows thrown in for good measure. The stone came from the local quarry at Aldour. The foundation stone was laid on 4th September 1883. A feature of the church is its fine organ, partly funded by a generous donation from Andrew Carnegie. The clock and bell were erected in 1887 in memory of Archibald Butter who had died two years previously, at the age of eighty.

In 1923, Mount Zion was designated as the second Parish Church, but was used only during the summer months. Later, heating was introduced and, after the Second World War, Mount Zion was used for each Sunday morning service, with evensong at Moulin. In 1989, when Moulin Kirk closed for good, all services were from then on held at Mount Zion. In 1991, it became the only Church of Scotland in Pitlochry after the closure of the East Church and so was renamed as the Pitlochry Church of Scotland.

The East Church

It is nowadays forgotten that the Disruption of 1843, which split the established Church of

East Church, Lower Oakfield, Pitlochry before its conversion to flatted dwellinghouses in 1993

Scotland right down the middle, was one of the most momentous domestic issues in nineteenth century Scotland. The decision was reached on 18th May that year (at a meeting in St Andrews Church, George Street, Edinburgh) with thirty-eight per cent of the ministers entering the Free Church. They were joined by about forty per cent of the total membership and even more of the elders. The Disruption was a turning point in Scottish social life, ending for ever the parish-orientated administration of schools and relief of the poor.

Shortly after the Disruption, the original Free Church of Moulin was formed. As no landowner would grant the congregation a feu of land, they held their first meetings in a barn at Auchlatt (between Moulin and Kinnaird) and, in the same year, built a church nearby at what is now Kirk Lodge. As a result of a growth in numbers, caused in part by those from Tenandry Parish merging with those of Moulin Parish in 1848, it was decided to build a new Free Church. This was located at Lower Oakfield, near the centre of Pitlochry, where a feu was at last provided, and was consecrated in 1863.

After the Church moved to Lower Oakfield, its original building at Kinnaird was used for ten years as the Free School, until the new Pitlochrie Public School was opened in 1873, after which it was converted into a dwellinghouse, with a first floor being added and the long windows being divided to provide for both floors; it has since been sub-divided into three two-storey houses.

The East Church, as the one in Lower Oakfield became known after the Reunion of the Churches (effected at a meeting in a bus garage in Edinburgh on 2nd October 1929), continued as a place of worship until the end of 1990, after which Mount Zion was left as the only Church of Scotland where previously there had been three.

The East Church had been home to the successful seasonal 'Gallery' festival of painting, handicrafts, music and drama. This ran for five weeks or so each August,. Having started in 1968, it ran for twenty-four seasons there. In 1993, the East Church befell the same fate as its predecessor at Kinnaird, being transformed into dwellinghouses. As a result, Pitlochry lost its unofficial community arts centre and the 'Gallery' festival was without a regular home.

Holy Trinity Church

Episcopalians have been in this district since before 1275, but as far as can be ascertained, the first services in Pitlochry began only in about 1855, perhaps fittingly in a joiner's shop. At times, services were dependant on whether a clergyman happened to be passing through on the stage coach. If so, he would be greeted by a little reception committee, assembled on the off chance, who would lose little time in offering him lodging as a break in his journey and persuading him in exchange to conduct a service for them.

The Episcopal Church, known as Holy Trinity, is situated at the eastern end of Pitlochry. It was designed by Mr. Charles Buckeridge of Oxford when he was only 24. The church was dedicated in

1858 and at that time the chosen spot was quietly situated up a muddy lane away from the main road. Only five years later the railway line came very close by and, with it, a forced realignment of the main road which was brought much closer too. The Church stood its ground and was enlarged in 1889. A lych-gate, now listed as a structure of architectural importance, was added in memory of Colonel Herbert Foster of Faskally.

Pitlochry Baptist Church

The Baptists are part of the Evangelical movement, but hold two different tenets which distinguish them from other sects. The first of these is that only true Christian believers should be members of the Baptist Church and part of their local religious community. The second is that each individual church is independent, in not being beholden to any central ecclesiastical body.

The Baptist movement in Pitlochry arose out of the success of those in Blair Atholl and particularly Tulliemet. In 1844, Tulliemet boasted almost twenty per cent of all Baptists in Tayside and was the largest of all the congregations, including Dundee. The Pastor at Tulliemet began to hold services on Sunday afternoons in Pitlochry, initially in a joiner's workshop (which seemed to be a religiously appropriate vogue!).

The congregation in Pitlochry was formally constituted as a church in December 1881. By July 1884 a fine church building was opened in the main street, where it still stands. The wheel came full circle when, for a time before its closure in 1973, the Tulliemet church was looked after by the minister from Pitlochry.

In 1971, the Atholl Centre was built behind the original church buildings, as a youth centre, as a denominational training centre and as a resource centre for the disabled, with accommodation for up to sixty. This was largely the brainchild of Watson Moyes, minister at Pitlochry between 1965 and 1983.

Roman Catholic Chapel of St. Bride

This Church was built in 1949, principally to cater for the many Irish men employed in the construction of the Hydro-Electric scheme. Indeed, it was constructed largely by their voluntary labour. Tragically, this building was burnt down one Sunday in August 1955. However, a new Church was soon built on the same wooded knoll near Loch Faskally.

A Tour of Churches and Religious Sites Elsewhere in the District (conducted clockwise)

Logierait Church

Logierait Church was founded by St Cedd in about 650 AD. Those at Grandtully and Foss were founded at about the same time by his brother St Chad. The brothers were on their way home to Lindisfarne from instruction in Iona, under the patronage of Oswald, the Saxon Northumbrian King (who himself had fled to Iona in about 630 and whilst there had been converted to Christianity).

The present church dates from 1805 and underwent renovation in 1928 and alterations (to create two anterooms and lower the ceiling) in 1971.

Because the foundation is so old, there are many interesting stones in the graveyard, including two Pictish ones (one recumbent and one standing) dating respectively from perhaps 825 AD and 900 AD. There are also three mortsafes [see Chapter Ten].

Killiechangie Chapel

On the south side of the River Tummel, about two miles west of Logierait, is Killiechangie. It was in use, linked to Logierait, until about 1700. It fell into ruin and in about 1850 the tenant farmer pulled down the remains, but two old stones with incised crosses were placed against a dyke at the bottom of a big field below the road, where they still remain.

Dunfallandy Chapel

A mile and a half further west is Dunfallandy, where there was an old chapel, probably connected to Logierait Church and perhaps founded at about the same time. Nothing remains of it, although a graveyard lies between the Mausoleum and the Mains of Dunfallandy which may have been associated with it.

Bloody Stone of Dunfallandy

Dunfallandy means 'the mound of blood'. About one hundred metres from the north side of the public road, above Wyandotte Cottage, there used to be a boulder (about two metres by one and nearly a metre high) known as 'the Bloody Stone of Dunfallandy'. It was a rough block of black schist, blackened by fire, with a deep cup near one end.

An old photograph of the Bloody Stone, now buried within a roadmakers' quarry

In explanation of its name, there is a tradition that, in the fourteenth century, Adam Fergusson hid behind the Stone to kill his neighbour Baron Stewart with an arrow. Fergusson was aggrieved that Stewart had not permitted his daughter to marry Fergusson's son. After this murder, the embargo was lifted and the marriage went ahead. Ironically, at the beginning of the twentieth century, the Stewarts became lairds of Dunfallandy, the current surname of the family being Stewart Fergusson.

The Bloody Stone was probably a 'cresset' stone, on what was the line of an old road between Logierait and Dunfallandy. As such, it would have been used to light the way to the chapel at Dunfallandy, its hollow cup being filled with tallow into which a wick was inserted. Unfortunately, in about 1979 the Stone was incorporated within an infilled quarry at Dunfallandy which had been used in connection with the new A9 Pitlochry bypass.

Within the wood to the south of Wyandotte Cottage, near the river bank, is the wishing well known as *tober traigh*, which bubbles endlessly.

Clachan an Diridh

On Carra Beag (Fonab Hill), about fifty metres to the north of the path between Pitlochry and Strathtay (which is one of the oldest routes in the district) and close to the ridge, is the celebrated *Clachan an diridh* ('stones of the ascent'). Two complete stones remain as well as the remains of one of two others. They are at about 1,150' (350m) above sea level and are now within the forest, although they were still, dramatically, on open moorland until the Second World War [see Chapter Three].

These *clachan iobairt* ('stones of worship') were visited on 1st May each year, the religious rite being to go round the stones *car deiseal*, that is, from east to west with the sun (as opposed to *car tuathal*, that is from west to east, which was the "unlucky" way travelled by the Druids whenever they wished to pronounce a curse).

A little to the north-west is a Pictish cemetery with small hut circles and a circular cattle enclosure nearby.

Chapelton of Clunie

The next religious foundation westwards, still on the south side of the Tummel, was Chapelton of Clunie (from *cluain*, meaning 'a pasture'), near the Clunie Power Station.

The Praying Stone of this chapel is called 'the Priest's Stone' and is situated just to the south of the public road to Foss. The stone, a red sandstone slab, has a raised cross on both sides with bosses at the junction of the arms, indicating that it dates from about the seventh century. In case it was flooded by the Hydro-Electric Scheme in 1950, it was removed from beside the old road (a section of which is still visible nearby, just above the waterline of Loch Faskally) and relocated to its current position above the new road.

The foundation of the chapel itself can be seen about one hundred metres to the north of the stone, in front of the cottage which used to be known as Chapelton, but now as Wester Clunie. About twenty metres to the south of the stone lie the remains of an old clachan.

Duntanlich Church

The next church westwards was at Duntanlich (from *dun an laich*, meaning 'fort by the still water'), on the south shore of Loch Tummel, almost opposite the Queen's View. The church was situated on the east side of the field, but nothing now remains of it and only some mounds indicate the ancient graves.

Foss Church

The westmost church on the south side of Tummel was the earliest. It is at Foss (which derives from the Gaelic *fasaidh*, meaning 'a dwelling place'). The present church dates from about 1820, but is built on the site of the church founded by St Chad in about 650. The churchyard contains the walled enclosures of the three oldest families of the Foss and Kynachan district, all of whom were Stewarts.

Borenich Burial Ground

On the north side of Loch Tummel, a mile to the east of Strathtummel, is a quaint burial ground on a mound in a field to the south of the road. The house nearby is known as Chapelton. About two miles west is another graveyard, above Grenich, which is no longer visible.

Fincastle

In 1843 a chapel was built at the entrance to Glen Fincastle, beside the new road between Pitlochry and Tummel Bridge. This was as a result of the Disruption when the minister and much of the congregation from Tenandry switched from the Established Church of Scotland to the Free Church. This new chapel was built for them, although they also linked up with the Free Church in Moulin parish. From 1877 the chapel was used also as the local primary school, 'the glen school' as it was known.

Near the head of the Glen is a burial ground which is also known as Chapelton. No church now exists, but there were ruins there until about 1770. The stone was removed at about that time, perhaps to be incorporated in the building of houses nearby. There were occasional burials at Chapelton until the early twentieth century.

About two miles to the east of Edintian (which derives from *aoann an t-sithean*, meaning 'face of the fairy hill'), at the head of Glen Fincastle and a mile to the east of Loch Bhac, are four standing stones in a group, situated beside the ancient path which ran from Blair Atholl, passing the head of Glen Fincastle to Loch Tummel. They are called *na clachan aoraidh* ('the stones of worship'). They vary in height from three-quarters of a metre to a metre and a quarter. They are situated at about 1,300' (400m) above sea level and are now immersed within the Allean Forest.

Less than a mile from Fincastle is Bonskeid House, built around 1800 and greatly enlarged in 1859 and 1863. From 1922, the house was tenanted by the Young Men's Christian Association. The YMCA became owners of the house and policies in 1951 and enlarged it further in 1960.

Tenandry Kirk

Situated above and to the south-west of the Pass of Killiecrankie is a church of the Church of Scotland, which serves the communities of Strathtummel, Fincastle, Bonskeid, Faskally and Killiecrankie. It was built in 1836, originally as a 'Chapel of Ease' for the benefit of those for whom the Parish Church was too far distant. In 1851, after a reorganisation, it became a Parish Church.

King's Island Church and St. Andrew's

About half a mile to the south-east of Bridge of Tilt is an area still known as the King's Island (originally *eilean an righ*), which until the early twentieth century lay midstream, rather than bypassed by the River Garry as now. It was so named because King Robert the Bruce is reputed to have rested there on his way to Rannoch (presumably on a different occasion from his visit via Coille Brochain [see Chapter Five]).

On the island a Free Church was constructed of wood in 1844, a year after the Disruption. It remained in use for about twelve years before the damp and danger of floods prompted the congregation to build a new Church within Bridge of Tilt. Now there is a house on the area known as King's Island, built in 1993.

That new Free Church was St. Andrew's, built in 1856 this time of stone, which could seat some

four hundred. It remained in use until 1950 and then both church and tower were demolished in 1971; only the vestry still remains. The site of the church is now a small garden fronting the main street, between Bridge of Tilt's two shops. It is remembered in the name of St. Andrew's Crescent in the middle of the village.

There was a Baptist Church in Bridge of Tilt until 1886, which was situated in what is now Annat Cottage.

Kilmaveonaig

Kilmaveonaig sits at the edge of a field now within the village of Bridge of Tilt. The church was founded by St Adamnan (softened to *Eonan*) who was the ninth Abbot of Iona. He was born in Ireland in about 624 AD and began his missionary journeys in about 665 AD, becoming the ninth Abbot of Iona in 679 AD. Prior to his arrival at Bridge of Tilt, St. Adamnan founded the church at Ardeonaig ('Eonan's height'), the mill at Bridge of Balgie (known as Milton Eonan, where he died in 704 AD) and the Monastery with Collegiate Church at Dull (where he is buried).

Kilmaveonaig Church at Bridge of Tilt

In Boiamund's *Taxatio Beneficiorum* there is mention in 1275 of *"Ecclesia de Kylnevenet: 1 marc"* and in 1276 of *"Ecclesia de Kilmevonoc: 1 marc"*. A merk was about two-thirds of a £1 Scots.

Kilmaveonaig was rebuilt in 1591 by the Robertsons of Lude, once they had moved to Lude House nearby. At that time there was a village of Kilmaveonaig, just to the west of the church, which remained in use until about 1834. Wade's military road ran just to the south of the church on its way to Old Blair, until its line was altered in 1820.

The church was rebuilt again in 1794, when the congregation was free to worship once again, after the repeal in 1792 of the Penal Acts which had been in force for the previous ninety-seven years. Those Acts had forbidden worship by more than five persons together. Restoration work took place in 1866 and again in 1898; on the latter occasion the building was enlarged. The Church is still in use, linked to the Episcopalian Church in Pitlochry.

Kirkton of Lude

St. Adamnan founded another church in what is now a remote spot about three miles to the north of Bridge of Tilt, near the head of Glenfender. Some of the walls of that church and chancel are still standing and the font is in its place. An annual service is held there in the open air.

Near the church was the original house of the Robertsons of Lude. This was vacated in about the middle of the sixteenth century, when they moved closer to Kilmaveonaig, to a house called Balnagrew. This was occupied until about 1823 when the present house, called Lude again, was built nearby. When the Robertsons moved, the Kirkton was abandoned and fell into disrepair.

Old Lude House in about 1821

Old Blair Church

At Old Blair is St. Bride's Church, which may have been founded by St. Adamnan also. Certainly it was an old foundation and was mentioned in Boiamund's *Taxatio* of 1275 as due to pay four merks which, being four times more than Kilmaveonaig at that time, indicates its importance. Here lies the grave of John Graham of Claverhouse, Viscount Dundee, who fell at the Battle of Killiecrankie on 27th July 1689.

By 1769 it was, according to Daniel Defoe, a *"poor old kirk, the pews all broken down, doors open, full of dirt where the minister preached once a week."* In spite of the Duke of Atholl's wish to relocate the church midway between Blair and Struan, St. Bride's was rebuilt in 1824, but it remained in use only until 1828.

Blair Church

Only three years after St. Bride's Church was rebuilt in 1824, it was decided to build a new church. This reflected much debate in previous years as to whether there should be one church for both Struan and Blair Atholl, but the prompt for a new church in Blair seems to have been that Old Blair had just been by-passed. Whilst General Wade's Great North Road had passed through Old Blair on its way behind Blair Castle, a new Parliamentary road was built, at the Duke of Atholl's wish, to the south of the Castle, close to the Mill and along its present line. With the new road, the new village of Blair Atholl began.

The church was one of the first buildings within the new village, designed by Edinburgh architect Archibald Elliott, situated on the haugh by the new Castle gates and opened in 1828. It then became the new Parish Church, to the final eclipse of St. Bride's.

Queen Victoria attended the church for a service on Sunday 15th September 1844, in a specially raised 'royal' pew situated in front of the pulpit and listened to a sermon which, at her request, was no longer than twenty-five minutes.

Struan Church

Old Struan was another ancient religious settlement, situated at the confluence of the River Garry and the Errochty Water. It was dedicated to St. Fillan and was also mentioned in Boiamund's *Taxatio* of 1275. An old preaching stone lies in the graveyard, as probable testimony of even earlier worship at this hallowed spot. By 1820, the Church was falling into disrepair and it was therefore decided to replace it with the present Church, which was built in 1828. Considerable internal alterations were effected in 1938. Its fine old bell, known as St. Fillan's Bell, can now be seen in Perth Museum.

Thus, within one year the Parish found itself possessed of two brand new churches, one at Struan and the other at Blair Atholl. In the same year, a fine new Manse was constructed (now known as the Old Manse) at Baluain, by the now disused West Lodge of Blair Castle. Thus situated, the Manse was precisely midway between the Minister's two churches, to satisfy both 'wings' of such a large and well-spread Parish. The local heritors, who paid proportionately for all three buildings, experienced an expensive year.

A wooden Free Church was built in Old Struan in 1855, opposite Clachan Farm on the main road from Calvine to Trinafour, which served sufficiently for a time. It was later rebuilt in stone, when it was known as Clachan of Strowane, and continued to be used as a church until the nineteen thirties. It is now a house known as Dail na Sagairt ('field of the priest').

Aldclune Chapel

There was a chapel at Aldclune, but nothing remains, in spite of its having reportedly been in good order until 1770. The remains of graves were also evident, although no longer. In a wood north of Aldclune (indeed, now north of the A9 too) lies a recumbent tombstone, which is dated 1760, with the initials "CS" and a Lochaber axe inscribed upon it.

Church at Druid

There are remains of a small stone church (about eleven metres by six) on the hill to the north of Killiecrankie, above Old Faskally House and below Druid Cottage. There seems little doubt that the church was built intentionally on the old heathen mound, which was a Druidical site of worship. A stone socket, which at one time held the cross or praying

Tombstone north of Aldclune, depicting Lochaber axe

stone, used to be evident a little to the north of the ruin. There are memorials to the Robertsons of Faskally for whom the Church may have become a private chapel.

Knolls in Pitlochry

On the west side of West Moulin Road is a small knoll, where the Craig Mhor Lodge now stands. This used to be known as *tom chluig* ('the knoll of the bell') as here a bell used to be rung for the citizens of Pitlochry and Toberargan who could not hear the actual church bell at Moulin.

There is another knoll almost exactly opposite, immediately to the north of the Pitlochry Hydro Hotel and within its grounds. This was called *cnoc dhubh*, or 'the black knoll' and is reputed to have been an old site of pagan worship.

The Fourich

On the north side of the River Tummel, just to the east of Pitlochry, St. Catherine's Chapel was built on the knoll behind Dalshian, to the west of the road leading to Croftinloan and Donavourd. It was built in the very centre of the old Pictish fort known as the *fourich* ('place of watching'). It is now a poor roofless ruin, thick with nettles within a circle of rhododendron. The remains of memorial stones within the building are still evident.

Tulliemet

A Baptist church was founded at Tulliemet in

1808, down a lane from Tighrioch, near Dalcapon, in what previously had been an Independent Church. The Independent minister was baptised into the Baptist faith and many of his congregation followed suit. Those who did not faced a seventeen mile return walk to the nearest Independent Church in Dunkeld. The building at Tulliemet, already the second on that site, was roofed in thatch and lasted only until 1847, when the present building was erected, which remained in use as a church until 1960.

At a time when Tulliemet was reasonably well populated, the congregation there in 1844 was over one hundred and thirty, which was an exceptionally large number when compared with one hundred and nine at Meadowside in Dundee, twenty in Aberfeldy, seventeen in Rannoch and a total of six hundred and sixty-two in the whole of Tayside.

A private Roman Catholic chapel was built in 1855, at yet another place called Chapelton, to the south of Tulliemet House. Services were conducted there for about forty years, after which the chapel became derelict.

(Above) The Fourich photographed in about 1925, showing the 'foss' or ditch on the north side (Below) and St. Catherine's Chapel, overgrown, in 1993

Bibliography

Angus Railway Group: *Perthshire (Steam Album, vol 3).* Broughty Ferry: Angus Railway Group, 1983.

Atholl Illustrated: New Popular Tourist Guide. Pitlochry: L. Mackay 1925.

Aytoun, William Edmondstoune: *Lays of the Scottish Cavaliers and other Poems.* Edinburgh: Blackwood, 28th ed., 1881.

Baker, Joan & Arthur: *A Walker's Companion to the Wade Roads.* Perth: The Melven Press,1982.

Barbour, Margaret F.: *Bonskeid: The Story of the House and its Owners.* Privately published, 1986.

Barnett, T. Ratcliffe: *The Road to Rannoch and the Summer Isles.* Edinburgh: R. Grant & Sons, 1924.

Bebbington, D. W. (ed.): *The Baptists in Scotland: A History.* Glasgow: Baptist Union of Scotland, 1988.

Boswell, James: *The life of Samuel Johnson, LL. D* and *The Journal of a Tour to the Hebrides.* London: Bliss, Sands & Co, 1897 reprint.

Bowstead, Christopher John Kaye: *Facts and Fancies, Linked with Folk- Lore about Kilmaveonaig.* Edinburgh: R. Grant & Son, 1912.

Breeze, David J.: *Why did the Romans Fail to Conquer Scotland?* Proceedings of the Society of Antiquaries of Scotland 118 (pp 3-22), 1988.

Buchanan, Lachlan D.: *Stories from Perth's History.* Perth: The Melven Press, 1978.

Coles, John M.: *Scottish Early Bronze Age Metalwork.* (Reprinted from the Proceedings of the Society of Antiquaries of Scotland 101 (1968-69, pp 1-110), 1969.

Cunningham, A. D.: *A History of Rannoch.* Rannoch: The Author, 1984.

Daviot, Gordon: *Claverhouse.* London: Collins, 1937.

Dewar, Annie: *Logierait Church and Parish.* Logierait: The Author, 1989.

Dingwall, Christopher: *The Falls of Bruar: A Garden in the Wild.* Dundee: The Author, 1987.

Dixon, John Henry: *Pitlochry Past and Present.* Pitlochry: L. Mackay, 1925.

Durie, Alastair J.: *The Scottish Linen Industry in the Eighteenth Century.* Edinburgh: John Donald, 1979.

Firsoff, Valdemar Axel: *In the Hills of Breadalbane.* London: Hale, 1954.

Fraser, Duncan: *Highland Perthshire.* Montrose: Standard Press, 1969.

Gillies, William Alexander: *In Famed Breadalbane:* The Story of the Antiquities, Lands and People of a Highland District. Perth: Munro Press, 1938.

Gordon, Seton Paul: *Highways and Byways in the Central Highlands.* London: MacMillan, 1948.

Gordon, Thomas Crouther: *Beautiful Pitlochry.* Pitlochry: L. Mackay, 1955.

Gordon, Thomas Crouther: *Robert Louis Stevenson in Athole.* Kirkcaldy: J. Davidson & Son, 1935.

Grant, Isabel F.: *Highland Folk Ways.* London: Routledge & Kegan Paul, 1961.

Groome, Francis Hindes (ed.): *Ordnance Gazetteer of Scotland: A Survey of Scottish Topography, Statistical, Biographical and Historical.* 6 volumes. Edinburgh: T. C. Jack, 1884-85.

Haldane, A. R. B.: *The Drove Roads of Scotland.* London: Thomas Nelson & Sons, 1952.

Haldane, A. R. B.: *New Ways through the Glens.* London: Nelson, 1962.

Hetherington, Alastair: *Perthshire in Trust.* Edinburgh: National Trust for Scotland, 1988.

Huie, Crawford: *Century of a Village Church.* Privately published, 1984.

Jackson, Anthony: *The Pictish Trail.* Kirkwall: Orkney Press, 1989.

Jamieson, John: *An Etymological Dictionary of the Scottish Language,* revised by John Longmuir. 5 volumes. Paisley: Alexander Gardner, rev. ed., 1879-87.

Kay, Billy & Cailean Maclean: *Knee Deep in Claret: A Celebration of Wine in Scotland.* Edinburgh: Mainstream, 1983.

Kerr, John: *Highland Highways: Old Roads in Atholl.* Edinburgh: John Donald, 1991.

Kerr, John: *Old Grampian Highways: Comyn's Road, Minigaig Pass.* (Reprinted from The Transactions of the Gaelic Society of Inverness, Vol 49). 1977.

KERR, JOHN: *Old Roads to Strathardle*. Keltering: The Author, 1981. (Reprinted from The Transactions of the Gaelic Society of Inverness, Vol 51).

Kerr, John (ed): *Queen Victoria's Scottish Diaries*. Moffat: Lochar, 1992.

KERR, JOHN: *The Robertson Heartland: Glen Errochty*. Pitlochry:Atholl Experience, 1992. (Reprinted from The Transactions of the Gaelic Society of Inverness, Vol 56).

KERR, JOHN: *Tummel Forest Park Guide Book*. Dunkeld: Forestry Commission,1990.

KERR, JOHN: *Wade in Atholl*. Blair Atholl: The Atholl Experience, 1986. (Reprinted from The Transactions of the Gaelic Society of Inverness, Vol 53).

LAING, LLOYD R.: *Celtic Britain*. London: Routledge & Kegan Paul, 1979.

LENEMAN, LEAH: *Living in Atholl* 1685-1785. Edinburgh: Edinburgh University Press, 1986.

LENMAN, BRUCE: *The Jacobite Cause*. Glasgow: Drew,1986.

Locus Breadalbane Ltd.: *'Locus' Route Packs*, 1991 (et seq.)

LOGAN, JAMES: *The Scottish Gael: or Celtic Manners, as Preserved among the Highlanders*. 2 volumes. London: Smith, Elder & Co., 1831.

LYNCH, MICHAEL: *Scotland: A New History*. London: Barrie & Jenkins, 1991.

MACKIE, JOHN DUNCAN: *A History of Scotland*. London: Penguin, 1964.

MACLEAN, A.: *Dunkeld: Its Straths and Glens*. Dunkeld: Charles McLean, 1857.

MACLENNAN, MALCOLM: *A Pronouncing and Etymological Dictionary of the Gaelic Language*. Edinburgh: John Grant,1925.

MacLeod, John (comp.): *A Dictionary of the Gaelic Language*. Edinburgh: Highland and Agricultural Society of Scotland, 1828.

MACMILLAN, HUGH: *The Highland Tay from Tyndrum to Dunkeld*. London: H. Virtue & Co., 1901.

MANN, JOHN C. & DAVID J. BREEZE: *Ptolemy, Tacitus and the Tribes of North Britain*. (Proceedings of the Society of Antiquaries of Scotland 117 (1987) pp 85-91).

MARSHALL, WILLIAM: *Historic Scenes of Perthshire*. Edinburgh: W. Oliphant, 1880.

MARTIN, WILLIAM: *Atholl in the Ice Age*. Pitlochry: L. Mackay, 1966.

MILES, HAMISH: *Fair Perthshire*. London: John Lane, 1930.

MITCHELL, DUGALD: *A Popular History of the Highlands and Gaelic Scotland from the Earliest Times to the Close of the Forty-Five*. Paisley: A. Gardner, 1900.

MITCHELL, HUGH: *Pitlochry and Neighbourhood*. Pitlochry: L. Mackay, 1911.

MITCHELL, HUGH: *Pitlochry District*. Pitlochry: L. Mackay, 1923.

MOLYNEUX, EMMA: *Recollections of William Stewart Irvine*. Edinburgh: D. Douglas, 1896.

MONCREIFFE OF THAT ILK, SIR IAIN: *The Highland Clans*. London: Barrie & Rockliff, 1967.

NELSON, GILLIAN: *Highland Bridges*. Aberdeen: Aberdeen University Press, 1990.

NORIE, WILLIAM DRUMMOND: *The Life and Adventures of Prince Charles Edward Stuart*. 4 volumes. London: Caxton, 1903.

North of Scotland Hydro- Electric Board: *Power from the Glens*. Edinburgh: The Board, 1973.

North of Scotland Hydro-Electric Board: *The Tummel-Garry Hydro-Electric Scheme*, 1950.

North of Scotland Hydro-Electric Board: *Tummel Valley Hydro-Electric Schemes*. 1950.

NOWN, GRAHAM: *Edradour: The Smallest Distillery in the World*. Melksham: Good Books, for the House of Campbell, 1988.

Perth & Kinross District Council: *The Pitlochry Archives*, 1975 (et seq.)

The Pitlochry and District Tourist Association: *The History and Heritage of Pitlochry and District*. Pitlochry and District Tourist Association, 1974

REID, A. G.: *Strathardle: Its History and Its People*. Blairgowrie: The Author, 1986.

RICHARDS, ERIC: *A History of the Highland Clearances*. 2 volumes. London: Croom Helm, 1985.

RIDEOUT, JAMES: *Carn Dubh, Moulin, Perthshire: Survey and Excavation of an Archaeological Landscape 1987-1990*. (to be published by AOC Scotland Ltd.)

RITCHIE, ANNA & DAVID J. BREEZE: *Invaders of Scotland*. Edinburgh: HMSO, 1989.

RITCHIE, ANNA: *Picts*. Edinburgh: HMSO, 1989.

Robert Louis Sevenson: The Man & His Work. (Bookman series). London, 1913.

Robinson, Mairi (ed.): *The Concise Scots Dictionary*. Aberdeen: Aberdeen University Press, 1985.

ROLLESTON, THOMAS WILLIAM HAZEN: *Myths and Legends of the Celtic Race*. London: Harrap, 1911.

Royal Commission on the Ancient and Historical Monuments of Scotland: *North-East Perth: An Archaeological Landscape*. Edinburgh: Royal Commission, 1990.

SALMOND, J. B.: *Wade in Scotland*. Edinburgh: Moray Press, 1934.

SCOTT, RONALD MCNAIR: *Robert the Bruce: King of Scots*. London: Hutchinson, 1982.

Sinclair, Duncan McDonald: *By Tummel and Loch Rannoch*. Perth: Northern Print Services, 1989.

Statistical Account of Scotland: *The Statistical Account of Scotland 1791-1799, vol. XII: North and West Perthshire*. Wakefield: EP Publishing, 1977 reprint.

Statistical Account of Scotland: *The Statistical Account of Perthshire*. Edinburgh: Blackwood & Sons, 1846.

The Stephenson Locomotive Society: *The Highland Railway Company and its Constituents and Successors 1855-1955*. London: Stephenson Locomotive Society, 1955.

Stewart, Alexander: *A Highland Parish: or, The History of Fortingall*. Glasgow: A. MacLaran, 1928.

Stewart, Elizabeth: *Dunkeld: An Ancient City*. Perth: Munro Press, 1926.

Sutherland, D. J. S. & Charles Robertson: *Historical and Statistical Account of Pitlochry and the Parish of Moulin*. Pitlochry: Pitlochry Town Council, 1958.

Sutherland, D. J. S.: *A History of Moulin and Pitlochry West Church*. Pitlochry: Typescript ms, 1959.

Sutherland, D. J. S.: *The History of Pitlochry High School*. Pitlochry: Pitlochry High School Parent-Teacher Association, 1977.

Taylor, D. B.: *Circular Homesteads in North West Perthshire*. Dundee: Abertay Historical Society, 1990.

Taylor, William: *Glen Fincastle 1841-1901: A Study of a Perthshire Glen*, Edinburgh: Oliver & Boyd for Dundee College of Education, 1967.

Thompson, Frank: *Gaelic: Looking to the Future*. Longforgan: Andrew Fletcher Society, 1985.

Tomasson, Katherine & Francis Buist,: *Battles of the '45*, 1962.

Tomasson, Katherine: *The Jacobite General*. Edinburgh: Blackwood & Sons, 1958.

Vallance, H. A.: *The Highland Railway*. Newton Abbot: David & Charles, 3rd ed., 1969.

Victoria, Queen: *Leaves from the Journal of Our Life in the Highlands from 1848 to 1861*, edited by Arthur Helps. London: 1868.

Waddington, Patrick: *Turgenev and England*. London: MacMillan, 1980.

Weir, Tom: *The Scottish Lochs*. London: Constable, rev. ed. 1980.

Williamson, David: *Kings and Queens of Britain*. (New ed. of *Debrett's Kings's and Queens of Britain*). London: Promotional Reprint Co., 1991.

Wordsworth, Dorothy: *Recollections of a Tour Made in Scotland AD 1803*, edited by J. C. Shairp. Edinburgh, 1874.

Yuille, George (ed.): *History of the Baptists in Scotland from Pre-Reformation Times*. Glasgow: Baptist Union of Scotland, 1926.

Acknowledgements

Very many thanks to each of the following:

- His Grace the Tenth Duke of Atholl (from his collection at Blair Castle, Perthshire); Bert Cameron; the late Col. Oscar Dixon; I.A. 'Toll' Fergusson; Fisher's Hotel; the photographs by Frank Henderson within *Pitlochry Past and Present* (by Mr. J.H. Dixon); Louis Flood; John Kerr; Ian McDougall; Tom Millar; the Perthshire Tourist Board; Margaret Pirnie; the Pitlochry Archive; the Pitlochry Estate Trust; Perth Museum; the photographs by Francis Smart within *The Summer of 89* (by Bob Charnley); Lt. Col. Ralph Stewart-Wilson; and Sandy Wilson: for providing photographs and maps.
- Janice Moles of Photocall, Pitlochry, for providing the cover photograph.
- Alastair Walker of Pitlochry for providing the photograph of the author.
- Scottish Enterprise Tayside for kindly giving permission to use a detail from their aerial panoramic map of Highland Perthshire.
- Jamie Stormonth-Darling for drawing the sketch maps throughout the book.
- The Reader's Digest Association Limited for kindly giving permission for the reproduction of the plan of the district from their Driver's Atlas, which is based upon the Ordnance Survey map with the permission of the Controller of Her Majesty's Stationery Office – Crown Copyright.
- The Scottish National Portrait Gallery for permission to reproduce the painting of John Graham of Claverhouse, Viscount Dundee, by an unknown artist.
- James Rideout of AOC Scotland Ltd. for permission to draw upon his archaeological research at Carn Dubh, Moulin between 1987 and 1990.
- The Pitlochry Archive, 26 Atholl Road, Pitlochry for all their sources and material.
- John Kerr; Hamish Liddell; Katrina Liddell; Donald McKenzie; Dr. Jean Munro; the staff of Perth Museum; Perth & Kinross District Libraries; Sylvia Robertson; Alastair Steven; and Tessa Till: for their help in various ways.

Almost all of the modern photographs were taken by the author, who also provided some of the older photographs.

About the Author

A descendant of the MacDuffs of Strathbraan (near Dunkeld), Colin Liddell was born in 1954 and spent his childhood in Pitlochry. After an education at Cargilfield School and Fettes College in Edinburgh, he read Jurisprudence at Balliol College, Oxford, and Scots Law at Edinburgh University. He returned to Pitlochry in 1980 to become the third generation of his family in the Highland Perthshire legal practice of J. & H. Mitchell, W.S. He is married with two daughters.

Index

A

A9: 35, 104, 107, 110, 116, 125, 127, 131, 137

Abbeyfield Home: 104

Aberfeldy: 12, 18, 99, 116, 122, 133

Access to hills: 98

Agnew, Sir Andrew: 57 - 59

Agricola, Emperor Gnaeus Julius: 14, 27

Agriculture: 14, 17, 20, 30, 67, 70 - 71, 82 - 83, 98 - 99, 127, 128

Alba Place: 82, 85, 88, 89, 106

Aldclune: 34 - 35, 52, 139, 146

Alder: 17 - 18

Aldour: 12, 59, 87, 99, 108 - 109, 140

Ale: 67, 72, 82, 126, 131

Allt Essan: 134

Allt Girnaig: 12, 125

Alpin mac Eachach: 36

Amber: 31

Ambulance, Scottish Service: 104

An Dun: 33

An galar mor: 43

Angles: 27, 30, 37

Angus, Raid of: 47 - 48

Annat Cottage: 145

Antonine Wall: 28

Antoninus (Pius), Emperor: 28

Ard-fhuil: 38, 125

Ardoch: 28

Argyll, Earl of: 50, 56

Armoury: 107, 109

Ash: 17 - 18

Aspen: 17 - 18, 125

Athole frigate: 18

Atholl Aerated Waterworks: 87

Atholl Auction Mart: 82

Atholl Brigade: 57 - 59

Atholl Brose: 123

Atholl Centre (Atholl Baptist Centre): 142

Atholl Country Collection: 126

Atholl Curling Rink: 101, 102

Atholl District Laundry: 90, 107

Atholl Highlanders: 126

Atholl Leisure Centre: 105

Atholl Mercantile Association: 117

Atholl Palace Hotel: 26, 40, 88, 110

Auction Mart: 82

Axe(s): 20, 21, 26, 146

B

Badenoch, Wolf of: 47 - 48

Badvo: 23, 69, 132

Baledmund: 24, 39, 56, 69, 70, 85

Balfour Stone: 54

Balghulan: 86, 96

Ballinlochan: 40, 64, 84, 85, 98

Ballinluig: 100, 114, 115, 121, 122, 133

Balliol, John de: 43, 46

Ballyoukan: 41, 70, 74, 131, 133

Balnabodach: 32

Balnacraig: 86

Balnadrum: 43

Balnagrew: 145

Balnakeilly: 12, 24, 33, 40, 70, 85, 86, 89, 132, 134

Bank of Scotland (and Union Bank): 86, 105, 108

Banks: 79, 86, 105, 108

Bannerfield: 55

Bannockburn, Battle of: 33, 43, 46

Baptists: 123, 142, 145

Barley: 42

Barley, (bere or bear): 30, 67, 71

Baron's Court of Moulin: 72

Barrow(s): 22 - 23, 26

Barytes: 12

Battle of Bannockburn: 33, 43, 46

Battle of caislen credhi: 36

Battle of Culloden: 45, 56, 59 - 60, 65, 67, 72

Battle of Drumderg: 34, 36

Battle of Dunkeld: 54 - 55

Battle of Falkirk: 57

Battle of Glasclune: 47

Battle of Innerhadden: 46

Battle of Killiecrankie: 24, 50 - 55, 145

Battle of Methven: 46

Battle of monaidh craebi: 36

Battle of monith-carno: 36

Battle of Mons Graupius: 27

Battle of Preston: 56

Battle of the Clans: 48

Battle of Tulloch: 38

Bayonet: 52, 55

Beinn a' Ghlo: 125, 137

Bell barrow: 23

Ben Skievie: 23, 30

Ben Vuirich: 12, 14

Ben-y-Vrackie: 11 - 12, 21, 48, 77, 86, 88, 89, 93, 137
Bhac, Loch: 127, 128, 144
Birch, (and silver birch): 15, 17 - 18
Black Castle (of Edradour): 16, 31, 40
Black Castle (of Moulin): 33, 43
Black Castle (of Strathgarry): 33
Black Spout: 16
Black Wood of Rannoch: 17
Blackie, Professor James Stewart: 96
Blair Athol Distillery: 109
Blair Atholl: 11, 13, 34, 85, 100, 102, 115, 125 - 126, 133, 135, 144, 146
Blair Castle: 13, 19, 35, 48, 51 - 59, 63, 67, 73, 76, 90, 93 - 95, 99, 116, 126, 127, 131 - 133, 135, 137, 146
Blairmount: 84
Bloody Stone of Dunfallandy: 143
Bloomeries: 12
Boar of Badenoch: 110
Boat of Dunkeld: 50
Bobbin Mill: 107
Boiamund de Vicci (Boiamund's Taxatio): 140, 145, 146
Bombs: 110
Bonnethill Road: 63, 79, 82, 87, 90, 102, 107, 108
Bonnie Prince Charlie (see Stuart)
Bonskeid: 70, 74, 144
Borenich: 32, 134, 144
Bowling: 102
Brerachan, Glen: 13, 21, 23
Brerachan, River: 132
Bridge of Allan: 22
Bridge of Tilt: 125 - 126
Bridge, Tummel: 93
Bridges: 40 - 41, 57, 92, 93, 124, 126 - 128, 133 - 136
Britons: 27, 30, 37
Bronze Age: 25 - 26, 42
Brooch (Aldclune): 35
Brook Place: 115
Broom, Loch: 33, 36
Browning, Robert: 95
Bruar: 16, 33, 57, 67, 76, 126 - 127, 135
Bruar Falls: 56, 76, 93 - 94, 127, 133
Bruce, Robert the: 43, 46, 144
Burgh, creation of: 64
Burial mounds: 22 - 23, 35 - 36
Burnlea: 115
Burns, Robert: 76, 93, 127
Burt, Captain Edmund: 65, 68
Butter Memorial Fountain: 103

C
Caesar, Emperor Julius: 14, 26, 139
Cairn(s), chambered: 22
Calvine: 127
Cammoch: 111
canoe (dug-out): 14
Caracalla: 29
Caravan sites: 116, 129
Carn Dubh: 21, 41
Carra Beag (see Fonab Hill)
Casteals (see castles)
Castle Menzies: 54
Castlebeigh Hotel: 31, 104
Castles (and forts): 16, 25, 28, 30 - 33, 35, 40, 43, 56, 57, 121, 147
Ceilidh: 68
Celts: 26 - 27, 29 - 30, 132
Chaggs: 72, 73
Chain boat (at Logierait): 135
Chapelton of Clunie: 143
Chariots: 26, 35, 132
Chequers Eventide Home: 104
Christmas: 139
Churches: 42, 54, 121, 125, 126, 129, 140 - 147
Cinema: 105
Clach na brataich: 33
Clach-na-faire: 62
Clachan an diridh: 24 - 25, 33, 132, 143
Clan Donnachaidh: 32, 33, 47, 65, 127
Clan Donnachaidh Museum: 33, 56, 127, 134
Clans: 46 - 50, 65
Clans, Battle of the: 48
Claverhouse, John Graham of, Viscount Dundee: 51 - 54
Claverhouse Stone: 24, 53, 76
Climate: 14, 17, 20, 30, 69, 78, 102, 114, 128, 133
Clunemore: 22
Cluneskea: 70, 132
Clunie Bridge: 114, 135 - 137
Clunie Dam: 111 - 112
Clunie footbridge: 114
Clunie Monument: 111
Clunie Power Station: 15, 111
Cluniemore (see Pitlochry estates)
Coaches: 77, 85, 133 - 134
Coille Brochain: 46
Colm, Saint: 42, 64, 140
Columba, Saint: 37, 139 - 140
Commonty: 71
Comyn's Road: 131
Contour lines: 75

Coronation Bridge: 15
Courthouse at Logierait: 122
Cows and cattle: 20, 49, 65 - 66, 122, 134
Craig a Barns: 14
Craigiedun: 25, 32, 33, 40, 131
Craigower: 12
Crannogs: 30, 33, 39, 43
Creag nan Caillich: 20
Crieff: 65, 134
Croftinloan: 100, 131
Croftmechaig: 99, 102
Crusader graves: 42
Cuil-an-Daraich: 122
Cuilc: 16, 19, 82, 132
Culloden, Battle of: 45, 56, 59 - 60, 65, 67, 72
Culture: 68, 72, 83, 99, 103 - 105
Cumberland, William Augustus Duke of: 57 - 59
Cup-marked stones: 23, 26, 139
Curling: 79, 101

D

Dalchampaig: 29, 61, 99
Dalchosnie: 46, 48
Dalguise: 95
Dalnacardoch: 93, 133
Dalnacarn: 48
Dalriada: 36 - 37
Dalshian: 23, 133
Dam (Pitlochry): 15, 105, 111 - 114
Danes: 27, 30, 38
Dane's Stone: 24, 69
Deer: 12, 20, 30, 82, 98
Defoe, Daniel: 146
Dhubh, Donald: 122
Dirnanean: 21, 38, 70, 125
Disarming Act: 83
Disarming Act, 1747: 71, 72
Disruption, The (1843): 84, 124, 141, 144
Distilleries: 71, 86 - 87, 109, 124
Doctors' Surgery: 104
Donavourd: 40, 104
Dowally: 73, 114
Drochaid na h'uinneige bridge: 127
Drosten: 34, 36
Droves (cattle): 65
Drowning, death by: 33, 37
Druid (place): 74, 139, 146 - 147
Druids: 36, 143
Druim alban: 30, 37
Drumderg, Battle of: 34, 36
Drumnakyle: 18, 32

Drumochter Pass: 11, 94, 131
Duff, Dr. Alexander: 92
Dunadd: 36 - 37
Dunalastair: 15, 20, 46, 50, 110, 114
Dundarach: 40, 90
Dundee, Viscount (see Claverhouse)
Dunfallandy: 23, 29, 34, 70, 79, 142 - 143
Dunfallandy stone: 34
Dunkeld: 14, 37 - 38, 54 - 55, 95
Dunmore, Loch: 32, 101
Dunne, John: 109
Duntanlich: 144

E

East Church: 140 - 141
East Haugh (of Dalshian): 40, 133
East Moulin Road: 85, 102
Edintian: 128
Edradour: 70, 74, 87, 100, 124, 131
Education Act, 1872: 83
Edward I: 46
Edward II: 46
Edward III: 132
Eigheach, Loch: 15, 110, 114
Elizabeth I (of England): 51
Employment: 69, 82, 98 - 99, 128
Enochdhu: 38, 100, 110, 125
Ericht, Loch: 110
Errochty, Loch: 15, 110 - 111, 114
Errochty Water: 126, 146

F

Faire Mhor: 41
Faire na Paiteag: 24
Falls of Tarf: 94
Falls of Tummel: 15, 94, 107, 111
Farragon: 12
Faskally: 18, 70, 76, 93, 94, 116, 144
Faskally House: 108
Faskally, Loch: 15, 16, 20, 29, 61 - 62, 83, 102, 110 - 114, 116, 132, 137, 143
Faskally Woods: 18, 63, 101, 133
Feadail: 110
Feill Machalmaig: 42, 82, 140
Feill Sraid: 82
Fender, River: 16
Fergusson, Adam: 122
Ferries: 14, 66, 69, 121, 134 - 135
Ferry capsize: 69, 135
Ferry Road: 83, 86, 90, 107
Fincastle: 24, 31, 74, 95, 128, 131, 144
Fire Brigade: 107

First World War: 99, 109, 110
Fish and fishing: 15, 82, 89, 108, 112
Fish Ladder: 15, 105, 112, 114
Fisher's Hotel: 63, 77, 82, 87 - 89, 95 - 96
Flax: 70 - 71
Flints: 20
Floods: 115
Fonab: 66, 132, 134, 140
Fonab Hill: 25, 110, 132, 143
Fonab House: 109
Fonab, Overton of: 30
Football: 72, 101, 105, 123
Forestry Commission: 18, 108, 125
Forestry (*see* Trees)
Fortingall: 29
Forts: 16, 25, 28, 30 - 34, 40, 121, 132 - 133, 147
Foss: 121, 129, 144
Foss, Braes of: 18, 32
Four poster stones: 23 - 25, 128
Fourich: 40, 147
Fraser, James: 135
Free Church: 84, 141, 144 - 146
Frenich: 18
Freshwater Fisheries: 108

G
Gaelic: 37, 73, 83, 99
'Gallery' festival: 141
Gallows' Knoll: 121 - 122
Game: 82, 99
Garrons: 30
Garry Bridge: 17, 128, 131, 136
Garry, Loch: 110
Garry, River: 15 - 16, 21, 35, 69, 83, 102, 111, 125 - 128, 135 - 136, 144, 146
Gas: 85, 91, 107, 117
Gatehouse: 32, 33, 62, 134
Gean: 18
George I: 55
George II: 56 - 57, 59
Gladstone, William Ewart: 95
Glamis Manse Stone: 34
Glen Brerachan: 13, 21
Glen Lyon: 29, 32
Glen Sassunn: 46
Glen Tilt: 13, 20, 66, 94, 109, 131, 137
Glenalmond: 28
Glenfender: 20, 127, 132
Glenfernate: 70, 125, 132
Glenfruin, Slaughter of: 49
Glorious Revolution: 51
Goats: 20, 30, 49, 82

Golf: 88, 102
Grampians: 27, 66, 125, 131
Grand Gutcher Stone: 43
Grandtully: 95, 121
Graves and gravestones: 33, 36, 42 - 43, 46, 48, 54, 121, 140, 144, 146
Gray, Thomas: 75
Great North Road: 44, 64, 77, 86 - 87, 124, 126 - 127, 132 - 134, 137, 146
Great ox: 19
Green Park Hotel: 116
Greengates: 25
Grenich: 32, 144
Grouse: 82, 95, 99
Guides: 102

H
Hadrian's Wall: 28 - 29
Haer Cairn: 27
Hammer of the Scots: 30, 46
Hard tartan: 30
Haugh of Tulliemet: 21, 33
Hazel: 14, 17
Health: 67, 69, 78, 93, 103 - 104
Heartland FM: 99, 102
Heritable Jurisdictions (and courts): 66, 67, 72, 121 - 123
High Drive: 124, 131
Higher Oakfield: 14
Highland Clearances: 66 - 68, 73
Highland Games: 83, 100, 126
Highland Perthshire Development Company: 108
Hogmanay: 97
Holy Trinity Church: 141
Homesteads: 31 - 33, 40 - 41
Hotels: 44, 55, 57, 61, 63, 77, 87 - 89, 93 - 96, 115 - 116, 122 - 124, 126 - 129, 131, 134
Housing problem: 97 - 98
Hut circles: 21 - 22, 30, 33, 36, 40 - 41
Hutton, Charles: 75
Hydro-Electric Scheme: 14 - 15, 33, 110 - 114, 127, 137, 143

I
Ice Ages: 13 - 14, 19 - 20
Inchtuthill: 27 - 28
Institute: 104 - 105
Iona: 37, 139, 140
Iron (bog iron): 12
Iron Age: 23, 27, 29
Irvine, Dr. W. S.: 78, 92, 95, 104
Irvine Memorial Hospital: 62, 103 - 104

J

Jacobite Rebellion, 1689: 45, 50 - 55, 58, 125
Jacobite Rebellion, 1715: 18, 45, 55 - 56, 71, 123, 132
Jacobite Rebellion, 1719: 56 - 60, 71
Jacobite Rebellion, 1745: 56
James III: 121
James IV: 73
James V: 73
James VI and I: 45, 49, 50
James VII and II: 51, 55

K

Kenneth mac Alpin: 37
Killiechangie: 32, 142
Killiecrankie: 12, 17 - 18, 22, 24, 33, 50 - 54, 59, 74, 100, 115, 125, 132 - 136, 139, 144, 146
Killiecrankie, Battle of: 50 - 55, 145
Kilmaveonaig: 126 - 127, 131, 145
Kinardochy, Loch: 101
Kindrogan: 70, 95, 125
King's Ford: 46
King's Hall: 46
King's Island: 144 - 145
King's Palace: 34 - 35
King's Stables: 121
Kinloch Rannoch: 46, 114
Kinnaird: 13, 40, 70, 71, 84, 86, 96, 131 - 134, 141
Kirkton of Lude: 145
Knock Barrie: 32
Knockard Road: 31, 116
Knockfarrie: 40
Knox, John: 66, 133
Kynachan: 32, 59

L

Lady's Dell: 83, 102
Lagreach: 20, 116, 132
Language: 9, 30, 73, 83, 99
Larch: 12, 17, 18
Larchwood Road: 61 - 64, 106, 107
Lassintullich: 18
Laundry: 84, 90, 107
Lemonade: 87, 90, 115
Lettoch Farm: 17, 88, 132
Limestone: 13
Lindum: 39
Linen: 17, 70
Linn of Tummel: 15, 50
Litigan: 31

LMS railway: 115
Local Authority offices and Library: 86, 105
Loch Tummel Sailing Club: 129
Lochs: 12, 14 - 15, 33, 36, 110 - 112, 114, 128 - 129
Logierait: 70, 72, 121 - 122, 134 - 135
Logierait prison: 50, 122
Lower Oakfield: 14, 101, 105, 106
Lude: 35, 36, 56, 70, 126, 145
Luggie: 99

M

MacBean, Donald: 53, 125
MacDonald, Flora: 60
MacDuff Institute: 123
MacKay, Major-General Hugh: 51 - 55
Mackenzie, Hon. Alexander: 122
Macnaughton, A. & J. Ltd.: 86, 101, 108
Macrae, Iain: 52
Mail coach: 77, 85
Mar, Earl of: 55
Marble: 13
Margaret, Queen 'Maid of Norway': 46
Marjorie, Princess: 48
Markets (and fairs): 42, 69 - 70, 72, 82, 107, 140
Marl: 16, 19, 82
Mary, Queen of Scots: 19 - 20, 48
Maskelyne, Nevil: 74 - 75
Matrilinear succession: 34, 37
McGregor, Rob Roy: 50, 122
McGregors' Cave: 50
McGregors, persecution of: 49 - 50
Mendelssohn, Felix: 94
Menzies, James of Culdares: 17
Mid-Atholl Hall: 123
Militia Riots, 1797: 74, 128
Millais, Sir John Everett: 77, 90, 95
Mills: 16, 40, 63, 70, 86, 89, 107, 108
Minerals: 12 - 13
Minigaig Pass: 131
Mitchell, Joseph: 91 - 92, 126
Mitchell, Messrs J. & H.: 86
Mons Graupius, Battle of: 27
Monzie: 22
Moraig, Loch: 35
Mortsafes: 121, 142
Moulin: 39 - 44, 133
Moulin Bowling Club: 102
Moulin Burn: 63, 86, 89 - 90
Moulin City Football Club: 102
Moulin Kirk: 42 - 43, 140

Moulin Market: 42, 69 - 70, 82, 140
Moulin School: 84
Moulin-Pitlochry Central School: 85, 99
Moulinearn: 55, 57, 63, 123
Mount Zion (Church): 42, 92, 140 - 141
Mullinavadie: 20
Murray, Lord George: 56 - 60

N

Na clachan aoraidh: 24, 128, 144
Nechtan mac Derilei: 36
Neolithic (man): 20 - 23, 26, 41
Newholme Avenue: 84

O

Oak: 17 - 18, 59
Oats: 30, 42, 71
Oengus mac Fergus: 34, 36
Old Bank Buildings: 86
Old Blair: 57, 126, 131, 145
Old Bridge of Tilt: 126
Old Faskally: 22
Old Fincastle: 74
Old Struan: 127, 146
Orchilmore: 52
Overton of Fonab: 30

P

Paddling Pond: 105
Palaeolithic Man: 20
Park Terrace: 86
Parkcroy: 64, 70
Parliament (English): 51, 55, 56, 132, 134
Parliament (Scots)(see Privy Council also): 84
Pass of Killiecrankie: 11, 13, 20, 46, 49, 52,
    55, 58, 76, 91, 93, 125, 128, 131,
    134 - 136, 144
Pass of Thanksgiving: 48
Peat: 17, 39, 71, 79, 107
Pennant, Thomas: 31, 68
Penny's Supermarket: 86, 108
Pictish art: 34
Pictish Dwellings: 30
Pictland: 27, 29, 31, 33, 34, 35, 37, 125
Picts: 27, 29 - 38, 61, 132, 140, 143
Pigs: 20, 79, 82
Pilate, Pontius: 29
Pine: 12, 14, 17 - 18
Pine Trees Hotel: 40, 116
Pipe Band, Vale of Atholl: 100
Pit dwellings: 21, 30

Pitagowan: 110, 127
Pitcastle: 32, 73
Pitclochrie: 62
Pitfourie: 74, 131, 132
Pitlochrie: 62, 84
Pitlochrie Public School: 84, 140, 141
Pitlochry & District Tourist Association: 116
Pitlochry & Moulin Community Council: 103
Pitlochry Baptist Church: 115, 142
Pitlochry bonnet: 63, 79
Pitlochry Bowling Club: 102
Pitlochry Church of Scotland (see Mount Zion)
Pitlochry Development Association: 116
Pitlochry Estates: 33, 56, 70, 85, 102
Pitlochry Festival Theatre: 99, 101, 105 - 106,
    116
Pitlochry Gas Company: 107
Pitlochry Golf Course: 102
Pitlochry High School: 40, 64, 99
Pitlochry Highland Games: 83, 100
Pitlochry Hydro Hotel: 13, 88, 116, 147
Pitlochry Leisure Company: 105
Pitlochry Protest Committee: 111
Pitlochry Town Council: 105, 108, 117
Pitlochry Town Hall: 83, 99, 105, 110
Pitnacree: 22, 66
Plague: 43 - 44
Police: 107
Population: 40, 66, 68, 77, 78
Port-an-Eilean: 33, 129
Portnacraig: 90, 106, 134, 137
Post Office: 62, 85, 106, 108, 111, 122, 123,
    125, 126, 129, 134
Potter, Beatrix: 95
Priest's Stone: 143
Prince Charlie House: 56 - 57, 63, 89
Prince Charlie's Bridge: 57, 123 - 124
Prisoner-of-war camp: 110, 127
Privy Council: 49, 66, 67
Ptolemy: 29, 39, 75
Putting Green: 102

Q

Quarry, Aldour: 12, 140
Quarry, Glen Tilt: 13
Quarry, Shierglas: 13, 32, 126
Quartz: 12
Queen Anne: 51, 55
Queen Victoria: 15, 90, 94 - 95, 123, 135, 146
Queen's Drives: 26, 34, 35, 132
Queen's Pool: 46
Queen's View: 31, 46, 95, 128, 144

R

Raid of Angus: 47 - 48

Railway: 134

Railways: 9, 64, 77, 79, 88, 90 - 92, 95, 115, 122 - 127, 134

Rannoch: 12 - 14, 19, 30, 37, 110

Rath: 121 - 122

Recreation Ground: 61, 64, 83, 99, 102, 105, 111, 114, 132

Regality Court of Logierait: 93, 121 - 122

Reiving: 50, 66, 122

Religion: 37, 139

Roads: 9, 25, 35, 106, 116, 123, 124, 126, 128, 131 - 134, 137, 146

Robert de Athole: 47

Robert, Earl of Fife and Duke of Albany: 47, 121

Robert II: 47 - 48, 121

Robert III: 47 - 48, 121

Robert the Bruce: 43, 46, 144

Robertson Crescent: 17

Robertson, Duncan of Carie: 75

Robertson Oak: 59

Romans: 14, 17, 26 - 30, 61

Rowan: 17

RSPB sanctuary: 125

Ruith Castle: 32

Runrig: 67, 70 - 71, 82

Ruskin, John: 15, 77, 90, 95

S

Salmon: 15, 89, 108, 112

Salmon ladder (*see* Fish Ladder)

Sawmill: 89, 107, 108

Schiehallion: 11, 26, 50, 54, 75, 101

Schist: 12 - 13, 143

Schools: 83 - 85, 99 - 100, 124, 128, 129, 141, 144

Scotch mahogany: 17

Scotland's Hotel: 85, 87, 116

Scots: 20, 27, 29 - 30, 36 - 38, 72

Scots firs: 17 - 18

Scottish Field Studies Association: 125

Scout Hut: 84, 102

Scouts: 102

Second World War: 98, 105, 110, 127

Severus, Emperor Septimus: 28 - 29, 61

Sheep: 17, 20, 30, 49, 66, 70, 82, 98, 134

Shielings: 66, 70, 82

Shierglas: 32, 63, 126

Shinagag: 132

Shinagag Road: 132

Shinty: 72, 102

Shops: 86, 106 - 109, 116 - 117, 122, 123, 145

Siege of Blair Castle: 57 - 59

Sithean: 23, 26, 35

Skiing: 101 - 102

Smithy: 64, 107, 108, 122, 126, 129

Soldier's Leap: 53, 125

Souter, John: 23, 69

Sport and recreation: 72, 83, 100 - 106

Sporting: 82, 98

Spruce: 12, 17 - 18

St. Andrew's Church: 144

St. Bride, R.C. Chapel of: 142

St. Bride's Church: 54, 146

St. Bride's Wishing Well: 64, 134

St. Cedd: 121, 142

St. Chad: 121, 142, 144

St. Colm: 42, 64, 140

St. Colm's Well: 64

St. Fillan's Bell: 146

St. Vigeans, Arbroath: 36

Stage coach (*see* Coaches)

Stalking: 82

Standing stone(s): 23, 34, 38, 53, 69, 76, 143, 144

Star Inn: 85, 87

Stevenson, Robert Louis: 96

Stewart, Duncan of Garth: 47 - 48

Stewart, Patrick of Ballechin: 51

Stone circle(s): 23 - 25, 33, 128, 143

Stone of Destiny: 46

Stones: 23 - 26, 33 - 34, 38, 53, 61 - 62, 69, 76, 128, 139, 142, 143

Stones, cup-marked: 23, 26, 139

Stones, four posters: 23 - 25, 128

Stones, paired: 24

Straloch: 24, 70, 125

Strathardle: 21, 23, 38, 55, 72, 93, 125, 132

Strathgarry: 24, 33, 70, 99

Strathgroy: 35 - 36, 139

Strathtay: 121, 132, 143

Strathtummel: 32, 33, 69, 95, 127, 131, 144

Strathview Terrace: 62, 86

Stronchavie: 23, 69, 70, 132

Struan: 32, 92, 100, 110, 115, 126 - 127, 146

Stuart, Prince Charles Edward: 56 - 60, 63, 123 - 124

Stuart, Prince James Francis Edward: 51, 55 - 56

Succession: 34, 37, 46

Succours Inn: 127

Sunnybrae Cottage: 63

Surgery: 104

Suspension Bridge: 64, 114, 135 - 137
Swinburne, Algernon: 95, 96
Sycamore: 18

T
Tacitus: 27
Tack/tacksman: 70
Tanistry: 46
Tarf, River: 94
Tartan: 30, 72, 83, 100 - 101, 108
Tarvie: 23, 48, 70, 125
Tay, Loch: 12, 33
Tay, River: 16, 27 - 28, 37, 39, 46, 48, 134, 137
Taymouth Castle: 67, 94
Telephone Exchange: 106
Telford, Thomas: 68, 134
Tenandry: 17, 32, 82, 134, 141, 144
Tennis: 88, 105
Terracing: 14
Theatre (see Pitlochry Festival Theatre)
Thomas the Rhymer: 69, 135
Throckmorton Coat: 108
Tigh a Cladaich: 89, 99
Tigh Glas Inn: 126
Tigh-na-Cloich Hotel: 61
Tigh-na-Drochait Inn: 94 - 95, 128 - 129
Tigh-na-Geat: 49, 135
Tighrioch: 123, 147
Tilt, Glen: 13, 20, 66, 94, 109, 131, 137
Tilt, River: 92, 126
Toberargan: 64, 70, 104, 106
Tom an tigh mor: 127
Tombreck: 32
Tomnamoan: 85, 99
Tomphubil: 18
Tourism: 64, 78, 87, 97 - 98, 105, 115 - 117, 126
Town Hall (see Pitlochry Town Hall)
Trees: 14, 16, 17, 18, 59, 71, 110
Tressait: 33
Trinafour: 20, 133
Trooper's Well: 52
Trysts: 65, 134
Tulchan: 36
Tullibardine, Marquis of: 55 - 56
Tulliemet: 122 - 123, 131, 142, 147
Tulloch: 21, 23, 38
Tummel Bridge: 70, 93, 95, 115, 116, 128 - 129, 133
Tummel, Falls of: 15, 94, 107, 111
Tummel, Linn of: 15, 50
Tummel, Loch: 15, 32, 46, 76, 110 - 114

Tummel, River: 15 - 16, 21, 32, 34, 46, 61, 93, 114, 134
Turgenev, Ivan: 95
Turner, Joseph Mallard William: 93
Turnpikes: 134
Tynreich: 25, 57, 122

U
Union Bank of Scotland: 86, 105, 108
Urrard: 24, 52 - 53, 70, 76
Urus: 19

V
Vale of Atholl Football Club: 102
Vale of Atholl Pipe Band: 100
Victorian Pitlochry: 12, 77 - 78, 97, 117
Vikings: 27, 30, 37, 38, 139

W
Wade, Major-General George: 44, 53, 124 - 134
War Memorial: 110
Water: 14, 89, 107, 111, 125
Waterfalls: 15 - 16, 76, 126
Weather: 14, 20, 69, 78, 102, 114, 128
Weaving: 66, 70, 86
Well Brae: 64, 82, 102, 116
Wells: 12, 52, 64, 134, 143
Wellwood Hotel: 89
West Church (see Mount Zion)
West Haugh: 134
West Moulin Road: 14, 79 - 82, 85 - 86, 89, 102, 105, 108, 147
Whisky: 71, 72, 86 - 87, 97, 109, 124
William III (William of Orange): 45, 49, 51, 55
Wine: 67, 72
Wolf of Badenoch: 47 - 48
Wolf/wolves: 17, 19 - 20, 31, 71
Wood (see Trees)
Wordsworth, William & Dorothy: 93
World War I (see First World War)
World War II (see Second World War)
Wyntoun: 48

Y
Yellow London Lady: 75
YMCA: 144
Youth Hostel: 116

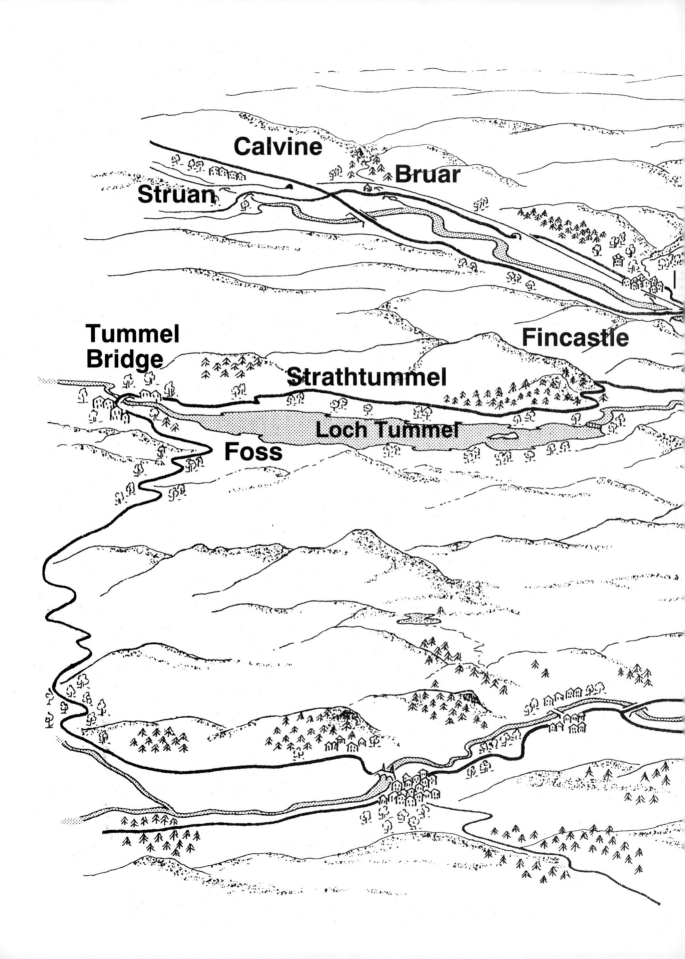